To Bud – Christmas 1970

from

Bernice and Raymond

COACH

A Season with Lombardi

COACH

A Season with Lombardi

by TOM DOWLING

W · W · NORTON & COMPANY · INC ·
NEW YORK

SBN   393   08622   4

Library of Congress Catalog Card No. 79-128615

ALL RIGHTS RESERVED

Published simultaneously in Canada
by George J. McLeod Limited, Toronto

PRINTED IN THE UNITED STATES OF AMERICA

3 4 5 6 7 8 9 0

For Janet

Preface

When I wrote this book in the winter and spring of 1970 Vince Lombardi seemed indestructibly alive.

Now he is dead. Looking over what I have written I find casual phrases and common incidents that seem to prefigure the terrible fate that none of us — Lombardi, his family, the Redskins, the fans, or myself — could have sensed or accepted. Yet, as with any life, the hints of mortality were there. Perhaps more so with Lombardi, for to him wins and losses were matters of life and death.

I see in what I have written the pains and exhaustion that overtook him toward the end of the season; the ferocious need to win each game, as if there could be no next Sunday, no new season. Lombardi was, of course, the sort of man who conserved nothing of himself for the future — not his overriding will, his energy, his sheer indomitable strength, or even his wrath. He put it all on the line day in and day out. Not even death, in the end, could cheat him and us of what he had already done, only what he could still do.

I remember too that he told me last December that he had returned to football coaching because no one wanted to be a dead legend, and that having come back he would no longer be a legend, because then he would be suffering defeats. When he said that, he had already suffered four defeats, more than a man of his nature was meant to endure. But, he added, he was glad he had come back, because it meant he was still alive. Now he is dead, and a legend once again.

It was my fate to record Vince Lombardi's last season, his farewell to football, a season that would end with the same 7–5 record he had had in his first year as head coach in Green Bay in 1959. In all he had had eleven years at the top. He had come to eminence late in life. And he left it early. Yet they were an extraordinary eleven years. He dominated sports in the 1960's, and not merely as a coach but as a man, oversized at times, but nonetheless a man.

In many ways, I like to think, 1969 with the Redskins was Lombardi's most challenging year, the most rigorous test of his combative nature. It was six months of conflict, pressure, insecurity, and fear. The Packers had time to get used to him, the Redskins didn't. He bent men to his will, and it was not always a pleasant thing to witness — not for the players, the observers, or even for Lombardi. I have tried in this book to tell what that year was like — the good with the bad, the glory with the humiliation and defeat. No one's death can change that, can alter the way Vince Lombardi and the Redskins were in 1969. And I would not change what I have written. From Coach on down the Redskins were an honest and honorable collection of men, and their experience together cannot be diminished by the truth, as one man saw it.

Finally, I would like to say flat-out what I hope this book makes clear: that I admired Vince Lombardi and was personally fond of him. He was a man who knew what his job was, knew how to do it surpassingly well, and went about it with his whole being. You knew where you stood with Lombardi. He said he was going to be tough and ruthless, and he was. He said he was going to be honest and fair, and he was. He could also be shy, uncertain, generous, and compassionate. He was wary of those qualities, and he suffered in their exercise. He thought, I suppose, that they were impediments to the job he had to do. Characteristically, he went about suppressing them as best he could. Characteristically, they were too deeply imbedded in his nature for him to succeed at it.

Coaches, as Lombardi liked to say, are only as good as their records. There have been others in his profession who had better won-lost records over a longer period of time. Yet Lombardi existed in a realm beyond the hackneyed athletic pantheon of wins and losses. He was, for all his ego and harsh, autocratic nature, a great man. Never less than that. He is dead now, but for me, at least, no dead legend.

COACH

A Season with Lombardi

Chapter 1

In sports the winners seldom retire, so it surprised no one when rumors began flowing from Green Bay in 1968 that Vince Lombardi was restive in the Packer front office, was brooding over his self-banishment from coaching, was open to the right proposition elsewhere. He had acquired a certain taste for the limelight, might be expected to hunger for those winning Sunday afternoons riding from the field on the shoulders of his linemen, that big toothy smile flashing across the TV screens of the nation.

For nine years he had been head coach and general manager of the Packers. He had brought the team two straight Super Bowl championships and five National Football League titles, including a record-breaking three in a row from 1965 to 1967. Lombardi had made the Packers the dynasty of professional football. He had marked each annual triumph by distributing "world-championship" diamond rings to his team, baubles almost oriental in their size and ostentation, like a Turkish sultan rewarding his loyal pashas after a successful campaign against the infidels.

When the Packers ran over the Oakland Raiders at the 1968 Super Bowl in Miami, Lombardi gave the Packers rings encrusted with three diamonds for the three straight NFL championships and announced his retirement from coaching.

The two jobs were too much for one man, he said, retaining the general managership for himself and turning over the coaching chores to Phil Bengston, his chief defensive assistant since 1959. But, as 1968 wore on, Lombardi discovered that if the two jobs were too much for one man, the one he had kept for himself was clearly too little.

Lombardi said he expected to have his hands full with the threatened players' strike and the final NFL-AFL merger talks. Both were potentially nettlesome issues, but in the end the strike didn't take place, and the merger did, which left him the normal responsibilities of an NFL general manager—trading with other teams, negotiating player contracts, conducting the college draft, and administering the team's business affairs.

No one in the league showed much inclination to swap players with Lombardi, none of the Packers squawked much at contract time, the college-player draft was a largely computerized operation that occupied a few days in January, and business ran itself with a sold-out stadium and guaranteed television revenues. Beyond this, the scope of general managing was limited to banquet appearances, negotiating hot-dog concessions, selling ads in the game programs, and reordering shoulder pads and office supplies.

So Lombardi was left plenty of time to polish up his golf game on the sporty 18-hole course at Green Bay's Oneida Golf and Riding Club. But breaking 80, while a worthwhile goal, was not a challenge cast in the Lombardi mold. Breaking 80 was like general managing: a lot of men could do it. Real success was like coaching championship football: only a rare few had the gift.

So Lombardi was on the market. There were rumors that he would be the next Commissioner of Baseball. Then, it was politics, with the statehouse in Madison as one possibility. Big Business? After all, he had been voted Salesman of the Year in a poll of one million American salesmen and his presence in the board room of any corporation would perk up company morale. The speculation over his future finally came full circle, all the way back to coaching.

The Atlanta Falcons offered Lombardi a $1-million package, but they were spurned and had to settle for Norm Van Brocklin midway through the 1968 season. Next, owner John Mecom, Jr., hankered to have Lombardi at the helm of his New Orleans Saints. Was Lombardi looking for equity? Well, the

Boston Patriots of the AFL were ready, almost desperate, to accommodate him with a piece of their club.

Toward the close of 1968, Lombardi was reportedly heading a group that planned to take over the Philadelphia Eagles, whose owner, Jerry Wolman, had gone bankrupt and needed $35 million in a hurry to stave off his creditors and retain possession of the franchise. Wolman airily told the press that a $35-million loan was in the bag; a statement whose ignorance of the money mart went a long way toward explaining how he had gone bankrupt in the first place. The Lombardi-Philadelphia deal faded from view.

Then, Lombardi was reported to have bought a house in Virginia, right across the Potomac from Washington, whose Redskins had just lurched to a 5–9 season under coach Otto Graham. The house turned out to belong to another man named Lombardi, but the Washington story still looked good. Lombardi had met with the Redskin president, Edward Bennett Williams, in Miami during the 1969 Super Bowl, and a Washington reporter recalled that when the Packers had played the Redskins during the 1968 season, Lombardi and Williams had breakfasted together. Later, in the owner's box at RFK Stadium, Lombardi was heard to remark, "Washington is really a great place, isn't it? *This is where everything happens.*" An idle expression of pride in the nation's capital? Or a phrase that had sunk in deeply during that breakfast salestalk by Williams?

Certainly there was abundant evidence that Williams, a trial lawyer not given to dallying with lost cases, was disenchanted with Graham. "We are looking for a crackdown coach with a winning background," Williams had said on hiring Graham from the Coast Guard Academy in 1966. Three seasons later, Graham's "winning background" had dwindled to a 17–22–3 record. Far from cracking down, he had ruled the Redskins with an affable disregard of discipline, asserting himself only when the mood seized him.

The Redskins had even asked quarterback Sonny Jurgensen to call a closed team meeting with Williams to grouse about the coaching staff. The team had lost its nerve by the time

Williams confronted them in the locker room, but the meeting itself, the shuffling feet, the averted eyes, and the ghastly silence that followed Williams's "Well?" were not without effect. Graham had lost control. He sat tight, hearing the rumors about Lombardi, but shrugging them off; to him nothing was seriously wrong that couldn't be rectified in 1969 with a few trades and some good draft choices. Besides, Graham had two years to go on a five-year contract that paid $60,000 a year, plus a stipulation for a $150,000 settlement if the contract were not renewed for another five years. Nothing creates misconceptions faster than money. To Jerry Wolman $35 million was a trifle, an obstacle to be brushed aside. To Otto Graham $270,000 was a fortune, an ace-in-the-hole to keep Edward Bennett Williams standing pat.

In late January, the rumors of Lombardi's imminent appointment to lead the Redskins were gaining momentum. As the college-player draft continued at Redskin headquarters, Graham's coaches and scouts gathered in the conference room, festooned with cardboard tags listing the positions and names of the eligible 1968 collegiate crop. The draft proceeds slowly under the best of circumstances, but for the Redskins, who had traded off three of their top five picks, it was even slower than normal. Finally Graham said, "I think I'll call Lombardi in Green Bay and see if he wants to trade Donny Anderson and Jim Grabowski for A. D. Whitfield. If he says yes, I might as well go home." The assembled coaches and scouts, whose jobs were linked to Graham's tenure as head coach, responded with mirthless stares. "You got to have a sense of humor," Graham said. They would all need it in the next few weeks.

Once the college draft was concluded, Otto Graham left for a golfing holiday in California. Williams had said nothing to him, and to the end he remained one of the few men in America who had no inside information on his impending ouster; some of the others belonged to the seven-man executive committee of the Green Bay Packers. It appeared that, like Williams, Lombardi was playing his hand as cozily as possible.

By the first of February, the papers carried reports of Redskin stock transfers that would allow Lombardi to buy into the club. On February 3, the Washington papers said Graham was out. The Packers executive committee called an emergency morning session, presumably to release Lombardi from his contract, which ran through 1973. On February 4, Packer president Dominic Olejniczak said the executive committee would defer an announcement on Lombardi's release until the matter could be put before the whole forty-five-man Packer Board. Olejniczak was said to be miffed at learning of Lombardi's private and extensive discussions with Williams. In Washington, tackle Jim Snowden became the first Redskin to comment publicly on the story: "The prospect of playing for Lombardi frightens me," he said. And in Green Bay, Lombardi told the press, "Everyone wants to own something. The challenge is not in maintaining, but in creating."

On February 5, Lombardi flew from Green Bay to New York to receive the Catholic Youth Organization's John V. Mara Memorial Award as Sportsman of the Year. Later that day, the Packer management made a sporting gesture of their own and released Lombardi from his contract.

Lombardi arrived in Washington by private jet on February 6. The event was dubbed "the second coming" in the Washington press, and one sports columnist claimed to discern a " slight puff of smoke," rising Vatican-like from Edward Bennett Williams's law office. At 2:30 that afternoon, Vince Lombardi, now head coach, general manager, and five-percent owner of the Washington Redskins, strode to the rostrum installed in the gold Chandelier Room of the Sheraton-Carlton Hotel and peered into the bank of TV arc lights. A thicket of twenty-three microphones protruded above the rostrum's edge. "In spite of what you've heard," said Lombardi, "I can't walk on water. Not even when the Potomac is frozen."

Someone wanted to know how Lombardi had disentangled himself from Green Bay.

"You're wondering what Washington got for Chuck Mercein? Well, I'm it," Lombardi grinned. It was a typical Lombardi answer: a *non sequitur*, austere, somewhat masterful. For not only did it side-step the still fresh turmoil and bitterness of the Packer executive committee meetings, but in its self-effacing way it recalled the wizardry on which Lombardi's football reputation rested.

Mercein was the journeyman fullback Lombardi had plucked from the Redskin taxi squad halfway through the 1967 season. In the eighth game of the season, the Packers had gone to Baltimore still in quest of their third straight NFL title and had been beaten by the Colts, 13–10. Both Packer fullbacks—the veteran Elijah Pitts and Jim Grabowski, half of the $1-million backfield Otto Graham was jokingly to use as a litmus test of Lombardi's availability—were injured in the Colt game, leaving the Packers with no inside runner for the homestretch drive.

Mercein, with a no-cut contract from the New York Giants, had been sent to Washington on a make-the-team basis. He had signed a Redskin contract, but not the binding NFL document that would have made him official Washington property. Lombardi, remembering Mercein's good days against the Packers when he had been a Giant, got on the phone. Mercein disappeared from the nation's capital and surfaced a few days later in a Packer uniform, the signatory of an official NFL contract with Green Bay. Otto Graham yelled that Mercein had been "snatched"; Edward Bennett Williams talked limply about getting a Packer player in exchange.

Later, in 13-below-zero weather on a frozen Green Bay field, with the NFL championship at stake, Mercein was to have the greatest day of his football career. The score was Dallas 17, Green Bay 14, with a minute and a half to play. The Packers had the ball first and ten on the Cowboy 30-yard line. As the cliché would have it, the time was ripe for "the big play," and Mercein came up with two of them in a row.

First, he got behind Dallas linebacker Dave Edwards and took a Bart Starr swing pass 19 yards, down to the 11-yard line; he then punched 8 yards off tackle to the Cowboy 3. Donny Anderson carried to the 1 for the first down and ran the ball twice more, picking up another half yard on the icy goal-line. It was third and one-half yard, with sixteen seconds left on the clock—time for a quick pass and, if that failed, a field goal to send the game into sudden-death overtime. In the huddle, Starr called a quarterback keeper over Dallas tackle Jethro Pugh. Jerry Kramer and Ken Bowman double-blocked Pugh, and Starr wedged in for a touchdown, with Mercein's hands buried in his rump, pushing him across the goal-line.

"It was a dumb call," Cowboy coach Tom Landry said afterwards in the Dallas dressing room, "but now it looks like a great play." And perhaps that quarterback sneak was imprudent, even cock-eyed, for if Starr had failed to go in, the Cowboys could have run out the clock before the Packers, their time-outs exhausted, could have gotten their field-goal unit on the field. But, however dubious that final call might have been, the two calls that moved the ball from the Cowboy 30 to the 3-yard line had been impeccable. They were the backbreakers, and they had been extracted from a fullback who had not made the Redskin forty-man roster.

If Lombardi could get that kind of a day from Mercein, what might he exact from the regular Redskin runners? There was hope, then, for the Redskin running game, up to now the disgrace of the league. Such was the implication in Lombardi's jovial, if sly, rejoinder to the press. Lombardi's secret was that even when he said nothing, he suggested everything. Yes, he was saying, he had left Green Bay and come to Washington; yes, he was suggesting, he had brought the formula for the Packer success along with him: himself, to be blunt about it. Like it or not, he was the prisoner of his legend and his record. He was a man whose phrases, looks, and gestures triggered strong associations and stirred either admiration or execration. Quite naturally a newsman stood up in the Chandelier Room and said, "You're supposed to be a real tough guy. Are you going to put on a different face here in Washington?"

"I don't know if it's possible," Lombardi said. "It's the same old face. Actually, I'm a pretty soft guy." That inspired a brief snort of derisive laughter, an obeisance to Lombardi's reputation as the meanest man in football.

Why had Lombardi returned to coaching?

"Because my wife said I was a damn fool for quitting the side lines. And on that note, gentlemen, I thank you."

The floodlights dimmed, and Lombardi was on his way, back to the Redskin offices for five months of seclusion to study the films of the team he had inherited.

Yet the questions that had been posed in the news conference lingered. What sort of a man was Lombardi? A meanie or a softie? Did he deserve the credit for making the Packers champions? And if so, how had he done it? Why had he left Green Bay? Why had he come back to coaching? Why Washington? And above all, why were these questions worth answering? In a sense, this last question was a prologue to the others. Certainly, there was no other coach in pro football whose comings and goings inspired such curiosity, whose nature, real and alleged, merited such scrutiny. Perhaps the reason lay in the way Lombardi had become entwined with the sport he coached.

Lombardi's rise and the unfolding of the Packer dynasty paralleled the extraordinary rise of pro football to the pinnacle of American spectator sports. The game itself was cut along the lines of the American grain: it was savage, violent, militaristic in its meticulous organization, moralistic in its celebration of performance and high purpose, remorseless in its contempt for failure and its adulation for success. Above all, it was a drama more perfect in its suspense than the reality of armed combat or the romance of the movies and TV. The final score was the climax of the drama, but within the sixty-minute framework was a series of miniature dramas. The series climaxed in the first down, the first down in the drive, the drive in the touchdown. The series built up to the suspense and resolution of the third-down situation, the ends of the two halves peaked in the suspense of the blitzkrieg that followed the two-minute warning. The game's architecture was perfect, balanced between the *yin* of the fragile quarterback and the *yang* of the defensive front four. Moreover, the game was ideally suited for television: the barrage of cameras, the zoom shots, and the instant replays revealed subtleties the fan in the stadium could not see and penetrated the hand-offs, traps, pile-ups, wedges, and other concentrations of mass that obscured the action. The 1958 sudden-death championship game between the Colts and the Giants is generally regarded as pro football's great television breakthrough, but whenever the exact moment, there could be no doubt that the game dominated television sports throughout the sixties, its audience in the tens of millions and its future apparently limitless.

When so many Americans are fascinated, even obsessed, with an event, it ceases to be frivolous, can no longer be regarded as a mere game. If escapism and the urge to be entertained are American characteristics, so too is the call of the Puritan ethic, with its need for moral uplift and the reassurance that time was spent usefully. Thus as the nation's pastime, pro football had to be endowed with an ethical function, a sense of high purpose.

These values had long been associated with college football, where young men were said to learn enduring lessons to prepare them for later life—sportsmanship, fair play, teamwork, second effort, and so on. The college game was a sort of rite of passage, a young man's introduction to manhood in the panoply of a public spectacle. Moreover, the point of the college game was that it was played by young men who received no pay for their exertions and injuries. Money corrupted the moral content of the game, and it was this concept that blunted the success of the professional game for years. From the 1930's on, the pros were playing rougher, more exciting, and more adroit football than the colleges, but they were getting paid to play, and they were grown men, often in their thirties, who were acting out the transition to manhood years after the event was expected to have occurred. The pros lacked identity and moral worth; they were merely actors. Consequently, they failed to win mass acceptance. They were fun to watch, but they lacked a deeper purpose.

But not Lombardi. He exuded fervor, the conviction that he was up to something of the utmost gravity and importance. He conceived of football as a man's job: it was a profession like dentistry, the law, public accounting, the military, or the pulpit. Like professional men, pro football players were expected to be well-groomed, well-dressed, well-spoken, well-thought-of in the community, and above all, they were expected to work diligently at being successful. In these terms, college fulfilled the same function for a professional football player as it did for the other professions, for it taught him the basic skills of his job and gave him the social respectability that membership in the professional class required. Accordingly, Lombardi's first fiats at Green Bay prohibited players from roaming the streets in bermuda shorts and T shirts, from drinking liquor leaning on the bar rail of a public tavern. In addition, the team would travel first-class in suits and ties, carrying slender attaché cases with a change of linen. Soft drinks would be served on the flight out, there would be two cans of beer per customer coming home, and the stewardesses were not to be pinched or molested on either leg of the trip.

The reasoning for this was simple. A fragment of the American public might watch rude stevedores and millhands banging away at one another on the gridiron, but a great mass of them would watch and identify with *professionals* struggling on the field, with men who behaved like gentlemen off the field, who had some sartorial style, and who sipped their liquor, if they must, in the discreet booths of cocktail lounges. The fans needed to be reassured that the pros had class, just as the collegiate players did. Lombardi was not the only coach to recognize the essential seriousness of pro football, the fans' hunger for instruction as well as entertainment. But his arrival on the professional scene coincided with the sport's huge television exposure. He was immensely telegenic and articulate, and he had a great gift for intensity. Above all, he coached a team that could and did win. And winning was what the game was all about, what America was all about, when it came to the point. And it could not be discounted that the Packers won precisely because Lombardi sensed the pro player's innate urge to be a professional man, a man of dignity who worked at an important job.

Lombardi announced that his credo was "excellence." To be excellent was to win. "Winning isn't everything," he said, "winning is the only thing." No words minced there. It was a moral code the certitude of which would do honor to the Prophet Elijah. And, of course, it was Lombardi's prophetic, even messianic streak that stirred that vast band of football believers and gave the taste of spiritual satisfaction to a Packer victory.

The Packers were small-town America—solid, simple, proud of themselves, hard-working, and dedicated. Week after week, when it was all put on the line, the Packers were able to thrash the big-city teams: Green Bay was tougher than Chicago, New York, Los Angeles, and all the other big cities of America. The Packers vindicated a way of life, and Lombardi was its representative man. Like everything else in America during the 1960's, it was a way of life that was threatened, its values attacked by what Spiro Agnew called an "effete corps of impudent snobs." The defenders of those values rallied around Lombardi and rejoiced in his denunciations of the cancerous laxness that was eating at the American fiber.

By the same token, there were those who were appalled at the costive narrowness of the Lombardi code and its values, which had led to what Senator Fulbright called "the arrogance of power": the American need to win and succeed whatever the cost, whomever it hurt, and to justify the process as a moral crusade.

Attorney General John Mitchell was to tell Edward Bennett Williams that the Nixon high command in early 1968 had toyed with the idea of inviting Lombardi, a lifelong Democrat, to join the Republican ticket as the presidential running mate. The comment is more symbolic than real in all likelihood, but one that nonetheless hints at the constituency the Republicans sought and Lombardi could reach. He was, after all, a household word.

The questions Lombardi raised, then, did seem worthwhile, and in May 1969, I flew to Green Bay, Wisconsin, to look for the answers. I hoped to find out what Lombardi was like and why he had returned to coaching, to see how much of the Lombardi legend was black and how much white, to study the code he had set for himself, and to find out whether he had lived up to it. It was a journey that turned out to occupy the better part of a year, and in the end it all hinged on what pro football, or at least the Redskin team, was like. Lombardi was only as good as his record, and if his future was in **Washington**, his past was in Green Bay.

Chapter 2

Spring comes late to northern Wisconsin. As the plane closed on Green Bay, I could see the trees budding and fresh green in the farmland below. The man next to me, a businessman from a small town north of Green Bay, was assuring me that "the Pack would be back," that the team's dismal 6–7–1 record in 1968 without Lombardi in command was just one of those things.

As for the Redskins, Lombardi would shape them up in a hurry. Had I read about the off-field carousing of Redskin quarterback Sonny Jurgensen in the *Saturday Evening Post* a year ago? I had. Had I noticed Sonny's jellybelly on the TV games? I had. Well, he ventured, Sonny would be well advised to do something about that gut. Diet. Go on the wagon. That spare tire was not something Coach Lombardi would warm up to.

Jurgensen's stomach was to prove a continuing *leitmotif* during my Green Bay stay. Some Packer fans regarded it as a direct personal affront to Coach Lombardi, others as a minor indiscretion that would have to be dealt with understandingly, yet firmly. From the viewpoint of the Green Bay citizenry, themselves built on almost Bavarian proportions, Jurgensen's stomach was apparently the most familiar landmark in the nation's capital—no wonder the nation was in deep trouble, the younger generation going to the dogs. What could you expect when the quarterback, the field general, the leader of the football team in the very capital of the nation had run to seed, like a pudgy general in some Latin American junta?

It was in this xenophobic atmosphere that Lombardi's winning brand of football was nurtured. Yet, there was the irony that Lombardi himself was an Easterner, a city boy from Brooklyn. This fact nagged at many. Green Bay wanted a winner, but they were loath to have an outsider, an Easterner, produce it for them. So they pretended Lombardi was a home-grown boy, deliriously happy down on the farm.

Sometimes, though, the truth stared them in the face. A friend of Lombardi's told me that once he had been in Coach's room in the Drake Hotel in Chicago before a Bears game. Lombardi was standing at the window, looking down at the Outer Drive and the city lights reflected on Lake Michigan. "C'mere," Lombardi grunted. The man walked over to the window. "Look at that," Lombardi commanded. "What about it?" the man asked. "You don't have anything like that in Green Bay," Lombardi said. "You're damn right we don't," the man said. "What do you mean?" Lombardi asked, startled at the counterattack. "Vince," the man said, "you've never had it so good, never been so happy anywhere as you've been in Green Bay." Lombardi hung his head, but the truth was out. Coach had a hankering for the outside world. Green Bay's Fox River with its iron ore scows was all right, but it wasn't the Outer Drive, with the lights of the sky-scrapers glittering in Lake Michigan.

My seatmate on the plane chortled to himself as he continued to ponder Sonny Jurgensen's stomach. Lombardi will take care of Jurgensen, he concluded. Coach always gets 110 percent from his players.

This, of course, was the essence of Lombardi's method. He did demand 110 percent, seemed to believe the figure meant something. He had convinced millions of Americans that his ominous, growling requests for 110 percent had been met in full and that enemy lines parted like the Red Sea when his players smelled the goal-line. The credibility gap had never been a problem for Vince Lombardi. "Football is a game of clichés," he had written, "and I believe in every one of them."

When Lombardi took over the ailing Green Bay Packers in 1959, he was forty-five years old and was known nationally, if at all, as one of the original "Seven Blocks of Granite" in the Fordham line during the mid-1930's. He had played right guard at 172 pounds. He was not an All-American.

After leaving Fordham Law School one year short of graduation, Lombardi coached from 1938 to 1946 at St. Cecilia's High School in Englewood, New Jersey; at one point his teams won thirty-six straight games. From 1946 to 1948 he was an assistant coach at Fordham, and for six more years an assistant at West Point under Colonel Earl "Red" Blaik, of whom Lombardi has written, "Whatever success I have must be attributed to the 'Old Man.' He molded my methods and my whole approach to the game . . . if there is a number one coach of all time, in my opinion, it is Colonel Blaik."

In turn Blaik observed of his protégé, "Lombardi is a thoroughbred with a vile temper."Assistant coaches under Blaik had a way of moving up as head coaches elsewhere—Stu Holcomb to Purdue, Andy Gustafson to Miami, Bob Woodruff to Florida, Bobby Dodds to Tulsa, Murray Warmath to Minnesota. But it didn't work out that way for Lombardi, who left West Point in 1954 to become an assistant coach once again, this time with the New York Giants.

"I wanted to be a head coach at a large university," Lombardi wrote three years ago. "The offers I had were from schools that were too small or from larger ones that were de-emphasizing football. I know I lost some jobs because of my Italian heritage." So it happened, whether through discrimination, vile temper, or bad luck, that Vince Lombardi was forty-five when he became a head coach for the first time.

The Green Bay Packers were 4–8 in 1956; 3–9 in 1957; 1–10–1 in 1958. In 1959, their first year under Lombardi, the Packers finished 7–5. In the first game of that season they beat their traditional rivals, the Chicago Bears, 9–6, and the Packer players carried Lombardi off the field on their shoulders. While Lombardi was head coach, the Packers scored 3080 points in season play, their opponents 1874. That works out to a Packer average of 25.3 a game and 14.5 for the opposition. Thus the Packers were eight-tenths of a point better than the classic ten-point spread a coach must play for as the margin of protection in the closing minutes of the game. There is something almost Newtonian in the clockwork sense of cosmic order contained in that eight-tenths of a point. Small wonder Las Vegas bookies used to say that Lombardi meant "two points" when the odds on a Packer game were figured.

Among football fans, there is divided opinion over the finest football team of all time; some believe it was the 1962 Packers, others, the Packer squad of 1966. Both were destroyers, remorseless in the fourth quarter, but though the players were largely the same, the teams were vastly different. The 1962 Packers were young and overpowering; the 1966 squad experienced, cunning, and resourceful. They were both trained, like jungle cats, to possess what Lombardi had called "this ravenous appetite for success"; they were teams that had the mark of the lion's paw, the Lombardi touch.

In Green Bay, I found that the myths, platitudes, and misinformation about Lombardi had already been codified into a sort of canon law. And why not? He was already referred to as St. Vincent and "God."

"How about the earthy side of the man?" I asked a member of the Packer executive committee.

"I never heard the man swear in my life," he said. I was to hear some strange things in Green Bay, but nothing stranger, more preposterous than that—not even the claim from the Packer linen concession man that the team used thirteen thousand towels during a muddy game with Cleveland. The man who never heard Lombardi swear was not alone in reshaping the legend. The real facts were rapidly sinking into the rich loam of small-town myth. Lombardi had ruled Green Bay with an iron hand for ten years, and now that he was gone his detractors and apologists were hard at work altering the legend to their own needs. Yet, I was to find out that even the detractors had to fall back on magnification in order to reduce Lombardi to size. There was only one way to belittle the man, and that was to raise him to a plane of absurdity, for to demean Lombardi was to tarnish the beloved Packers, to diminish doughty Green Bay, the All-American city of 75,000 plain-living citizens who had financed and fielded the greatest football team of all time. The Packers were the religion of Green Bay, and Lombardi, though gone to the Great Beyond of Washington, D. C., was still its saint.

"You should have seen the canonization when he left," I was told. "There must have been five thousand people at the testimonial dinner for St. Vincent. Max McGee (rake, prankster, twelve-year-veteran end, and a Lombardi favorite) walked out on stage with loaves and fish on a platter. Vince laughed like hell. Well, why wouldn't he? The truth never hurts."

The Lombardi home in Green Bay was sold to a local psychiatrist. "Vince asked $56,000 and got $56,000," said a man who knew the new owner. I expressed surprise at the purchaser's cowed bargaining. The man shrugged. "You don't dicker with 'God,'" he dead-panned.

My informant's wife broke into the conversation. "After the Lombardis moved out, the psychiatrist's wife had all her girlfriends come around and go over the place with a fine-tooth comb, from top to bottom."

"What were they looking for?" I asked.

"Relics," she said with delight, "holy relics."

Henry Jordan, the Packers' five-time All-Pro defensive tackle, sat behind the bare desk of his Green Bay mortgage company examining the progress of his portfolio in the *Wall Street Journal*. "You know," Jordan said, peering into the palm of his hand, "I'll tell you something about Coach." (Lombardi is called Coach. Not the coach, or Coach Lombardi, but Coach.) "A couple of years back I had this terrible rash on my hand, getting worse and worse. The Packers sent me to five specialists and they couldn't do a thing. I could see the bone, it got so bad. Even with bandaging I'd be doing pushups at practice and a blade of grass would touch that wound and I'd holler like a baby. One day Coach comes up to me. 'Here,' he says real gruff and hands me this little unmarked bottle of liquid. 'Use this.' So I figured, what the hell. Two days later the rash started to heal." Jordan thrust out the giant hand for me to see, a miracle prop in an Oral Roberts tent meeting.

"I'll tell you another thing," he went on. "One day it's raining at training camp. I'm sort of walking by Coach, minding my own business. Suddenly he looks up at the sky and says, "Stop raining, Goddamn it." There's a flash of lightning, some thunder, and then it stops. He looks at me and I look at him. Well, I've been eating fish on Fridays ever since, and I'm a Methodist."

A favorite Packer story about Lombardi is the night he went home after a long practice session in the cold, climbed into bed with his wife, Marie, and she said, "God, your feet are cold."

"Dear," he said, "in the privacy of the house you may call me Vince."

The greater the saint the sweeter the incense, the proverb goes. But the incense is, after all, burned in offering to the legend, to the saint's ultimate meaning to the faithful, to his followers' urge for enlightenment. And so it was that the Lombardi injunctions from the Book of St. Vincent were meant to polarize in their absolutism, bound to produce jeers or adulation. A few simple Lombardi admonitions:

"There are three important things in life: family, religion, and the Green Bay Packers."

"Fatigue makes cowards of us all."

"You've got to be mentally tough."

"There is no substitute for work."

"There is only one yardstick in our business and that is winning. Second place is meaningless."

"I will try to make of each of you the best football player he can possibly be. I will try with every fiber in me, and I will try and try and try."

Before going to Green Bay I had read all of the available book and magazine Lombardiana. As a fan I had watched the televised drama of the Packers' great championship games over the years—a drama, we were all reminded by zoom shots, that was staged by the sheer will power of the squat Italian-American standing on the side lines in the fur cap and camel-hair overcoat. It seemed that, on the record at least, Lombardi's central qualities were a monolithic ego and formidable intelligence, a spiritual hunger that bordered on religiosity, and a natural exuberance that he distrusted and refused to value except as an instrument to lead men.

The ego had forged his indomitable pride, his extraordinary

sensitivity about himself (matched by an equally extraordinary insensitivity to others), his ambition, his decisiveness, and his combative need to win. His intelligence had taught him self-control and had allowed him to fashion the fundamentals of football into a compact and highly organized system. His spiritual side was grounded in order and unyielding faith. It was not for nothing that Fordham taught its sons the texts of St. Thomas Aquinas and St. Augustine. He demanded loyalty and the acceptance of order. His spiritual faith led him to reduce moral issues to black and white, to give him a strong didactic streak, and to infuse him with an absolute disregard for pain and discomfort. His exuberance allowed him to communicate with his team, to bend them to his will, to make him in the end—for all his dictatorial qualities and pettiness—a "likable bastard," as one Green Bay front-office employee put it.

These are traits of both considerable virtue and potential danger, for circumstances can make them go either way. They are traits that can break men. Lombardi is a man, then, who truly seems to hinge on success or failure. If his teams are winners, they owe it all to Lombardi—their money, their fame, and their pride. If his teams are losers, it is Lombardi's doing as well and there will be jackals laying in wait. Forty football players will pay the Lombardi price of anguish, humiliation, and bodily punishment to win, but not to lose.

The Packers are the oldest franchise in the NFL, founded in 1919 by Curly Lambeau, with jerseys provided by the Indian Packing Company. Lambeau was to remain as head coach for thirty years. Some of his Packer teams were great ones and six were NFL champions.

When Curly Lambeau died in 1967, there was considerable local sentiment for renaming the city stadium after him. The team's nominal rulers, the seven-man executive committee, thought it a fitting tribute, but Lombardi demurred. Call it Green Bay Stadium, he suggested; no one knew who Curly Lambeau was anymore, and why have TV announcers mumbling "Curley Lambeau Field," when they could just as easily give Green Bay a little national exposure. Lombardi was overruled by the executive committee, however, and Lambeau Field it is. Cynics might say, and did, that it grated Lombardi to play on a field named after his illustrious predecessor.

I took a cab out to Lambeau Field, located at 1265 Lombardi Avenue, to talk to the players and coaches who had worked for Lombardi. Lombardi memorabilia were pointed out to me: the League's first wall-to-wall carpeted dressing room; the divot in the conference-room carpet where Coach had erected a golf net to perfect his game ("You know," he once said, "with my temperament I could have been a great professional golfer, except for one thing—I can't play golf very well"); the three-tiered sauna bath with benches like Roman banquet couches. Publicity director Chuck Lane took me for a tour of the stadium. The Packer management was talking about building an all-weather dome complete with astroturf; they had to come up with some money-squandering scheme to spend what I was authoritatively told was $3.2 million in liquid assets.

One such "improvement" was the new press box high above the stadium. The windows on all but one of the boxes were louvered. "The window that's sealed up is where Coach used to sit last year when he was general manager," Lane explained. "Why is that," I joked, "so Lombardi wouldn't jack open the window and yell down, 'Bengtson, you dumb son-of-a-bitch, you shouldn't have used a 4–3 defense on that play' "? Lane gave me one of those looks that said you're not as thick as you look.

"Whom the Lord loveth, he chasteneth." It was on Lambeau Field that Lombardi had put this Biblical precept to work, where he had driven his players through the endless repetition of grass drills, windsprints, calisthenics, and the finely honed routine of blocking and tackling that was his style of football.

"There's shape and there's Lombardi shape," Henry Jordan told me. "Lombardi shape's when there's no sweat on your jersey in the fourth quarter when you've been in all afternoon. Shape's the guy across the line from you—the sweat dripping and the eyes glassy."

"Coach drives players hard, himself harder," said assistant coach Dave Hanner, a Packer tackle when Lombardi had taken over in 1959. Hanner should know; he had his appendix cut out some years ago, and Lombardi had him suited up on the football field twelve days later. Gale Gillingham, a Packer guard, broke his hand in the college All-Star camp and was released from the squad as injured. Drafted by the Packers, he reported to their training camp and started practicing the next day.

"Hurt is in the mind," Coach says, quoting his father, Harry Lombardi. This is the Lombardi legend, the tyrant with the rictal grin torturing his post-collegiate innocents, rallying the crippled and dying for one last goal-line stand.

I was told that when Paul Hornung and Max McGee were roommates, they used to stage a ritual game of breaking Lombardi's curfew rules. One night they drew their single beds together, undressed, and when Lombardi made the 11 P.M. bed check, he found the pair of them grinning up at him, naked in one another's arms. "Jesus Christ," Lombardi is supposed to have said, "you guys do need a night on the town." Freudians may gasp but the point is that football players live in a realm that is beyond guilt and the suspicion of sexual ambiguity. "You've got to be mentally tough," Lombardi says, and when a football player loses his supreme confidence in his super-masculinity, he is in deep trouble.

"When Vin gets one he thinks can be a real good ballplayer," Marie Lombardi said, "I feel sorry for that boy. Vin will just open a hole in that boy's head and pour everything he knows into it, and there's no way out of it. I don't want to watch it."

What Mrs. Lombardi does not want to watch is Vin the psychologist at work. His psychological mastery of others suggests a quality of guile, deliberation, and mandarin patience. It is a quality far removed from the stereotyped picture of Lombardi as the impetuous castigator striking out at players at random.

One of the staples of the Lombardi legend is the trade that sent the Packers' seven-time All-Pro center Jim Ringo to the

Philadelphia Eagles. Ringo arrived to talk contract with Lombardi, accompanied by a lawyer. "This is my lawyer," Ringo said. "I brought him since I don't know much about business." "Excuse me for a moment," Lombardi said, leaving the room. Five minutes later he came back and addressed the lawyer. "I am afraid," Lombardi said, "you have come to the wrong city to discuss Mr. James Ringo's contract. Mr. James Ringo is now the property of the Philadelphia Eagles."

Although a good story, it puzzled me. First of all, Ringo was a Lombardi-style player—hard-nosed, 110 percent, all desire. He was an aging All-Pro, but still good market value; he was said to be moody, something of a clubhouse lawyer, the sort of man who might let it be known that he was planning to stick it to Coach when contract time came around. Lombardi, who maintained a sort of oriental espionage network in the dressing room, was probably a step ahead of Ringo. Would it not be crafty to trade Ringo while he was still good value, thereby petrifying any other contract bandits on the team, and then capping the whole affair on an aphoristic exchange with Ringo's lawyer that would make good press copy for years to come? I asked Lombardi about the Ringo trade—if it had happened in a five-minute time span. He gave me a Fu Man Chu scowl. "Hell, no. That's no way to general manage a football team." Might not the Jim Ringo trade have been signed and sealed before Ringo and his lawyer tapped on the general manager's door, I inquired. He gave me a grin. "Yeah, something like that," he said.

Henry Jordan provided still another insight into Lombardi's endless patience and plotting. One day Jordan was passing by Coach's office before a practice session and, peering in, saw Lombardi at his desk making hideous grimaces. "I poked my head in, trying to figure who he was looking at. Damned if he wasn't all alone, trying to get himself mad at us, I guess. That sort of thing takes a lot out of Coach."

The Packers are about 40 percent black and 60 percent white, and they are an integrated society at ease with one another. Rookies are assigned roommates in alphabetical order; Lombardi saw to that. Marv Fleming, a black tight end, arrived at training camp in 1967 and with a big grin flashed calling cards that said Muhammad Fleming. That was the summer of Newark and Detroit. Later that summer the Packers were playing an exhibition in Cleveland, where racial tensions were flaring. In the dressing room someone had pasted bumper stickers proclaiming "Polish Power" over the locker of Zeke Bratkowski, white, and Elijah Pitts, black. The Poles were a dirty word in Cleveland's black ghetto that week, the blacks a dirtier one in the city's East European blue-collar neighborhoods. The Packers roared with laughter. And why not? The team had once given Lombardi a T shirt to take on a hunting trip with a bull's-eye on the back bearing the words "Italian target." And hadn't Coach laughed like hell in that hunting lodge in upper Michigan when he opened the surprise package?

With his players, Lombardi had no obligation to observe the small civilities of life. There was no room for equality between player and coach, underling and boss, so I talked with members of the Packer seven-man executive committee, Lombardi's friends, and Green Bay sportswriters. These were men, I thought, for whom he had no need to practice those solitary grimaces, men who might have seen him waver from the single-minded code of self-discipline and success.

Lombardi's intimate friends were known locally as the "trained seals." I found them approachable, generous, and articulate, radiating self-confidence and success and invariably obsessed with the Great Man. Stories abounded of their washing his golf balls on the links, of Coach yawning at a TV program and his friends outdoing one another to switch channels and denounce the fatuousness of the fare they had been chuckling at moments earlier. "When Vince laughed, the seals roared," a member of the entourage told me.

Yet, there were special dispensations where Lombardi and his friends were concerned. They were small-town men and proud of it, and while they were rich and successful, they were still a little astonished to be buddies with one of the greatest men in America. Lombardi was a windfall none of them could have predicted for themselves, and so they counted their blessings and brought out the worst side of his monumental ego. They laughed at his jokes, applauded his gall and called it charm, washed his golf balls and called it friendship.

I wondered if Lombardi's special affection for Paul Hornung and Max McGee didn't have something to do with the fact that both were lip-offs in a boyish sort of way. Also, by their very wildness, Hornung and McGee brought out Lombardi's reformist zeal, the old Italian *paterfamilias* pride in the prodigal sons who drank raw red wine throughout the night at the village cantina and rose promptly at dawn to attend mass before trudging off to the fields for ten hours of backbreaking work. Lombardi loved their irreverence toward him. Perhaps he felt that boys should have spunk, and that grown men should be serious, even worshipful. His grown friends were all of that and tenaciously loyal as well. There are not many men who command loyalty to the degree Lombardi does, and for that matter, not many who preach it with his Savonarolian intensity. Loyalty is the very heart of the Lombardi code.

Before I went to Green Bay I had heard that Lombardi's abrupt departure to Washington was regarded as a betrayal or at least a deviation from this rigid code of loyalty. I had heard that Lombardi's friends were heartbroken at the furtive manner of his departure and at the back-room arrangements worked out with Edward Bennett Williams and Pete Rozelle.

"To Oley—for his contribution to the Packers and his sympathy and loyalty to me, Vince." So reads the inscription on the smiling ink portrait of Lombardi on the office wall of Packer president Dominic Olejniczak.

"How about the loyalty issue?" I asked Olejniczak, a real-estate entrepreneur and former Green Bay mayor. "Wasn't it true," I said, "that in 1961, when Wellington Mara of the New York Giants wanted Lombardi for head coach, he contacted you as president of the Packers to get permission to sound out Lombardi for the job?"

"That's right," Olejniczak said. "That was the way it

happened in 1961. Vince wanted to take the Giant job, the executive committee turned him down, and he stayed on and continued to do a great job for us."

"Well, then," I said, "when Lombardi asked to be released from his Green Bay contract to go with the Redskins there was no consultation with the executive committee, as there had been in the Mara feeler in 1961. Lombardi had pretty clearly hammered the arrangement out in advance with Edward Bennett Williams and Pete Rozelle before seeking his release."

"Vince was not disloyal. He was general manager of the club, and as such could be approached legitimately by Williams."

"He was also general manager when Mara asked for him," I reminded him.

Olejniczak glared at me and then with a thin smile said, "Let's just say that Wellington Mara is one kind of man and Edward Bennett Williams another."

Still, the loyalty issue hung in the air. I remembered that Jimmy Taylor, the Packers' great fullback and all-time ground gainer, had played out his Green Bay contract to become a free agent and sign with the New Orleans Saints for more money. "Lombardi regarded what Taylor was doing as disloyal to him and the Packers—in that order," I was told. And when Green Bay held a civic testimonial dinner to honor Taylor and Paul Hornung, Lombardi was unaccountably absent—"in New York on business"—in spite of the depth of his feeling for Hornung. Coach did, however, send a telegram; it contained a passage from Cicero on loyalty, obviously meant for the astounded Taylor. It was one of those excruciatingly narrow gestures that make fair-minded men wince.

Packer coach Phil Bengtson sat behind a spheroid-shaped desk in the stadium long office he had inherited from Coach.

"Why did Lombardi go the Redskins?" I asked Bengtson. "Was it a chance to own part of a ballclub, a need to get back into coaching, combined with the knowledge that to do it here would mean you would have to go, a sort of spiritual need to redeem another failure of a team, a sense that the nation's capital was a place that could use a winner at long last?"

"Yeah, those are some pretty good reasons," he said. For a

fraction of a second he shook his head, as if to say, "They're damn good reasons all right, but for Lombardi they just aren't adequate."

Bishop Aloysius Wycislo is the prelate of Green Bay, which is 75 percent Catholic. I was late for my appointment. It was the Bishop's day off, and he was taking the air in the back yard of the immense caboose-red brick residence. It was one of those heavy Victorian piles thrown up across the Midwest in the late nineteenth century. Inside, the institutional carpeting, Morris chairs, antimacassars, Victorian chests, and huge wardrobes proclaimed a Catholic world where the Pope was still infallible, pill and all.

I met the Bishop in his study; he wore a blue short-sleeved shirt, had a high-buffed color in his face, and had gray wavy hair. "I didn't know Vince all that well," he began, "though I've seen him socially and we've worked together on charitable causes for the Church. I suppose you read what I said at the airport when I arrived?"

I admitted I hadn't.

"There was a crowd of welcomers there, and as the TV cameras started to grind, Vince stepped up with a sealed envelope. Inside was a Packer season pass. So I said, 'Apparently, judging from the enthusiasm shown over this season pass you bring to me, you must consider it more important than the Papal Bull that the Holy Father in Rome gave me to bring here to you.' It occurred to me they may have had a good laugh over that sally back at the Vatican, but in Green Bay, with twenty thousand fans on the waiting list for season tickets, you could swap three Papal Bulls and two Apostolic Briefs for one ticket in the end zone."

Having established the primacy of the Church over the Packers in his own mind, the Bishop relaxed. He had obviously done a lot of thinking about Lombardi and was fond of him. "Vince was an old-fashioned Catholic," he told me. "When he'd see me, he'd ask to kiss my ring. I'd joke and say, 'You don't have to do that. It'll only get you ninety-days' indulgence, and football season won't even have begun by then.' 'No,' Vince would say, 'I still want to do it.'"

I noted that Lombardi had once been a seminarian, studying for the priesthood, and asked if he would have made a good priest.

"Yes," the Bishop said. "There is an underlying compassion in the man. This is going to sound peculiar in light of his ego and his temper, but there is a manly humility about him as well. He is a man of tremendous will. He is able to control his life, yet able to let go, to reveal himself—perhaps deliberately —so that people sense some extra quality about him. Before he left I was going to ask him to talk to the priests going through an identity crisis. They respected him."

"Was Lombardi a happy man?" I asked.

The Bishop swiveled in his chair and regarded the wall. "No," he finally said, "I don't think so." He turned back to stare at me. "I think in the whole time I knew him I only saw him happy, truly at ease, just once. It was at a party after a football game, and I can't even recall whether the Packers won or lost, but some friends from his Fordham days were in town. They were playing a word game in Latin, in which the declined endings were cleverly disguised to score points at one another's expense. Your Latin had to be first-rate to play the game and Vince was reveling at it. His Latin was excellent."

I pressed ahead on the problem of loyalty. The Bishop didn't think Lombardi had acted with disloyalty. There were, he said, people in Green Bay who judged Lombardi harshly, who harped on the loyalty theme, who were suspicious of Lombardi as an Easterner.

Finally he said, "You know, a boy serving mass told me, 'I guess he should go to Washington, but how can he be disloyal? It's a good thing for him, my parents say, but I can't believe he'd do it.'"

The Bishop and I mulled that one over. It had a certain finality. Out of the past came the voice of the small boy staring up at Shoeless Joe Jackson after the Black Sox scandal and saying, "Say it ain't so, Joe."

The Bishop seemed serene, unruffled. After all, the Church existed because men were flawed.

It occurred to me that if Lombardi had wanted to get off the loyalty petard he had hoisted himself upon in Green Bay there would have been a graceful way: politics, with its "call to higher duty." Lombardi was clearly a man with a volcano inside him, a sense of destiny, a capacity to move and deeply influence men. He had been offered the lieutenant governor's nomination on the Wisconsin Democratic ticket in 1968, and some said he was even building a state power base for the governorship by entering the public-housing field in Milwaukee. Politics must have tempted Lombardi, a man interested in the exercise of power, the intellect, and the spirit, a man who in his way was the Cardinal Richelieu of the gridiron.

My own hunch is that Lombardi, like most of us, is uncomfortable in a milieu that is strange to him and that he cannot knowledgeably dominate from the outset. Perhaps this is why he went into coaching in the first place, rather than finishing the law degree, which would have been an uncommon asset in the mid-1930's for a poor Italian boy from Brooklyn.

Then, too, there was the image of Lombardi high in the Drake Hotel scanning the Chicago lakefront. "I was at a party with Vince once," a friend told me. "It had been going on for an hour or so, everybody having a good time. Then this sudden look came over Vince's face. 'I think I'll have that first drink now,' he said. You can't imagine the intensity of that look, as if somehow he had been holding himself back, holding himself back all of his life." Was Washington—the capital of the world, as Lombardi has called it—what he had been holding off for?

After I returned from Green Bay, I went to the Redskin offices to meet Lombardi for the first time. My telephone conversations with Redskin officialdom, while arranging for the interview, were punctuated with the familiar yet still unnerving "Coach is ... " and "Coach says ... " and "Coach informs me. ... " "Coach" was always a reverential tone lower than the other words in the sentence. Sonny Jurgensen was making a telephone call in the office next to Lombardi's; the papers said Sonny had referred to Coach as "Mr. Lombardi."

Did he look 110 percent fit and trim? Was there a trace of that spare tire to be seen? I couldn't tell. He had his back to me.

If Lombardi's office in Green Bay resembled a presidential suite in a midwest motel, his Washington hideaway seemed the Hilton Hotel's version: the Prussian blue fabrics and darkly stained Danish furniture created a forbidding atmosphere. Lombardi was a man of character, and it struck me as peculiar that he would choose to work in offices devoid of character, each in its own way.

Lombardi was working at his desk in shirtsleeves when I came in; there was a blue VTL monogram over his breast. He had a modest pile of papers on his desk, which he continued to scratch away at throughout the interview. I had the impression they were not documents of any moment and that by laboring over them he was fulfilling some Puritan need to make wise use of his time.

His teeth and his eyes are his strongest features. From pictures I had expected him to be gap-toothed, but his teeth are set fairly close together; they are just so large and dice-shaped that you tend to see them as individual units rather than as a set. Behind the glasses the eyes are unusually volatile and expressive. His changes of mood are dramatically sudden, and you can read them instantly in the eyes.

He is not an easy man to talk to. He answered my questions directly, often at length, often with style, and always, I felt, with honesty. Yet, there was a quality of reserve and suspicion, greater than the guarded habits of a public man fearful of being misquoted in the press.

When he spoke of football, of Green Bay, and of his background, he was forceful and eloquent—too much so, as if these were answers reeled off many times before. When he spoke about the young, the racial situation, the turmoil everywhere, he was surprisingly humane and reflective.

I asked why he had left the seminary, half-expecting some bombast about his always regretting not being a priest. Instead he said, "You've got to have a vocation. That's why I wasn't a priest. As for why I went to Fordham, I was trying to

get a football scholarship to college, and they gave me one."
I asked what he had learned in his years at West Point. "West
Point taught me discipline, regularity. I guess you'd say order.
Red Blaik taught me the meaning of organization." And then
what? "And then Green Bay taught me to be successful."

"You've got to make a choice between winning and losing,"
he said. "It's a funny thing in football that when a team has a
weakness it always stays with them. There have been NFL
teams that could have been champions except that they lacked
good offensive guards. They trade for them and they draft them,
but year after year guards are always their weakness. And year
after year they're losers."

Everyone in Green Bay had said, perhaps with the gift of
hindsight, that they knew Lombardi was a winner the moment
they laid eyes on him. I asked if he had had any doubts on that
score, if he was apprehensive about taking over a dispirited ball
team. "I've never been apprehensive in my life," he said.
"You've got to do things according to your own personality, and
being apprehensive isn't part of mine."

I asked about a speech he had given to business groups several
years ago in which he had said that the clamor for individual
freedom had been twisted to mean a disrespect for authority. He
had said that 95 percent of men wanted to be led rather than to
lead, and that the call for too much freedom would cut these
people adrift from the stability and values they needed to survive. It was a thesis that had been developed with the usual
Lombardi intensity, the flat assertions of black and white, the
noticeable absence of even the slightest apprehension.

"Long hair doesn't mean anything," Lombardi said. "It may
be dirty-looking and I may not like it, but it doesn't mean anything. But I am disturbed at what's happening. This idea of running free-lance and doing what you please is not freedom, but
license." Then he went on to say that because the old perceived
what the young are doing purely as "license," they feared it and
might seek to repress it with violence and brutality. It would be
a terrible failure, he said, "a sign that they couldn't communicate, because the kids and the discontented have something important to say."

We talked above poverty and racial tensions. "We are our brother's keeper, I don't give a damn what people say," he said. "If people can't find work, whether it's their fault or not, you've got to help them, clothe them, and house them properly, and try to get rid of the conditions that have held them back." He said he is an integrationist, that the problem with black separatism is that black people are not separate and independent. Like everyone else they are dependent on others and need the strength and the size of a whole community. "Any kind of separatism is bad," he said, "in football or anywhere else."

We turned to Green Bay and loyalty. "Don't forget," he said, "I was everything out there when I was coach and general manager. I made a horrible mistake when I stepped out of coaching, but to go back to it in Green Bay would have hurt people."

"Bengtson?" I asked.

"Him particularly. If I were coaching and someone else in the organization were questioning me, I couldn't take it. I could never do that to anyone else. So it's not true that I was disloyal to Green Bay. I think there is always a time when a man who has contributed his life and efforts to whatever should be a part of that whatever. And that's why I came to Washington."

His mouth clamped shut and his eyes said he was through talking. So I left and mulled over what I had heard and seen. My impression was that Lombardi was a man who believed in himself. There was the seminary training, the priest-teachers at Fordham, the eight years in the parochial high school, and West Point. They added up to thirty years in an ivory tower where doubts did not flourish, where there was the wrong way to do things and the Church's way, the wrong way to do things and the Army's way. These were years spent in the company of children, oversized waifs of one sort or another who needed the guiding hand of discipline, regularity, order. It was not a broadening environment, yet clearly Lombardi had transcended it, keeping what was essential in it to quiet his own insecurities and to still the doubts of others.

At bottom, the Lombardi code of excellence is a distillation of those thirty years in the company of children, priests, and soldiers. But it is a distillation with the added mixture of Lombardi himself—larger, subtler, more restless, more complex in a Shakespearean sense than the narrow bounds of the code, the simplistic rules of loyalty and winning. He is not blind to the fact that life is a larger proposition than is taught at Fordham, at St. Cecilia Prep, at West Point, or even in the Packer dressing room. Although he demands that others stay within the limits of the code, he himself will venture beyond it, to test the outer limits. He has described himself as a "conservative" coach. This is true of the "fundamentals" style of football the Packers played and the Redskins were to play, but it is not true of Lombardi. He is, in fact, a gambler, a risk-taker, a man who was willing to pit himself and his system against the long odds of the 1959 Packers. And now he was pitting it against the long odds of the 1969 Redskins.

Chapter 3

The nature of those odds finally dawned when eighty-two ballplayers reported to the Redskin training camp in Carlisle, Pennsylvania, on July 10. Fifty-one of them were veterans, men with an NFL record. Even if their past were largely undistinguished, Lombardi had a certain reputation for reclaiming derelicts and journeymen, for transforming mediocrity into excellence.

Besides, no one really knew whether the Redskins were better or worse than the record they had compiled under Otto Graham. In 1966, Otto's first year, the Redskins had been 7–7, then 5–6–3 in 1967, and finally 5–9 in 1968—a downward parabola certainly, but one that could be explained by circumstances. In 1967 a field-goal kicker, a scintilla of luck, and a handful of defensive plays would have left the team with a 10–4 record and the Capitol Division title. In 1968 Jurgensen had missed the exhibition season after an operation to remove calcium deposits in his throwing elbow. He threw four touchdown passes to win the season opener against the Bears, broke some ribs, and then played the bulk of the season in a protective cast that limited his effectiveness.

Jurgensen, the owner of the best arm in football, was the Redskins. Without him, they were quite possibly the worst team in football; with him, who could tell? He had thrown the ball for more than 400 yards five times in his career, and he had what was called "the quick release," so that on a given day he could beat anyone. As a result, the Redskins had developed a breathtakingly simple game plan: Sonny dropped back and unloaded the bomb. Either he put six points on the scoreboard, or the other team took over on downs; and that was the rub, for when the other team got the ball it did not need a Jurgensen at the throttle to move it on the Redskin defense.

In 1967, a healthy Jurgensen had broken his own NFL record for most passes thrown and most completed. Of 508 balls that went up into the air, 288 came down completed. On the receiving end that year were Charley Taylor at split end, Jerry Smith at tight end, and Bobby Mitchell at flanker. Between them they caught 197 balls and finished one, two, and four in the league's pass-receiving race, the first time in NFL history that three members of the same team had finished that high in the standings.

Such was the Redskin team Lombardi inherited at Carlisle. Offensively, it had an aging quarterback with a mended golden arm, who had the reputation of calling a bad game, of going for broke; a brilliant receiving corps, perhaps the best in pro football; a mediocre collection of running backs; a line that provided adequate pass protection, but lacked the speed to lead the way for the running game; and a weak bench. Defensively, it had a front four that was largely unseasoned and ineffective; one established linebacker; two solid defensive backs; and a weak bench. Above all, it was a team that was demoralized, weary from the debilitation of losing year after year, benumbed by the carping claims from public, press, and coach that down deep the Redskins were losers.

The Redskins and Lombardi had been together for forty-seven days when I arrived at training camp on August 26. Practice had just started when I showed up at the Dickinson College football field. The team was far across the field but I could hear their sighs and groans, as loud and sharp as canvas snapping in the wind. Lombardi watched them for a while, arms akimbo, and then climbed into his ivory electric golf cart and swept noiselessly across the field. He wore a red baseball cap, grey flannel knickers, and a white V-necked T shirt. As he drew closer I could see his teeth, but his expression was lost behind a pair of sunglasses. The golf cart stopped, and Lombardi climbed down from the running board. I walked up to him, and as we stared out over the playing field together,

I was unable to think of anything to say. Lombardi turned his head and looked at me. "I'm sick and tired of this publicity," he said in a tone of deep weariness. "It's gotten out of hand. I just want to be left alone to coach this football team."

I mumbled that he could not stop the publicity and that I wanted to write a book about the making of a football team. He gave me a faint smile and returned to the golf cart. "I'll see you tonight," he said and purred off.

A park bench had been set up in front of the dressing room for the convenience of the press, and I walked back to it, shaking my head, lamenting the banality of my remarks. But I was to find out I was hardly the first man to lose the thread of his thoughts when confronting Coach for the first time at training camp. Later in the season I confessed my failure to second-year linebacker Tommy Roussel. He was a Louisiana boy who'd played his college ball at Southern Mississippi and had been the Redskins' second-round draft choice in 1967. He had a look of collegiate innocence about him, with his jeans, suede saddle shoes, baby-face, curly black hair, and look of boyish befuddlement.

"Listen," Roussel confided, "at least you said something. I came up on the plane and was reading his book, *Run to Daylight*, and right off he's talking about meeting the rookies and he says something like, 'Every year these poor young lads come up to camp from their colleges and every year they're so afraid they won't even look me in the eye.' Goddamn, I thought, not look a man in the eye? It sure must be weird to talk to somebody and not look him in the eye. Not me. And I came to that first meal at the camp cafeteria and there he is standing down at the end of the food line, shaking hands and getting introduced to everybody. So I get my tray full and come walking up to him, and do you know, I couldn't look that man in the eye. I guarantee I couldn't. I just stood there thinking to myself, Goddamn, please don't jump on me right now. Please God, don't let him jump on me until after I eat my supper. Please, God, I got to have some food in my stomach for these drills tomorrow."

I sat in the sun and watched the pass drills some forty or

fifty yards up the field. At length the beat reporters from the Washington newspapers arrived and joined me on the bench. They had been banished from the field, I later learned, because Lombardi thought they were overhearing and printing too many of his legendary off-the-cuff remarks to the players. Before the day was out, this struck me as a futile precaution, since his voice carried with unmistakable clarity from the remotest corner of the field.

"What the hell kind of a play was that? What the hell is going on here, anyway?" Lombardi's voice boomed from fifty yard away.

"What are you?" a reporter asked. "The town crier? Are the British coming?"

"Wake up! You can't just die out there," Lombardi yelled.

"Why can't he die?" a reporter said. "It's a man's privilege."

A bald furtive-looking man, later identified as the team trainer, Joe Kuczo, tried to slip past the press bench unnoticed. Kuczo had been told to keep the team's injuries under wraps.

"How are your troops, Joey?" a reporter asked.

"All right," Kuczo nodded.

"All right? Christ, they're walking around like the Bataan death march. You telling me they're all right?"

Kuczo shrugged. "Well, whatdya ask for, then." He plodded on.

"Don't slow up in the hole. How many times have I told you, don't slow up in the hole," Lombardi sighed from afar to a running back.

"What is he? A gravedigger?" a reporter asked.

The hard news that morning, such as it was, was the impending arrival of the latest waiver prospect, Bob Wade, a defensive back, whom the Redskins had acquired from the Pittsburgh Steelers for one dollar.

Kelly Miller, the equipment manager, a tiny bantam of a man with a perpetual scowl, drove by in Lombardi's golf cart. There was a sea chest marked "fragile" loaded in the back end. "Here comes Wade," a reporter said.

Kelly stopped the cart and heaved the chest to the ground with a ferocity that produced the chief laugh of the day. Although a new arrival, I already sensed the possibility, however ludicrous, that Wade might actually be inside the sea chest. Lombardi, as I learned, would go to almost any length to throw the press off the scent of new personnel.

"You're trying to catch the ball with your wrists," Lombardi told an abject receiver. "In case you haven't heard, the idea is to keep your eye on the ball."

"Who's he talking to?" I whispered.

"Search me," a reporter said. "It must be some new guy. I don't know who they all are, they come and go so fast."

Out on the practice field, a receiver snagged a ball and in a sudden burst of energy legged it out for a touchdown, hoping that perhaps Lombardi would watch the numerals on the back of his jersey grow smaller as he disappeared downfield and remember him favorably when the next player cut was due.

But the race was not always to the swift, nor the praise to the receiver. Lombardi strutted out of the offensive backfield, ripped off his baseball cap, and stared balefully at a linebacker. He was Number 54, Tommy Roussel, according to my roster. "Right over your head, Tommy," Lombardi said in an exasperated voice. "You played that one with your thumb up your nose." This figure of speech was his favorite rebuke to erring pass defenders. Receivers were told they were "catching with their wrists." More than once, the authors of poorly thrown passes were informed they "could not hit a bull in the ass with a handful of peas." It was hard to know the origin of these quaint rhetorical flourishes, harder still to see why they would inspire dread, trembling, and the other Pavlovian responses Lombardi was said to induce when he raised his voice. The most frequent comment of all was, "You are *really* something, *you* are, Mister," which was delivered in a variety of moods, ranging from rage and disgust through amazement and mirth. Lombardi's next most frequent remark was the threat to keep the team on the practice field for varying periods of overtime—an hour, two hours, all day—until they did it right.

One of the team's few moments of triumph that summer had

occurred a little more than a week before my arrival. I was told that Lombardi, furious with the defense during a field-goal drill, had told them they would stay on the field all afternoon until they blocked a kick. On the very first kick, Spain Musgrove, a quick but phlegmatic 270-pound defensive tackle, broke through the line and blocked the field-goal attempt. Defensive back Pat Fisher led the team off the field, leaping up and down, pumping his arms in the air and yelling, "Way to go, Spain, you great big sonofabitch!" Wryly enough, that was the only field goal the Redskins blocked all year.

For the first three weeks of camp Lombardi had held practice sessions both in the morning and afternoon, pushing the team even more than was his custom because he wanted to find out who was "durable." In late August the team practiced in the morning and attended team meetings in the afternoon. The greatest enemy of professional sports is boredom, the aimless standing around that leads to mental flatness, and which Lombardi sought to avoid by his screaming and by the meticulous organization of practices. He followed a precise scenario: he brought the team together at 9:30 A.M. for loosening-up exercises, then split the team into units for special drills, and around 10:30 A.M. reunited the team for an hour's scrimmage. During the unit drills Lombardi spent the bulk of his time with the backs and receivers, but occasionally wandered over to visit the linemen, whipping off his baseball cap, raising his eyes to the heavens, and asking, "What the hell is going on here?" He usually took a daily turn on the seven-man sled, deriving what seemed a sensuous pleasure in being driven around the field. The pop of the linemen cracking into the sled's canvas pads, their gasps and grunts from pushing the device, the hissing release of air as they finally sank exhausted to their knees—these were all distinct and gratifying noises. But I was told that the only way to judge the authority of a block was to ride the sled and feel the sharp sting in your hands that came from the contact of a good block, the kind that would drive an enemy lineman a yard back from the line of scrimmage.

It was getting close to 10:30. "Bring them over," Lombardi

waved to the assistant coaches supervising the linemen on the far side of the practice field. The team trotted over to the regular gridiron for scrimmage. The defensive linemen donned yellow foam-rubber arm pads, as large and puffy as YMCA boxing gloves. The exaggerated whacking noises the pads produced and the sight of them flashing in the air gave the line play an ungainly, faintly comic air. But even though the pads cushioned the blows, and the players had been told to hit at three-quarters strength, the contact was violent enough to hurt. Lombardi stood behind the huddle, his arms folded, watching the action. At length he called a halt to practice; the yellow pads were flung to the side lines, and the team chugged by to the dressing room.

As I watched the players pass, wriggling out of their helmets, I realized that although I had been a Redskin fan for years, I couldn't recognize a single face, with the exception of Sam Huff and Sonny Jurgensen. The regular reporters were in a somewhat different predicament. They could recognize the old guard, the stalwart veterans still on hand from past campaigns. But these faces were dwindling daily as new ones took their place, men whose names and backgrounds were kept a tightly guarded secret.

"Do you suppose he has any new ones today?" a reporter mused aloud.

"How the hell many people is he allowed to have up here now, anyway?" a colleague said, studying the mimeographed roster.

"Maybe he'll give us something today," the first reporter grunted sourly.

Presently Lombardi came out of the dressing room, his flesh tanned, glowing from the shower. He crossed his arms on his chest, leaned a gray suede shoe against the cinder-block wall, and said, "I don't have anything for you today."

"What's the status of Epps?" someone asked. A defensive back from the University of Texas at El Paso, Gene Epps had been the Redskins' top college-draft choice that year.

"Epps got hurt in the All-Star game and doesn't count against the roster," Lombardi said, brushing a fly away from his face.

"How about McLinton?" someone asked of the big rookie linebacker from Southern University who had broken his wrist in the Senior Bowl earlier in the year.

"Same thing," Lombardi said.

"John Love?"

"Military service. Doesn't count either."

"How many people are there up here, anyway?" The flies were now invading in earnest, swarming around our heads. Lombardi brushed them away and transfixed the press with a cryptic smile. "*Nobody* knows how many players we've got," he beamed and walked off.

Sonny Jurgensen came bounding out of the clubhouse, looking as lean as a whippet in his civilian clothes. His paunch was hardly the thing to pester a decent tailor. Certainly it was not nearly as large as Sam Huff's or Joe Rutgens's, both younger men. The problem was that Huff and Rutgens played positions that demanded a little portliness, but Jurgensen was expected to be svelte; he was, after all, the quarterback, whose skills won or lost the game. But there was more than Jurgensen's stomach conspiring against his reputation. He was a personable, gregarious sort of man, who liked to talk and laugh and who had a talent for self-deprecating wisecracks. "All the bartenders in Philadelphia wore black armbands the day I was traded to Washington," he had told a reporter years ago, and it had been requoted in every story written about him since then. "I don't throw with my belly," he reeled off to another writer. I can drink with my left hand," he said when asked if the pain in the calcium deposit in his right elbow would cramp his style. They were good gags, but they had been used to make him seem too nonchalant and a trifle disloyal to the high purpose of football. Perhaps Jurgensen had made a resolution to shed a few pounds and knock off the wisecracks that no longer seemed innocuous. Perhaps, like St. Paul on the road to Damascus, he had been smitten by a vision back in February when he had had his first session with Lombardi and had emerged to tell the press that he had learned more about football in ten minutes with Coach than he had in the last twelve NFL seasons.

In any case, he came out of the Dickinson College dressing room like a shot, a man learning to slouch out of sight in a hurry. Jurgensen is naturally endowed with the mod splotches of color that most people can only acquire from their wardrobe. And there he was, with his tangerine hair, the clear blue eyes, the burnished ruby sideburns, the fair Nordic skin and bright red cheeks.

"I'd like to introduce myself, Sonny," I said, ambling over from the press bench. He took me in at a glance and slipped around the side of the building. As a party of autograph hounds stopped him, I tried again, expressing the hope we could get together soon for a little chat. "That's nice," he said, scribbling his signature frantically, almost desperate in his need to break away from all of us. He finally waded through the children and adults toward the gate, and I repeated my pitch once more. He gave me a look of uncomprehending cordiality and disappeared into a waiting car, a man with a sucked-in stomach and no taste for further publicity.

When practice was over and Lombardi had gone on his way, I asked someone from the Redskin office what Lombardi had meant by saying he would see me "tonight."

"Oh, that's the Five O'Clock Club," he said. "Sort of a happy hour where you have a drink, and the Coach, assistant coaches, the press, and whoever else happens to be in town sit around and talk over the day."

Chapter 4

The Five O'Clock Club was located in a run-down Victorian frame house across the street from the college dorm where the team was quartered. Later, in Washington, a writer who had spent about a week in Carlisle earlier in training camp told me that an artist from his paper had come up for a few days to render a sketch of the Five O'Clock Club, which he had entitled "The Happy Hour." It showed Lombardi sitting on a couch smiling from ear to ear, flanked by the press and the assistant coaches, all of whom wore looks of unrelieved misery.

I did not find the atmosphere at the Five O'Clock Club that forbidding. "The Happy Hour" took its mood from Lombardi, and he was a man who believed in pausing to relax for an hour before dinner. There were some days when he felt satisfied, even exuberant, over what had been done in practice; other days, he was weary, depressed, and pessimistic. But he was never completely at peace, for he was, above all, a man driven by intensity, driven to put his whole nature into the fourteen hours a day of coaching and planning and even driven to try to relax for his own good that one hour before dinner.

When I arrived, Lombardi and the other coaches were out on the back porch taking the air. The coaching staff he had put together had clearly been selected with an eye to bridging the gulf from Green Bay to Washington. Offensive coach Bill Austin, defensive coach Harland Svare, and linebacking coach Sam Huff had known Lombardi from the New York Giant days of the 1950's. The Lombardi system, especially the defense, was an adaptation of the old Giant system, and Huff, Svare, and Austin would have no trouble in teaching it to the Redskins. Austin and receiver coach Lew Carpenter had served with Lombardi at Green Bay, knew the Packer offensive system, and could attest to its success. Running-back coach Dickson was an outsider, with no previous connection with the Packers, the Giants, or the Redskins, but he had a reputation as a savvy football man. Mike McCormack, for the offensive line, and Don Doll, for the defensive backs, were generally regarded as the most able members of the Graham staff; they knew the Redskin personnel and could answer the questions Lombardi would raise.

Lombardi sat on the back-porch stoop, to all appearances as carefree as a coach who had just claimed Dick Butkus, Deacon Jones, and Leroy Kelly from that day's waiver list. Football talk was rigorously eschewed, and when it came time for me to contribute to the discussion, I surveyed the back yard and said, "Gee, that's a small garage out there, doesn't even look big enough to fit a model T." At best, it was a genial observation, certainly one that would not leave me open to the accusation of coming on too strong for my material.

"That's no garage," Lombardi said, bending and straightening his arthritic knee, "that's an outhouse." He looked down at the knee ruefully. "Boy, this thing is troubling me tonight," he said. It always struck me as odd that Lombardi, the apostle of the code that hurt is in the mind, would make such a fuss about his ailing knee and would even wear a voodoo copper bracelet that left green stains on his wrist to ward off the ailment. But as the season wore on and I became more used to seeing him cup that knee, flinch, and look around the room for sympathy, I began to regard the whole production as one of his more endearing mannerisms. After one such performance with his knee, Marie Lombardi is reported to have stared him in the eye and said, "You've got to be mentally tough." No doubt he saw the humor in that— he was not incapable of laughing at his own foibles.

"An outhouse, eh?" I said. "Looks too big for an outhouse."

"It's a double-seater," Lombardi said. "Take a look, if you don't believe me."

I walked over, and sure enough, it was. "Well, I'll say this," I remarked, "the Redskins travel first-class." Lombardi got a fair belt out of that line.

He was waiting for Tim Temerario, the director of player personnel, to arrive with that day's waiver list transmitted from the commissioner's office. Temerario was an owlish, harried-looking man in his fifties, who was expected to know the personal life and football merits of every veteran, rookie, and free agent in the NFL, so that he could tell Lombardi if the player was worth bringing to camp for a trial. Tim had the slow movements and the almost bereaved tone of voice that came from memorizing stacks of personnel dossiers. And he had to know them, because Lombardi was in relentless quest for people, players, bodies, horses—the ones he already had and the ones he might acquire.

More than anything else, it was the football players who had shaped his moods during the long summer. I was told that on some nights the daily waiver list would arrive on the TWX machine, Lombardi would stare glumly at Temerario, and without even consulting the list say, "Take the whole damn bunch." Other nights he would find the name of a Packer or an ex-Packer in whom he had seen some potential in the past, and he would crow with delight. Sometimes, there was a player who had had a good day against Green Bay in the past, and Lombardi would figure that a man who had shown he could run against the Packer line or break through to dump Bart Starr was a man worth having. And some nights, he would discern in the thin ranks of his own inheritance a momentary sign of greatness and would boast that he would make Willie Banks pull as fast and powerfully as Jerry Kramer, that he would tap Spain Musgrove's vast potential, that he would make tackle Frank Bosch as quick as Henry Jordan, and rookie linebacker John Didion as savage as Ray Nitschke.

Chapter 5

The Redskins were the first NFL team to open training camp, and of the eighty-two veterans, rookies, and free agents who came to Carlisle on July 10, only thirty-two of them would survive the year. Eight-year-veteran defensive tackle Joe Rutgens was one of the first players to arrive. He was a great favorite of the Washington fans, known for his flying shirt-tail, his quickness, and his lateral movement at the line of scrimmage —characteristics all the more improbable because of his spindly legs, sway-back, and truckdriver's belly. The day before practice was scheduled to begin, Rutgens wandered out to the Dickinson field to survey the training equipment Lombardi had brought: the tackling dummies, sleds, exer-genie, the universal gym, and the other miscellaneous gadgetry of football. He spied Lombardi's golf cart parked by the dressing room and said, "They'll throw the bodies in the back to haul them off after they collapse." It was a comment that set the mood of camp.

On the night of July 10, Lombardi called the team together and gave his traditional speech of welcome, an oration honed to crisp perfection in the Packer training camp at St. Norbert's College outside Green Bay, but one that now contained some new variations for changed circumstances. "I've never been with a loser, gentlemen," he began, "and I don't intend to start at this late date. You're here to play football, and I'm here to see you play as well as your God-given abilities will allow. And that means total dedication. I want total dedication from every man in this room, dedication to himself, to the team, and to winning. Winning is a habit, gentlemen. Winning isn't everything, it's the only thing. If you can shrug off a loss, you can't be a winner. The harder you work, the harder it is to lose. And I'm going to see that you work, I'm going to see that you execute, I'm going to push you and push you and push you because I get paid to win and so do you. Football is a violent game. To play you have to be tough. Physically tough and mentally tough. And you've got to have pride, because when two teams meet that are equal in ability and execution it's the team that has pride that wins. Gentlemen, let's be winners! There's nothing like it." At this point he raised his arms in the air, wriggling his fingers. The Redskins could notice the gleam of refracted light in the air, the glitter of not one "world championship" ring, but a whole fistful of them. He had worn them all, every one, and the Redskins were damned impressed.

Practice began in earnest the following morning, with forty ups-and-downs to test the springy legs of eighty-two fore-warned men. Sam Huff was reported to be the first to show signs of caving, rising to one knee and then the other, like a game but punch-drunk pugilist. "Lead 'em around the goalpost, Sonny," Lombardi barked out when the exercises were over, and a startled Jurgensen puffed toward the goal-line, followed by a pack of eighty-one ballplayers thankful to be at the heels of such a distinguished if sluggardly pacesetter. The performances of Huff and Jurgensen that day were to prompt the most inspired skit of the rookie show in late August. First year Negro linebacker Harold McLinton played Lombardi with false nose on. "Lead 'em around the goalpost, Sam and Sonny," he boomed, and rookies John Didion and Gene Epps, both padded with pillows, crawled across the stage, panting, stretching out one arm and then slithering forward, like thirst-crazed legionnaires in the desert.

In the first wind-sprint drill, Lombardi blew his whistle and strutted up to a player. "Hold it, Mister," he said. "What did I say? I said sprint. If you quit on me now, you'll quit on me in the last two minutes of a game."

The first cut of the season was then made. The player to win this dubious honor was a first-year running back named, of all things, Sir Prince Borton. Sir Prince was described by one observer as having "thighs so fat it looked like he'd have trou-

ble getting one out in front of the other." As I let that wonderful name, Sir Prince Borton, roll off my lips I had to think that
Lombardi had invited him to camp in the first place for the
exquisite pleasure of announcing to the press that his first cut
was a man named Sir Prince Borton. "Sir Prince Borton?" the
reporters would say, blinking. "Yes," Lombardi would grin,
" Sir Prince Borton." Sir Prince had had little opportunity to
show his stuff, such as it was. Lombardi had taken one look at
him and whispered to an assistant, "Get him out of here
before he gets hurt." And this of course was more than a
humanitarian gesture, since an injured player becomes the re-
sponsibility of the club and Lombardi as general manager and
part-owner would not relish signing a payroll check for a
recuperating ballplayer who had no chance to make the club.
Much as he enjoyed the memory of Sir Prince's presence in
camp, he preferred that regally named young man to work out
his own destiny in his own good time and at his own expense.

In the afternoon practice session, Joe Rutgens banged the
blocking sled and injured his knee. "Our best lineman," Lombardi muttered as Rutgens hobbled from the field, without the
benefit of the golf cart. That night at the training table Lombardi demonstrated another of his preoccupations: diet. The
Dickinson cafeteria staff had spent the afternoon skewering
up steak-kabobs—a mushroom, a baby tomato, a hunk of green
pepper, a tiny piece of steak, a mushroom, etc., etc. Five minutes before dinner was scheduled to begin, Lombardi in-
spected the kitchen, where the staff proudly flourished the
skewered delicacies, beaming at their handiwork. No, said
Lombardi; it was nice, but it wouldn't quite do. Didn't they
know that broiled tomatoes, mushrooms, and green peppers
were indigestible, would sit heavily on the stomach, and
would in fact, have a tendency to rise during grass drills? In
due course the team was served a Spartan meal of broiled
steak chunks. Fried foods were another Lombardi bête noir.
Once, having bitten into a hamburger at lunch, his jaw
dropped open, a steaming piece of hamburger meat on the
floor of his mouth. His tablemates thought perhaps he had
bitten his tongue by mistake, or accidentally touched the ex-

posed nerve in a cavity. "Goddamn it," Lombardi said, "it tastes fried to me," and stormed off to dress down the culprits in the kitchen.

The second day of practice, first-team defensive tackle Walter Barnes was dogging it during the grass drills, running in place while the other players were dropping. "What the hell is wrong with you?" Lombardi said. "I've got this thing in my knee," Barnes explained earnestly. "You can't play this game with things, Mister," Lombardi roared. Pat Richter was shown the "proper" way for a tight end to block, and he broke his nose on the first try. Later that day, rookie receiver Bob Shannon collapsed on the way to dinner, and Charley Taylor broke a bone in his hand; Lew Carpenter told Taylor that he had played for the Packers with a broken hand and not to worry about it.

The following day Taylor, Barnes, and Shannon were back at practice. Taylor, who had been something of a hypochondriac under Otto Graham, got through the day with no audible whimper. Barnes got sick to his stomach during grass drills, but kept on going. Lombardi came up to Shannon and told him, "Take it easy and don't kill yourself; you've got a good chance to make the team."

You could be cynical and say that Lombardi was anxious to avoid another medical bill, but there was, I came to believe, more to it than that. Lombardi's athletic code, his insistence on playing hurt were rigid beliefs. Trainer Joe Kuczo was to say that, in his twenty-five years of tending àthletes, he had never seen a coach who pushed injured players more than Lombardi. He was also to add that he had never realized before that athletes could play so well with injuries that seemed disabling.

There was room for distinction, however, within the Lombardi code. Athletes like Taylor and Barnes, both veterans and both first-string players the year before, were expected to practice hurt because they were expected to make the team, and if they made the team, they were expected to play hurt in a game. Lombardi made no exceptions for first-string players. But he did make allowances for players who showed some potential, who were on the border line of making the club or being cut. Shannon was such a player; John Hoffman, the big rookie free-agent defensive end who had pulled a leg muscle the first day of camp, was another. Lombardi believed in giving men a chance, and it was hard to generalize about him. If he was often harsh, he was sometimes also generous.

Professional football is not a world like the theater or the ballet, where sexual deviations are shrugged off. Love beads and long hair are considered depraved by the average football coach and homosexuality a crime of almost unspeakable dimensions. There was a player on the Redskin roster who was widely reputed to be a homosexual. I could not envy the man the physical skill that had led him into professional sports as a livelihood. His life would be one of ill-concealed smirks when he entered the shower room and of occasional challenges to fight like a "man." I was authoritatively told that the player's "problem" had come up at a coach's meeting in a less than charitable fashion. Lombardi was reported to have winced and said that he had never felt so strongly about a player making the club. He had said that if there was a chance for this player to prove he could do the job, he would lean over backwards to keep him on the roster, for he believed the man was a victim of prejudice. He had added that some of the Redskins wouldn't associate with the player and that he hoped he could help in some way by showing that he, at least, was in the player's corner. One of the assistant coaches had said that he thought placekicker Charlie Gogolak, a Princeton man, was probably treated worse by the team because of his Ivy League background. No, said Lombardi, Gogolak was a lawyer, a smart kid with everything going for him. The other kid had nothing going for him, and he worried what the player could do to make a living if he couldn't make it in professional football.

Football was a "man's" game, and as such its borders were sketched in boyhood with its small cruelties, its distaste for misfits and odd balls, and its herd mentality. There were not many men in professional sports who had spent a lifetime in that atmosphere and had risen above it. In many areas, Lombardi had.

Training camp was six days old when Lombardi faced his first crisis, a walkout by three rookie bonus babies, though none of the three had commanded much signing money. Of the three, only Bill Kishman, a fifth-round defensive back, had looked as if he had had a good chance to make the club. Lombardi told the press, "They didn't want to make football a career, they said. They loved the game a week ago and now they don't like it, but all three took bonuses. This is an example of the moral code of our country. This is what our colleges are turning out."

Kishman announced that he had left camp because he had decided in his senior year at Colorado State that football was no longer fun. He took offense at the insinuation that he had cheated, that he was a bum. "If we represent the worst in America for doing what we did, then I'd have to say the youth of America are in pretty good shape," he noted tartly.

In Lorain, Ohio, however, Bill's mother said that she and her husband were "bitterly disappointed" by their son's behavior. "I feel for him," Mrs. Kishman said. "He ought to be able to take it. He wasted a wonderful opportunity. Bill is no baby. He should have been able to take anything Lombardi dished out." Good old Mom! She knew how to stand by her son!

As July wore on into the dog days of August, Lombardi began to realize with increasing clarity that the team he had inherited showed only pale and flickering traces of the mighty Packers, who were never far from his thoughts. There was no Willie Davis or Henry Jordan breaking into the enemy backfield, no Fuzzy Thurston and Jerry Kramer to lead the Packer sweep, and no Paul Hornung or Jimmy Taylor to run it.

The defensive line was not as quick and mean as he had hoped he could make it. The offensive line lacked the mobility to flare off the line quickly and had trouble adjusting to Lombardi's blocking technique. The running game was better than in 1968, but still less than explosive. Rookie Larry Brown had been impressive from the start of camp, and Bob Brunet looked good, but they were both essentially halfbacks who lacked the size and straight-ahead power for the short, crucial inside yardage. The linebackers looked acceptable, the secondary adequate. Only the receiving corps and the quarterback had the aura of championships.

Lombardi also knew that a championship club needed an experienced backup quarterback. Zeke Bratkowski had come off the bench on more than one occasion to win a key ballgame in the great Packer years. At Washington, his backup quarterbacks were young and untested. Moreover, you didn't win a championship without a defensive line or without an offensive line. Most of all, you didn't win the kind of game Lombardi had always won without a ground game that could assure ball control.

The Redskin rookies had gone to Baltimore to play the Colt rookies on July 20, and won 10–7. Some years earlier Edward Bennett Williams had told Colt owner Carroll Rosenbloom that the Redskins would beat the Colts that year. Rosenbloom had snorted and said that there would be a man on the moon before the Redskins ever whipped the Colts. On the day of the rookie game, therefore, at 4:17 P.M., EST, two astronauts from Apollo 11 landed on the surface of the moon, and Rosenbloom was made to seem unusually prescient. There was satisfaction there, a symbol of grandeur perhaps to come. But Lombardi was looking for more than symbolic gestures, and even though the rookies had won and some of them had looked good, the two quarterbacks, Gary Beban and Danny Talbott, had not been overly impressive.

A week later, Lombardi and Ed Williams sat with the motion-picture crew on the roof of Dickinson Stadium and watched the annual intersquad scrimmage. Lombardi was not pleased with what he saw and trekked down to the field to chew out the offense, man by man. The regular NFL referee for the occasion, Bernie Ulman, wandered over to the bench to tell Lombardi that the two-minute warning was in effect. "I'll tell you when this game is over," Lombardi told the startled official. This announcement, delivered in a thin voice of menace, so galvanized the offense that they moved the length of the field to score on a series of sweeps and off-tackle runs.

The exhibition season opened in Washington against Lombardi's old rivals, the Chicago Bears. The game was played in a deluge of rain that turned the field into a swamp. The Redskins gained a total of 92 offensive yards to the Bears' 146, but Washington won 13–7 on two intercepted Chicago passes.

Sam Huff carried one in for a touchdown, and linebacker Tom Roussel picked off the other one and carried it down to the Bears' 31-yard line. Surveying the trampled, muddy field, Bob Short, whose Washington Senators still had two months of baseball to play in the stadium, threatened a lawsuit against the Redskins. He correctly claimed that the right field had been turned into a grassless dirt heap, but the suit never materialized, probably because, as one sportswriter told me, no jury would ever decide in Short's favor once the Redskins showed the court the movies of their running game.

Still the Bears game was a victory, and Lombardi believed in victories. Some were sweeter than others, to be sure, but even if the Redskins had looked less than dazzling, they were still 1–0. Winning was the name of the game. A habit in fact.

The Redskins went on to Buffalo, home of the Bills, whose 1968 record as the worst team in professional football had earned them the right to draft O. J. Simpson, but even without Simpson, who was holding out for more money, the Bills won 21–17. Jurgensen played virtually the whole game to no avail as the Redskin running game fell to pieces. A Charlie Gogolak field-goal attempt was blocked, and Bobby Mitchell dropped a touchdown pass alone in the endzone. The best Lombardi could muster for the press was the long-range prognostication, "We'll have a winner here eventually." Mrs. Lombardi was more candid. A member of the Redskin family had watched the game on TV and told her the camera work was so bad you couldn't even follow the Redskin runners. "It's probably just as well," she sighed. Well, if winning was the name of the game, losing one every now and then was the nature of the beast. But to the Bills? To the Buffalo Bills, a team that had won one game the year before in the American Football League, which Lombardi was known to hold in low esteem?

When the team returned to Carlisle, Lombardi told them he was going to stop being a "nice guy" and become a "sonofabitch." He told the coaching staff that night, "They think I'm kidding about being a sonofabitch, but I'm not. I'm going to become a sonofabitch for real." During the game movies in the student center the next day, the coed at the reception desk down the hall from the meeting room with its thick closed door cringed and held her ears. Later, when the meeting was dismissed, the players came out like zombies, and one stopped at the desk to tell the girl they'd only gotten through the first half of the films. "The worst is yet to come," he said, mindful that the Redskin collapse had occurred in the second half of the game.

It was a time for Draconian measures, and Lombardi had never shunned them when the need arose. Regular cornerback Aaron Martin fell on his face trying to tackle Larry Brown, and Lombardi hovered over his prone defensive back. "If you don't tackle, you don't play the game, Mister," he said, and gestured for another cornerback. Mike Bass, a free agent released from the Detroit Lions cab squad, came in and remained the regular cornerback for the rest of the season. Martin was ultimately waived.

As August wore on, Lombardi was still restlessly searching for the right combinations, hoping that somehow he had overlooked that thin vein of talent that would lead to the mother lode. He was worried, for his time was running out. He brought a rookie quarterback, Buster O'Brien, to camp for a trial. Why at this late date? he was asked. "Well, he completed 39 out of 51 in a bowl game, once," Lombardi said wistfully. "We can't complete that many playing catch." But the hard reality of making do with what he had on hand was facing him, and he began to pare away at the roster. Tight end Ken Barefoot was traded to Detroit for a draft choice; running back Vilnis Ezrens, in camp on a look-see deal with the Rams, was sent back to Los Angeles; Ray MacDonald, the 1967 first-round draft choice was waived; Walter Barnes, the defensive tackle with the bad stomach, was put on waivers, went unclaimed, and was released. They came and they went by the dozen.

On August 22, the Redskins went to Atlanta to play their third exhibition game, this one against the Falcons, a team whose 1968 finish had entitled them to pick second in the college draft, right on the heels of the Bills. Here was a chance to boost the exhibition record to 2–1, to be a winner once more, and the Redskins took it, beating the Falcons 24–7. Although Jurgensen hit on seventeen of twenty-two passes, most of them were quickies to backs, and the game was closer than the score indicated. After the game, Falcon coach Norm Van Brocklin, prominent for his blunt home truths, dropped by for a word with Lombardi. "Well," said the Dutchman, "you slopped through that one, didn't you?"

The line had the ring of an epitaph, but Lombardi was in no mood to pout over a victory. Bob Shannon, the rookie wide receiver who had been advised to take it easy the first day of camp, appeared at the team bus outside the stadium with his girlfriend and astounded everyone by asking Lombardi if she could ride back to the hotel with the team. "Sure, why not?" said Lombardi with a big smile.

The next morning, perhaps emboldened by Lombardi's jolly exchange with Shannon, four players overslept and missed the team bus to the airport. Nine-year-veteran defensive end Carl Kammerer was the first to arrive, his cab screeching up to the ramp of the chartered United jet. All eyes were forward as Kammerer's terrified face peeped around the front of the first-class cabin. "You ought to have a keeper," Lombardi said. "Yes, sir," said Kammerer, slinking down the aisle to the tourist class. The next three players, defensive halfback Pat Fisher, rookie defensive tackle Fred Sumrall, and linebacker Tommy Roussel arrived together. "You all got to have a keeper from now on," Lombardi told them. Roussel and Sumrall looked stupefied with fear; Fisher was grinning. "What the hell were you smiling about?" the team asked him later. "Because I knew he was going to yell," Fisher said. "Besides, I couldn't help thinking about Roussel's face." Roussel, in spite of his baby-face, had a heavy beard and was clean-shaven on one side, but bearded on the other. Fisher and Roussel had roomed together, and when the phone call had come to tell them to get ready and come down to the bus, Roussel started to go back to sleep. "We're going to miss the bus," Fisher told him, and Roussel sluggishly got up and went into the bathroom to shave. Fisher packed his bag hurriedly and yelled from the door, "I'm going down, see you later." At this Roussel suddenly came alive, his plight all at once dawning on him. "Don't leave me, don't leave me," he begged, heaving his razor in the bag and jumping into his clothes.

But Lombardi was not so amused and returned to Carlisle to reshuffle what he already had and scour the waiver list to find what he still needed. Gary Beban was moved from quarterback to flanker, Marlin McKeever from tight end to outside linebacker, and running back Henry Dyer was purchased from the Giants. The day before I arrived, Larry Rakestraw, Don Shy, Terry Fleetenberg, Bob Wade, and Leo Carroll appeared on waivers, and Lombardi claimed them all; the clubs involved recalled on all except Wade. Just the same, that day after practice, a reporter said, "There are some new faces around here today, aren't there?" "Yes," said Lombardi, "some new faces," and stalked off.

Chapter 6

Three days after I arrived in camp, the Redskins were to fly to Tampa, Florida, for a nationally televised Saturday-night game with the Detroit Lions. It would be the nation's first glimpse of the Lombardi Redskins, and the practice that Friday hardly seemed auspicious for its viewing pleasure. Running back Gerry Allen ran a side-line pattern, muffed the catch, and punched his palm in frustration. Lombardi came out of the backfield and paced off the route of the pattern, showing Allen where to make his cut, pointing down at the spot on the turf like a master indicating to his puppy where the newspaper was. Allen tried again, and instead of running the square-out Lombardi had just ordered, did a little button-hook. Lombardi was aghast. "That's just the opposite of what I told you," he said, his voice jagged with anger. "Someone was on me," Allen replied in a reedy voice. Lombardi sucked in some air and opened his mouth as if to explode. Then he suddenly stopped, blowing the air back out, apparently recalling some arcane instruction that gave Allen the option of changing his pass route. "That's right," he mused and then let out a big laugh. "Hey, that's right. That's good. Atta way to think in there, Gerry."

The team moved over to the regular gridiron, and the press corps ambled over to the stands. Presently we were joined by Marie Lombardi. She had never missed a game played by a Lombardi-coached team, was something of a self-styled den mother on the away-game flights, and had driven up from Washington to ride to Tampa on the chartered team flight. She is a slender woman in her early fifties, rather attractive with blond hair, angular features, and an ironic shrug and voice. The only times I saw her during the season were at games or on the way to them, and there was always the sense that she regarded those football weekends as more of an obligation than a pleasure.

As she sat down with us in the stands, she lit a cigarette and showed around a charm bracelet with gold footballs hanging from it. She explained that two of the golden pigskins were for Lombardi's high-school championships, two from his coaching days at Fordham, two from Army-Navy games, and the rest for Green Bay Championships. "I had to take some of the high-school footballs off," she said. "It got too heavy."

"Yes, when you win so many championships it gets vulgar," one of the reporters said.

She laughed and shook the bracelet. "There's a stone in here that's loose in its setting," she said. "I have to put cotton-batting in there to keep it from rattling. The noise drives HIM crazy." She seemed to take immense pleasure in this last revelation, as if savoring the knowledge that she held the key to her husband's sanity, could pluck out the piece of cotton if he got out of hand. As I came to know her better, however, I learned that the ironic manner she assumed when talking about Lombardi was pure smokescreen. At bottom she was ferociously loyal to her husband, and was a skilled infighter on his behalf. In the end it seemed to me that the Lombardis had achieved that rare American ambition, a happy marriage. On the face of it Lombardi did not seem to be the easiest man in the world to live with. Certainly I never heard even the most admiring Redskin express the hope that his daughter would grow up to marry a man like Coach. And yet, there it was: Lombardi had married a nice woman, and they seemed happy together.

Down on the field Lombardi grabbed a running back by the shoulder pads. "Goddamn it, can't you remember," he said, "That's not the way you shift. One, two, three," he roared, marching the man three steps.

Marie shrugged.

"Goddamn it, that's the worst running I've ever seen," he yelled a few plays later. "We're going to stay out here until four o'clock this afternoon."

"Hey, Marie, give us a tip," a reporter asked. "We going to make that plane on time?"

"Sure," she said.

A hearse at the head of a long cortege of cars came down the road along the side of the practice field. Mrs. Lombardi looked at the funeral procession, exhaled a long jet of cigarette smoke, and said, "Do you think they'll stop to watch practice?"

"That's the way the deceased would have wanted it," I said.

"Well, if they do," she dead-panned, "I hope Vin stops swearing."

The Lions game was another disaster. The Redskins drew first blood on a 15-yard Gogolak field goal. Then the Lions marched 80 yards for a touchdown. The Redskins ended the first half with an 80-yard scoring drive of their own, capped by a 25-yard Jurgensen-to-Jerry Smith touchdown pass. The Redskins added another field goal, this one a 34-yarder, early in the third period, then tried for another. It was blocked, and Lion cornerback Lem Barney scooped up the loose ball and went down the side line for a touchdown. The Lions added another score after a long drive, climaxed by a 24-yard pass to Mel Farr in the end zone. Then, with time running out, Redskin strong safety Brig Owens intercepted a pass that set up a touchdown run by Gerry Allen a few plays later. It was then Lions 21, Redskins 20, and that was the way it ended a few minutes later after the Redskin on-side kick failed. It had been a sloppily played game and a costly one for the Redskins. Free safety Tommy Brown suffered a shoulder separation, running back Bob Brunet got a concussion, and defensive end Jim Norton had his ankle fractured when teammate Carl Kammerer fell on top of him. It was to be a costly game for Charlie Gogolak as well. Lombardi was suspicious of soccer-style kickers, "sidewinders" as he called them, and felt that their trajectory was too low. He decided to deactivate Gogolak and to try rookie placekicker, Curt Knight, in the next two exhibition games. "Our kicking game," he explained, "is the laughing-stock of the league."

Lombardi, I was told, had delivered a ripsnorting phillipic in the clubhouse after the Lions game. On the plane he had doubled up with the chest pressure that assaults him after a loss, seething with agony as intense as that of any out-of-shape 270-pounder at grass drills. After his recovery he asked for a flight manifest and drew up a team depth chart on the back of the paper. He then turned the manifest right-side up and cut the squad on the spot, placing an "X" beside the unlucky names.

Nonetheless, it is an injustice to Lombardi to pretend that he is all excoriation and hot rage on the gridiron, in the clubhouse, and on the team plane. He is a man who yields to the pull of his emotions, but if he is often angry, he is also often cheerful. The difference is that the first mood is more noticeable than the second. His gift is for intensity rather than blandness, and he had trouble coming to terms with that fact about himself. Nothing pained him more deeply than the impression in the land that he was the meanest man in football, a profane, heartless despot tyrannizing youngsters with peach-fuzz on their faces. He blamed the press for creating this image, and he thought that writers pandered to the public need for more of it. What he overlooked was the nature of fame, which feeds on its possessor's strongest, most dramatic characteristics. And while Lombardi had ridden the crest of pro football's wave, had become one of the most dominating personalities in the pantheon of the American Dream, he was still a man who had been shaped by the obscurity of his own past, those days at St. Cecilia Prep, Fordham, and West Point. No one had noticed him then, and that must have grated, for he was surely a man who yearned for the sort of recognition that Red Blaik enjoyed. When Blaik had been a national figure in the 1940's and early 1950's, football had been cocooned in the illusion of moral uplift. Coaches were pictured as saintly men who beamed encouragement to their charges, taught them the good clean virtues of the American Way. The harshness of the coaching vocabulary, the violence of football, its unremitting pressure on fragile human vessels—this was all shrouded from view. Now football was a big business and all that had changed. No one was prepared to regard Lombardi as a saintly, gentle man. They saw him as a ruthless business tycoon who got ahead because he was tough and brooked no obstacles. Indeed, it was this toughness that delighted the Lombardi supporters out in Middle America. The country needed more screamers, more no-nonsense men.

I once asked Lombardi who his favorite sportswriters were. He thought a while and then said that most of them were dead. It was a lament like that of an aged literary man surveying the current titles from Grove Press and wondering what had happened to authors like Arnold Bennett, Hugh Walpole, and Galsworthy, fellows you could read aloud to the family after dinner.

Lombardi did not like the press, then, because, as Spiro Agnew pointed out, it had a tendency to dwell on bad news. The reporters led their stories with an account of the scream that punctuated a busted play rather than the unobtrusive pat on the rump that followed a well-executed one. In addition, he distrusted writers because he feared that in their need to say something every day, they would push back the boundaries football had erected to keep the public ignorant of the game's real nature. "You see too damn much," he had told one Washington reporter, who had noticed a shift of personnel in the first-string defensive unit at practice. In a nutshell, they saw too much and they asked too many questions.

Coming to Washington had exacerbated the problem. When Lombardi went to Green Bay in 1959 he was a nonentity nationally, but in Washington great things were expected of him, and soon. Like it or not, he was Vince Lombardi, and the news media were going to tell the country he was still the same old Coach everyone had heard about. So Lombardi had been under pressure to produce from the moment he had stepped up to the nest of microphones in the Sheraton-Carlton Hotel back in February, and the pressure had started to build from the moment the grass drills had begun on July 10. Lombardi was a great believer in pressure, in submerging yourself in it until you mastered it, but there was one difference now. In Washington he was working with ballplayers he did not know and who did not know him, except to hold him in awe because of what they had heard and read. In Green Bay he had had a team that was used to him and that had proved able to thrive on an extra turn of pressure each year. The pressure he exerted in Green Bay had been an evolutionary process, a decade in the making. But to have picked up in Washington where he had left off in Green Bay would have been a revolutionary change for the Redskins, a departure so radical as to risk the destruction of the team. For the secret of pressure was knowing when to stop, and the 1969 Redskins had a lower tolerance for it than the 1967 Packers had had. The question was, would Lombardi recognize this, realize that he was starting all over again from scratch as in 1959, not just picking up the 1967 reins again after a year on the side lines. The doubt that surrounded that proposition was the nature of the pressure that faced the Redskins. They ran the risk of being broken. The nature of the pressure that faced Lombardi was that he could never go back to 1959. His legend would never permit it.

In 1959 Lombardi took over the Packers and said he would have a championship in five years. People scoffed at him. In 1969 if he had said he expected a championship in five years, people would have scoffed once more, but for different reasons. Five years for a championship? Hell, Otto could have done better than that. Five years? What are we paying him all that money for if that's the best he can do? Is he Vince Lombardi, or isn't he?

Yes, Lombardi was in something of a bind. He had, in the words of the sports clichés, put it on the line, hung it all out. Time and personnel were not on his side. He had not inherited a young and malleable team, as he had in Green Bay. Trades had taken away his top draft choices for 1968 and 1969. He expected the press to remind the public of that, to acquaint them with the length of the odds, and he was annoyed when they didn't, but continued to dwell on the forthcoming *annus mirabilis*. Moreover, the handful of established Redskin stars was not, on the face of it, Lombardi-style players, who blended with his system. Jurgensen was not a ball-control quarterback, not a leader; Jerry Smith was too light to provide blocking strength at tight end; Charley Taylor was too loose, too erratic a catcher for the dependability the Lombardi passing game required; Chris Hanburger was too light and too much of a free-lance operator to give the Lombardi precision linebacking coverage on the outside. Among the stars, only Len Hauss at center seemed to have the credentials for Lombardi football; he was tough and quick, like Jim Ringo a little underweight for a pro lineman, but a 110 percenter.

Bobby Mitchell had not been a 1968 regular, but he was unquestionably one of the great athletes in NFL history. Like Charley Taylor, Mitchell was a gamebreaker, but a man who made a spectacular catch one play and dropped the ball all alone in the end zone the next; he lacked the consistency that Lombardi had always sought in his receivers, and he was getting old as well.

Sam Huff was the quintessential Lombardi player, but he had sat out a season and had even been in physical decline during his last two playing years in 1966 and 1967.

It was harder to assess the adaptability of the 1968 Redskin regulars. Athough there were some good ballplayers among them, they lacked star identity and the strongly marked personal characteristics that would indicate how well they would mesh with the Lombardi system.

In the aggregate, the Redskins were a team largely composed of low draft choices, free agents, and veterans acquired from other teams, sometimes at prohibitively high prices. It was a team that had a history of folding, of swooning at the last moment. In 1967, five games had been lost or tied in approximately the final minute of play; in 1968, the team went downhill from the opening kickoff. Was it a team that had been under too much pressure, or too little? Under the right sort of pressure or the wrong? Lombardi didn't know, and he once told me, "The most important thing a coach needs is the knowledge that his team can or can't play under pressure. If it can't, you need new players; if it can, you can make do with average ones." From the start, then, he was determined to put the team under more pressure than they were used to, or at least a different kind of pressure—Lombardi pressure. It was both a mental and a physical process: it was physical in the relentless grind of conditioning at training camp and the need to play in spite of injury and exhaustion; it was mental in the humiliation of harassment and screaming, the ever-present threat of being cut, traded, or waived, and the insistence that there was only one right way to do something.

"To stay or not to stay, that was the question of training camp for most people," Vince Promuto told me. "Sometimes it takes more character to walk out than to stay on." Promuto was not speaking for himself, because he was determined to stay, to make Lombardi respect him, just as he respected Lombardi; there was almost a touch of the aspiring Mafioso in Promuto's hunger to gain that respect. Like Lombardi, Promuto was a poor Italian boy from New York City. He had won a football scholarship to Holy Cross and was playing his tenth year as the starting Redskin guard. He felt strongly that football had made a vast difference in his life, had allowed him to go to college, to make a decent living, and to see him through law school in the off-season. This sense of indebtedness was fortified by periodic trips to his boyhood neighborhood, where men he had grown up with were engaged in lives of petty crime and menial drudgery. He once told me he had run into an old teen-age pal in the Bronx who had just been sentenced to two years in jail for stealing a car. "Gee, that's too bad," he told the man. "Ahhh, don't worry about it, Vinnie," the friend had replied, "nothing to it. I can do two years standing on my ear." Promuto described the exchange and shook his head with its square jaw and features as strongly etched as a pop-art painting of Mr. America. These two years in the stir might have been his own fate without football, he was clearly thinking, and he smiled, thinking that he would have accepted them with something of his friend's bravura. The Lombardi training camp was then something he figured he could do standing on one ear, for it was the ethic of his youth that winning respect was the name of the game.

"I'd heard Lombardi practiced for an hour and a half," he

said. "Well, I've practiced for two and a half hours in my day and I could make the trip. I figured I was a tough sonofabitch and nobody was going to get me down. That first day in Carlisle I found I was wrong, I was ready to say uncle. Lombardi don't stop until everybody gets bushed. And you weren't used to him, you never knew how much longer he'd make you do those damn ups-and-downs. You'd lie on the ground and say, 'This guy's a madman, he'll never stop,' and within fifteen minutes you were bushed, frightened to exhaustion, and you had to do the next one hour and fifteen minutes on courage alone. This is his idea of getting you ready for the fourth quarter. Not even the Chinese could do so well at breaking you that first week. And I was trying so hard to look good, to show a great coach that I could play for him that I burned myself out, lost twenty pounds, and was actually down to 230 and I hadn't weighed that since college.

"Well, I lasted it out, got some of my weight back and just as I started to feel real good, a halfback ran into my left knee and it swelled up with water the day before the Buffalo game and I knew I'd have to play that way and I did. After the game he comes up to me and says, 'How do you feel, Vincent?' I said, 'I'm all right, Coach.' He says, 'Atta way to talk.' I said, 'That's the name of the game; you got to play when you're hurt.' Jesus, you should have seen him light up. He says, 'Atta way to go, Vincent, atta way to go.'

"Well, playing in Buffalo set me back a month. My knee got so bad I could hardly walk. Then I broke three ribs and separated my shoulder. But it was the knee that bothered me. What you need in this game is your legs. Shoulders and ribs, they hurt when you get hit there again, but you don't need them to do your job. There are a lot of big people walking around this earth, and the value of a pro ballplayer over a big guy walking around is the pro can play hurt.

"I'll tell you, most people play this game because they want to be heroes. Sure they do. I do. You play it to be recognized, for one, by a man you respect, like Lombardi. And you play it so you can see it in yourself. The greatest moment for me is when you walk into the locker room after you've won and you've had a good day personally. You're beat up and bruised, but you don't feel hurt. And you get a couple of minutes sitting in front of your locker before you say the team prayer, and you're sitting there saying, 'Hey, I'm a bitch. I'm really something.'

"Well, I had some days like that this year, and I got to be pretty biased in favor of Lombardi and his system. I'll tell you why. Because I learned not to be afraid of him. If you play for him because he gets to you out of fear, then there's a defect in Lombardi's system, because the minute you're not with him anymore you'll fizzle out. You see, some guys feel they're only doing what he wants them to do to keep from being yelled at. They're losers. You have to make one more step and see that it's not him that's making you play better football, but yourself. That's a feeling worth having."

But if Promuto had found the Lombardi system a cause to believe in, there were other players I liked and admired who challenged the whole philosophical underpinning of the Lombardi method. And they were not losers, either. One of them told me, "He says if he sees forty ballplayers playing to the best of their ability he's satisfied. Maybe, but if they do, it's because they're afraid. He motivates through fear. It's a terrible feeling to know you're afraid of the man you work for, terrible. When I think personally of what I have gone through this year! The hell you go through making the team, and it was hell. And then the fear of having that taken away from you. The statements he makes when you're hurt, like if you don't play for me hurt I'll get rid of you. I've heard him tell that to people. Hell, he's told it to me. When you've got a family, is that right to be told you're fired because you're hurt? You ask yourself, would he really do something like that? I think he would. And this is why his theory of winning has to be questioned, because of the man you become, because of the man the coaches, like Lombardi, become. He's trying to be the father image. He's tough, he's mean, and he's hard, and then sometimes he'll do a decent thing, something that's more than fair. Yes, he's capable of that too. More so than most people in this business. But in the end it comes down to winning and losing, and I ask myself, is that fatherhood? Well, I have a kid and I don't want to be that kind of father.

"You know, I was talking to some guys I knew on the Packers before training camp began, and they laughed at me and said, 'Hey, you're going to get that dirty bastard,' and 'When he gets ahold of you guys he's going to have your tongue hanging out.' They were all laughing, you know. With glee! Yet you'd think they'd really want him back, would miss him, but they didn't seem to. Maybe human nature doesn't want to win all that bad. You accept things more than you really want them. You accept being the champions of the world, but when the man who made you champions is gone, it's a tremendous relief.

"So I said to these Packers, 'Okay, why'd you guys have the 6–7–1 season last year?' And they said because Lombardi wasn't here. Hell, maybe that's just an excuse they used because they got outplayed. Ballplayers will alibi you forever. But they seemed like they believed it, like they knew Lombardi's going was why they lost. I tell you, you lean on a guy like Lombardi. He *is* the reason. You take him out, and the motivation, the control, the drive is all gone. He walks into the training room and says, 'Nobody's hurt, get the hell out of here,' and everybody limps out.

"He can get it out of you. He can win anywhere, providing he has just halfway decent ballplayers. But the trouble is, if you do win with Lombardi, you have the feeling you, the *team*, didn't do it. HE did it. Hell, he told us to our face in Carlisle, 'All I need is bodies, gentlemen.' Well, dammit, I like to play this game. I feel like when I have a good day, that's me who's had a piece of winning."

As this particular ballplayer talked in my living room, my wife sat in a chair listening. A stranger to professional sports, she asked a question that certainly had not occurred to me.

"Is it possible," she asked, "that Lombardi is capable of arousing such hatred that the team would want to humiliate him so badly they'd welcome defeat?"

The player thought for a while and said, "This is true."

"In that case," my wife said, "you have to believe in Lombardi. You have to try and believe in him, anyway. It's such a thin line he's drawing that if you step over it, you'll ruin yourselves as well as him."

"Yes," the player laughed, "he's got you, doesn't he? There's no way out of it."

So the Lombardi pressure elicited different reactions. Both of these players had gotten through training camp, had made the forty-man roster, but they judged things differently.

There was, I thought, great risk in such divergence, for Lombardi was trying to make a team, and his notion of a team, as I understood it, was a group of forty men united in a common purpose and outlook who submitted their will to the larger demands of Lombardi-type football. It was hard to know whether frightened men and questioning men fitted into that scheme. It was too early to tell, in any case. And I supposed that, from Lombardi's standpoint, he didn't care whether he had doubters and detracters, for in the end they would either show they could play football for him or would be eliminated.

Chapter 7

Having been evicted from the Dickinson Campus at the beginning of the new academic term and denied occupancy of RFK Stadium because of the baseball schedule, Lombardi booked a wing of the Washingtonian Motel, near Gaithersburg, Maryland, for the last two weeks of training camp. The Redskins were preparing for their fifth exhibition game, against the Cleveland Browns, defending Eastern Conference champions.

"These must be Cleveland plays, they're working so well," one reporter said, watching practice at the Gaithersburg High School field.

"Who's Number 44?" I asked, trying to identify the back who had sped through a gaping hole.

"That's Leroy Kelly's number," someone said.

"Our guy runs just like Kelly too," another reporter said.

"Yeah, Kelly Miller," the first reporter said. Down on the field, equipment manager Kelly Miller was pottering about with a pile of pads and footballs, scowling as usual, as if he had overheard us high above him in the stands.

One night two days before the Cleveland exhibition game Lombardi told me, "This team is shaping up. We're getting tough, nothing esthetic, but tough. We may be a pretty good ball team by the end of the season. The Browns are going to be tough this week, but it wouldn't surprise me if we beat them in the regular season. We're coming on, I'll say that."

One of the things that had cheered him up was the arrival of Leo Carroll on waivers from the Packers. Carroll, a 6' 7" defensive end out of San Diego State, had been a second-round draft pick by the Falcons in 1967. He had been traded to the

Packers for wide receiver Bob Long, who was also now with the Redskins and would soon replace the forcibly retired Bobby Mitchell. Carroll was reputed to be an outstanding pass rusher, and Lombardi was intrigued with his great height. "How about this for a front four," he said, "Carroll and Hoffman at 6′ 7″ at ends, and Crane and Crenshaw at 6′ 6″ at tackles? With that kind of height all they'd have to do is penetrate four feet and wave their hands in the air and nobody'd be able to pass against us." He grinned, almost in delirium, rose from his chair and jumped up and down, waving his fingers in the air to intimidate an imaginary quarterback. "All they'd be able to do is throw the bomb," an assistant coach chimed in. "Or throw the short ones straight up into the air," Harland Svare added.

"You know," another assistant coach said, "We must have the tallest roster in the league right now."

"That's right," Lombardi gave his 5′ 9″ laugh. "I'm no Napoleon, whatever the writers think. You know, he used to have his colonels, or whatever you call them, a couple of inches shorter than him to make him seem bigger." He pointed to me. "You know your history; that's right, huh? With me, the bigger those colonels are, the better."

The Five O'Clock Club at the Washingtonian Motel was held in one of the Redskins' rented rooms, from which the beds had been removed. Straight-back chairs, upholstered in salmon-pink vinyl, were placed around the walls, as at a junior-high dance, and there was a matching leather ottoman, which Lombardi always commandeered to prop up his arthritic knee.

Talk turned to the desirability of "meanness" in a football player. Earlier in the week Lombardi had told me that, if you could get two big, mean, quick men in your defensive line, you could be a contender for the championship. "Los Angeles with Jones and Olson, Dallas with Lilly and Andrie, Minnesota with three, the Packers with Willie Davis and Henry Jordan— you got two of them with quick feet and great strength in their upper body, you're all set for a run at the championship." It was generally agreed in this company of former Giants that

New York had had its share of big, mean linemen in the 1950's. "The first of the big, mean, fast ones in my book," a coach said, "was Al Derogatis. That guy was so ornery and independent he'd bump people off the sidewalk onto the street. Listen, he used to ride down the escalator in Grand Central Station and take the hats off men's heads going up on the escalator next to him. He'd get down to the bottom with a big pile of hats and say, 'Look what I've got.'

As I listened to the coaching staff talk during those weeks at Gaithersburg, I was forcibly struck by their lapses in memory, by the way the past had blurred for all of them into a confusion of years, dates, and ballplayers. One night, for example, someone commented on Lombardi's Super Bowl ring.

"Well," he said, "I'm not the only one here with one. Lew's got his on, I see," he said, pointing at Lew Carpenter's finger.

"Mine's not a Super Bowl ring, Coach," Carpenter said.

"It's not? Weren't you playing for us then?"

"Nope, Coach, you made me retire before then."

When the laughter died down, Lombardi turned serious. "When *did* you retire?" he asked Carpenter.

"1963," Carpenter said.

Lombardi shook his head, unbelievingly. "1963? Are you sure about that? I thought it was later."

"Nope, 1963."

On another occasion, they mentioned a wild after-game party thrown by the Detroit Lions, a team well known in the league for its sybaritic life style. "Where was that party, Bill?" Lombardi asked.

"That was in San Francisco at the Mark Hopkins," Austin said.

"In San Francisco? What year?"

"I can't quite remember," Austin said.

"What the hell were the Lions doing in San Francisco?" Lombardi asked.

"Playing the 49'ers I guess," Austin said.

"Well, what the hell were we doing there then?" Lombardi asked.

Austin scratched his head for a while. "You got a point there," he finally said.

It took a while for me to realize that the men in that room had collectively lived through more than two thousand regular-season professional football games as players and coaches; as I thought of the number of players, games, and seasons that would have to be dealt with over that course of time, the confluence of events and names became understandable. For Lombardi, at least, the past was summed up in the memory of a few dozen key plays that won the games, which, in turn, won the championships. All the rest was jumbled and did not really matter.

The Browns game was upon the Redskins. After going to the RFK Stadium dressing room with a 10–10 tie at half-time, the Browns came back to dominate the second half and win 20–10. Both teams went with their best players, Jurgensen completing twenty-one of thirty-one passes for 241 yards.

The game was lost by the usual errors and bad breaks that seemed to dog the Redskins. Curt Knight hit on one of three field goals and had a fourth blocked. Rookie John Didion, an All-American center converted to linebacker, tipped a pass he probably should have intercepted, and the ball was caught by Leroy Kelly, who converted the mishap into a 47-yard gain. Didion, who was also centering for the kicking teams, lofted a punt snap over Mike Bragg's head into the end zone. A pass from Jurgensen to Jerry Smith was intercepted in the end zone by Brown safety Ernie Kellerman when Smith slipped in the grass. The referees awarded Kelly a touchdown on a plunge that appeared to stop several feet short of the goal-line. Added together, they were the breaks that made the difference. Had these breaks gone against the Browns instead of the Redskins, the score would have been reversed, but the Browns were in contention for the championship year after year precisely because they did not let the breaks go against them. The same had always been true of the Packers; it had never been true of the Redskins, and there was a lesson in that. "If you could have won, you should have," Lombardi was fond of saying.

As the press corps crowded into the coachs' dressing room in the basement of RFK Stadium, Lombardi gave us a baleful look and said, "You fellows are in the wrong dressing room.

The winner's dressing room is on the other side, huh, huh, huh?"

"No photographers please," an assistant coach said, scurrying naked from the shower to the dressing room.

Lombardi sighed, steeling himself for the "good losers" speech he had been compelled to make more frequently of late. "Well," he said in a flat, bored voice, "I think we're improving each week. We played a good football team tonight, and we made a few errors, and we got beat. Those are the breaks of the game. The defense improved tremendously, and it was a shame Kelly scored on that third-down plunge. A defense that held Leroy Kelly on the goal—that's the sort of thing that bucks a whole team up and turns ballgames around. But if the ref said it was a touchdown, what can I say? I'll tell you we need more offense, and if the defense stays good like tonight we'll be okay. That's easier said than done, I might add."

The aura of defeat was not overly detectable in the Redskins' temporary dressing room. The floor was heaped high with snipped tape, jocks, dixie cups, and the skins of orange quadrants. Flamboyant, bright suits were hanging in almost all of the lockers; even the underpants were brightly colored—fuschias, pinks, lavenders, claret reds.

I spied safety Tom Brown in a corner locker and asked him how he found it playing on another Lombardi team, after all his years with the Packers.

"Well, I guess it's no secret that a lot of people had the feeling I was the weak link in the Green Bay secondary. I don't think that's true, but I'm aware of the charge. Here I've been switched from strong to free safety, and I want to prove I can play another position and show everybody I'm no weak link. It's a hell of a challenge, and now I've got this shoulder that's popping out when I grab at people. As far as the shoulder goes, I'm going to have to learn to tackle all over again. I've always been an arm tackler and now I'm going to have to hit with my shoulder. And I'm going to have to learn to live with pain."

"How is it to play with pain?" I asked.

"I think about it all the time. I think to myself, I'm going to have to be tough. But I've got something to prove and I figure I'll be tough enough to do it. I played four years in the starting backfield on a championship team, and then at the end of that to be known as a weak link—well, that's something it's worth some pain to prove wrong."

"Any differences in being a Redskin and being a Packer?" I asked. He looked around the locker room, the players padding silently into the shower room, others dressed and ambling out into the night.

"Well," he said, "the feeling of being a winner is not in evidence here. Not yet, anyhow. Everybody wants to win, but doing it—" he shrugged. "Jurgensen wants to be a winner, but he's never been with a winning club, and it's very difficult for him to suddenly just become one. You've got to win to be a winner, and that's true of Sonny and everybody else on this team. It'll take fourteen games to find out."

No, at 2–3 on the exhibition season, the Redskins were clearly not yet winners—just the opposite, in fact. As the dressing room thinned out, I had the sense of observing no great disappointment on the part of its occupants, perhaps because they had suited up earlier in the evening with no great sense of expectation. The Browns were, after all, the class of the Eastern Conference, and a 20–10 loss to them was hardly surprising, certainly not disgraceful.

But the Redskins' last exhibition opponent, Philadelphia, was another matter. The Eagles had tied the Falcons for the worst 1968 NFL record: 2–12. They were a team the Redskins could be expected to outclass.

The game, to be played in Philadelphia's Franklin Field the following Sunday, brought the glow of a special excitement to Lombardi's cheeks. Franklin Field had recently been covered in glowing green astroturf, and when it came to football technology and gadgetry, Lombardi was a true zealot. Lombardi had hoped to convince his co-tenants of RFK Stadium, the Washington Senators, to go halves on the installation of astroturf, but had failed to reckon on the parsimony of Senator owner Bob Short and the baseball fundamentalism of manager

Ted Williams. If Short had little interest in pumping more money into a ballclub that was not a great success at the gate, Williams had a sort of sentimentality about grass. He had had no trouble playing on it during his seventeen years as an active major leaguer, and besides, there was a rumor that astroturf held the summer heat like a blanket, raising field temperatures by fifteen degrees.

To have had astroturf in his own stadium would have been sweet for Lombardi, but failing that, he drew some pleasure from playing on it in Philadelphia. That Tuesday at Gaithersburg practice, he had a carpet of astroturf laid out and kept his linemen and backs on the field afterwards to see what sort of shoe worked best on the new surface. There were four different soles available, featuring ridges, nubby cleats, plain surface, and regular football cleats. Naturally enough, there was a great deal of bickering, indecision, experimentation, and grumbling going on as the players tried to make up their minds about the shoes. The squabbling prompted some off-the-cuff philosophy from Lombardi. "Who knows what the right shoe is? Four different guys, four different shoes. Who can say what the right choice is? The problem is, there are too many choices in America. The answer to the shoe question is, don't give anyone a choice."

But the next Saturday morning, Lombardi paced around on the Franklin Field astroturf with springy steps, smiling benignly at everyone. I ventured out on the astroturf, which had the color and texture of the shredded green nests in which Easter eggs are found in drug stores. It was exceptionally bouncy for the first couple of steps until the foot adjusted to its feel.

Sunday was a beautiful fall afternoon, a little hot, but filled with promise. In the first half, the Redskins, especially Sonny Jurgensen, ran the Eagles off the field. Jurgensen passed for 199 yards in the first half, hitting on seventeen of twenty-five, picking the Eagles' secondary to pieces. It was ten minutes into the second period before the Eagles got their first firstdown. The offensive line was giving Jurgensen fine protection, even opening up creditable holes for the runners.

Incredibly, the Redskin brilliance and the Eagle ineptitude left Washington ahead only 10–7 at half-time. At that, the Redskins had gotten three of their points on a field goal from the 16-yard line with two seconds left in the half.

There were thirty-two seconds left in the game when the Redskins scored next, and in the meantime the Eagles had put nineteen points on the board to win 26–17. Lombardi had gone with his reserves during the second half. Harry Theofilides quarterbacked the club and moved it better than the score indicated. The substitute line gave him makeshift protection, and although he had three balls intercepted, only one could be categorically counted against him. Mike Bragg surrendered two points on a safety by stepping out of the end zone on a punt after a high snap from center from the erratic Didion. Two fumbles, one by tackle Jim Snowden on a short kickoff and the other by fullback Henry Dyer, added to the indignity of Theofilides' afternoon.

I watched Lombardi through binoculars during the second half. Normally, he went through an elaborate ritual of knee-bends on the side lines, as if unable to bear the suspense of each play. But now he was standing, his arms hanging limp and his chin shoved forward, watching the disaster, powerless as a result of some inner agreement with himself not to send the first team back in. He had made a compact with himself to let the bench show him its stuff; it was, and he couldn't believe it.

In the dressing room after the game I made the rounds, introducing myself to some of the players I did not know. I approached one young man in the corner, held out a hand, got a firm handshake in return, and began my spiel: " ... Writing a book about the team. ... I thought you had a good day out there today ... certainly looking forward to hearing your views as a player. ... " He gave me a baffled look and said, "I'm one of the equipment boys." There was a loud burst of laughter from an adjoining locker.

On the train trip back to Washington, Lombardi wore something of my own look of surprised embarrassment in the dressing room, as if he too had expected to meet with football players during that second half and had encountered equipment boys instead.

The exhibition season was now history: 2–4 history to a coach who believed in establishing the winning habit during the pre-season games. It must have crossed his mind that Otto Graham's Redskins had finished the 1968 exhibition season with a 3–3 record. It must have also crossed his mind that the 1969 Redskins bore a distressing resemblance to the Redskins of a past age.

Chapter 8

George Preston Marshall, a Washington laundry owner and an indefatigable sports promoter, acquired a Boston NFL franchise in 1932. That first year, his team played its home games at Braves Field and adopted the name of the stadium's baseball occupants. The following year, Marshall moved to Boston's Fenway Park and renamed the team the Redskins. A man always more interested in half-time spectaculars than in football, Marshall had no doubt already invested in wigwams, tom-toms, totem poles, and other ethnic paraphernalia that left him no choice but to retain the team's Indian motif.

In any event, the Redskins failed to catch fire in Boston despite all of Marshall's promotional abilities. In 1937 he moved the franchise to Washington and went about turning the team into a business success with the dash and extravagant salesmanship that were his hallmarks. Vice-president John Garner chucked out the first-game ball, ballet troupes performed at half-time, smoke signals issued from the huge canvas teepee in the bleachers, leaping Indian braves in loin cloths performed rain dances, and a 150-piece Redskin brass band strutted about the field in feathered headdress and buckskin uniform. When the Redskins journeyed to New York to play the Giants, Marshall led the band up Broadway all the way to the polo grounds, playing the team's rally song, "Hail to the Redskins."

Marshall lived in an era when locker-room jibes and the crudities of prejudice were accepted in the sports world. His animosities were directed against Catholics, Jews, and Negroes —in descending order—yet many of his closest business associates were Catholic and Jewish. He had, however, no business dealings with Negroes and enforced a ban against blacks playing for the Redskins. His last will and testament, in fact, made the Redskins a charitable foundation that was specifically excluded from using any of its assets to further racial integration. In the early 1960's, he was forced to retreat from his racial policy on Negroes when he signed a long-term lease to play in the new Washington, D.C., stadium, which was located on Federal property and was administered by the Department of the Interior.

Marshall claimed that his views on racial and religious matters were derived from Thomas Jefferson, whom he quoted tellingly on all occasions. Indeed, he kept the collected works of Jefferson on the library shelf in his office at the laundry. When he died, an aide removed the Jefferson volumes and discovered that none of the pages were cut.

Whatever Marshall's shortcomings as a civil libertarian, he was a shrewd operator. In 1950 he astounded the other NFL owners by signing a contract with the American Oil Company to televise all Redskin games. The other teams in the league didn't even televise away-games at the time. But home-games? That was like giving tickets away for free, Marshall was told, yet he alone of all the football owners had the vision to foresee the time a decade away when millions of people would tune in to watch the Sunday-afternoon games. Who needed to sell tickets, with a TV audience in eight figures and sponsors ready to pay for the honor of reaching them?

Marshall also saw that a sold-out stadium of 50,000 had more class and, in the end, more economic reward than an 80,000-seat stadium that was not sold out. It came down to status, a subject on which he had some wily notions. If you sold out at the gate, the event automatically became exclusive; there would be people who wanted to get in and who could not, thereby endowing a Redskin season ticket with status and privilege. And so, when the Redskins signed a thirty-year lease to play in the new Washington, D.C., stadium, Marshall insisted that the seats have back rests and that they be 20 to 22 inches in width, rather than the 16 to 17 inches favored by the stadium's baseball occupants, the Washington Senators.

That width would reduce the seating capacity of the stadium by thousands of seats, Marshall was told; status seekers, he replied, did not wish to "rub asses" with their neighbors. Besides, the smaller the seating capacity, the faster the stadium could be sold out, the more fans there would be who wanted a season ticket, and the bigger the television contracts would be.

But there was one factor Marshall did not reckon with: the decline of the Redskins' football fortunes. The team had won the NFL championship during its first year in Washington, beating the Bears 28–21 in Chicago. That team of 1937 had four of the five Redskins in pro football's Hall of Fame: Cliff Battles, Turk Edwards, Wayne Millner, and Sammy Baugh, then in his rookie season, who remained with the Redskins through 1952, hitting on 57 percent of the nearly three thousand passes he threw over the years.

In the nine years from 1937 to 1945, Baugh led Washington to two NFL championships, five Eastern Conference titles, and an overall record of 68–24–5. In the next fifteen years, from 1948 to 1961, the Redskins eked out only three winning seasons and compiled a 69–116–8 record. As the 1950's wore on, it became obvious that the Redskins owed their decline to Marshall's ban on Negro athletes.

The years after World War II witnessed the breakdown of the color barrier in pro football as well as in major-league baseball. Indeed, Paul Brown brought Marion Motley into the Cleveland Brown backfield in 1946, a year before Branch Rickey brought Jackie Robinson up to the Dodgers. So from 1946 on, black athletes constituted a progressively larger percentage of the rosters of professional teams—of all teams, that is, except the Redskins.

Edward Bennett Williams indirectly was to resolve the Redskins' racial ban, in the process buy into the club, and ultimately become team president after Marshall was incapacitated by a stroke in 1963.

Williams is in his late forties, with thinning curly brown hair, a faintly rumpled look, and a quizzical, good-natured face. In spite of its sterile modern furniture, his law office on the tenth floor of the Hill Building in downtown Washington has a lived-in look, with pictures of his children on the walls, the library shelves dominated by the brightly colored dust-jackets of ordinary books rather than legal tomes.

"I had been interested in buying Redskin stock way back in the fifties," Williams told me. "I used to go to the games with Marshall and in 1959 or '60 Harry Wismer's Redskin stock was for sale, so I got an agreement from Marshall to go negotiate with Wismer. Finally, in the Waldorf Astoria's men's bar on Washington's birthday in either '59 or '60, I made a deal with Wismer to buy his shares for $250,000, came back, and had my final meeting with Marshall. Well, it blew up, because I told Marshall what I had been telling him for years: that he had to abandon the racial policy. I told him that, from his point of view, it was suicidal because it was just certain there would be an economic boycott on his two TV sponsors, Marlboro and Amoco, and it was very clear to me that if he persisted in the racial policy they'd drop him like a hot potato. I said, 'George, I can't come in unless there's a change. I can't come in for reasons other than I've articulated to you. I just can't be part of an organization that's the last bastion of discrimination.' And with that Marshall jumped up and said, 'You're not going to change the world,' banged the table, and stormed out. My deal collapsed, and he didn't talk to me for years.

"In the meantime, I tried the Adam Clayton Powell tax case in New York, and Marshall knew I was friendly with Adam. In 1961 the Redskins went through a disastrous season. I think they won one game, so Marshall called me up one night, asked me for dinner, and said, 'Look, I want to get Ernie Davis [Syracuse's Negro consensus All-American halfback]. You can get Adam Clayton Powell to line up Ernie Davis.'

"And remember, even though the Redskins had the first pick in the draft, the chances were high that Davis wouldn't even come here because there was a great hostility to Marshall among Negro athletes. I said, 'Okay, George, let's have dinner with Powell.'

"Well," Williams continued, "the three of us had dinner in Duke Zeibert's, and it was one of the funniest nights I ever spent. Marshall kept calling Powell 'Parson' all evening. He'd say, 'Now listen here, Parson,' and Adam would say, 'Now listen here, George, I'm not going to get you any house-nigger. If you want to get several Negro ballplayers, I'll help you, but I'm not getting you any house-nigger.' 'You're not going to run my football team, Parson,' Marshall kept saying. But oddly enough, the dinner ended on a fairly harmonious note, and Powell and I went and got Ernie Davis to agree to sign with Washington when he graduated from Syracuse.

"Meanwhile, Paul Brown, who was disenchanted with Bobby Mitchell, coveted Ernie Davis. He thought that, with Davis and Jim Brown, he'd have the greatest backfield in the world. So Brown called Marshall and negotiated a deal of Mitchell and the Cleveland first-round draft pick in return for the Redskin first-round choice, since our record gave us first shot in the upcoming draft. And that's how the Redskins got Bobby Mitchell, how the Browns got Ernie Davis, how the racial ban was broken, and how, in the end, I got an interest in the team, since Marshall then sold me stock and had me join the board."

The Mitchell-Davis trade was to contain a grisly irony, since shortly after Davis was drafted by the Browns, he was found to have leukemia. Davis never played, while Mitchell came to Washington, changed from a running back to a flanker, and caught nearly 400 passes in the next seven years.

From the time Mitchell joined the Redskins in 1962, through the 1969 season, anywhere from 25 percent to 40 percent of the team roster was black, a racial composition more or less identical to that of other NFL teams. Nonetheless, as I was to find out, when the black players ruminated on the dismal Redskin record over the years, they ultimately talked of the "Marshall jinx," a sort of voodoo hex, a retribution that Marshall's racism had brought to Washington.

The ethic of pro football is that the best man at any given position plays. There will always be players who feel that they are better than the man they play behind, but an intelligent coach can manipulate this feeling to the team's advantage and can use it as an edge in sharpening the competitive rivalry for a first-team job. But when a player feels he is better than the man ahead of him, but has been relegated to the second team because of race, it withers his competitive urge, and the malady soon spreads to the rest of the team.

There had been rumors of such racial tensions in the 1968 Redskins, a charge that the white members of the team recalled with some bafflement. Dissension, cliques, an erosion of coaching authority, yes. Everyone was aware of that. But racism? That was a bum rap, the white players said, and their genuine puzzlement argued a clean conscience. Perhaps it amounted to this: although the white players had forgotten about the "Marshall jinx," the black players had not and were quick to pick up nuances that the white players did not sense.

"When Otto was here," Negro tackle Jim Snowden told me, "there used to be such things as 'mistakes' and 'mental errors.' It seemed like the black players were always making 'mental errors' and the white players made 'mistakes.' Snowden, a sensitive and generous-spirited man, gave a gentle laugh. "The black guys on the team used to say Otto figured we weren't smart enough to make mistakes. With us, it was a mental problem. I don't know. Maybe he didn't mean it that way, but that's the way it always seemed to sound."

You could say that Graham regarded a "mental error" as less pejorative than a "mistake" and only used the two terms to avoid the hint of any racial bias. But even so, the two terms implied a distinction, one the white players were oblivious to, but one that stabbed at the black players.

Although Lombardi had many prejudices, they were not racial. His temperament and his ego did not admit to any great distinction among men. As far as he was concerned, all men were lazy and would lie down on the job if they got the chance. Many coaches regarded this as a Negro trait, but Lombardi thought of it as human nature, as a failing that affected all men equally—with one notable exception. He expected to win every game, but he did not expect much help from his players. They would have to be pushed, driven, and whipped until they became extentions of Lombardi's own will, his own grim egotistic expectation of victory. He wanted a team of uniform habits, for the habit of execution on every play led to the habit of winning.

The multiple offense with its variety of formations was a football style meant for optimists, for coaches who had faith in the perfectibility of human nature. Lombardi, the pessimist, expected very little of human nature and kept his offense as simple as possible. In his view, simplicity won football games, and complexity lost them. Eleven football players could make a habit of executing a few simple things automatically, but the execution of a dozen things created a sense of freedom rather than habit. Too much freedom led to a breakdown and increased the probability of human error. Human errors lost football games, and habits won them. The Lombardi system was that simple and circular in its logic.

In addition, for Lombardi a team was not eleven individuals, some of them more dependable than others. It was one unit with eleven parts, and when one part ceased to function the whole unit broke down; the chances of that one breakdown were reduced when the responsibilities of each player were kept simple but interconnected.

For example, under the Lombardi offensive system, Sonny Jurgensen did not fade back and hit Jerry Smith on a third-down square-in because Smith had good hands; he did not throw the bomb to Charley Taylor because Taylor had the speed to get behind the secondary. That would be depending too much on Smith and Taylor. Smith might slip running his pattern; Taylor might be cut down at the line of scrimmage by a crafty cornerback. Jurgensen had no primary or secondary receiver to be counted on because that man's individual skills fitted a certain situation. All the receivers were primary targets, conceived of not as individuals but as "X's" on a play chart who had a simple pattern to run and who were expected to acquire the habit of being in a certain spot at a certain time. Jurgensen was expected to read certain defensive keys that would tell him which "X" was covered and which would be open. Bart Starr could pick a defensive secondary to pieces because of his ability to read keys; it was a habit with him. Jurgensen was probably the most accurate passer in football history. He believed he could hit a dime at twenty yards, and in twelve years of quarterbacking he had formed the habit of looking off his primary receiver every time, but it was a habit at variance with the Lombardi system and to break Jurgensen of it, Lombardi had played him virtually the whole exhibition season. Yet, with the regular season ready to begin, Jurgensen was still throwing to individuals, not "X's"; he was still in the habit of humming that pigskin to the receiver he had in mind for the play—but that was freedom and it was dangerous.

So while the Lombardi system was not based on a very flattering notion of human nature or a very lofty assessment of individual merit, it was equally fair in the demands it made on the players. "Coach treats the players all alike—like dogs," Henry Jordan once said.

Chapter 9

The late afternoon shadows were lengthening toward the pitcher's mound in RFK Stadium. "Hey, aren't you Charley Taylor?" a grounds-keeper asked, a wheedling smile on his face.

"Sure am," said the pride of Grand Prairie, Texas, happy to be none other, the inimitable, the one and only. Taylor gave the man his big smile, with the gapped teeth all the whiter for the obsidian color of his skin. He was a lithe man in form-fitting bell-bottom jeans, looking lighter than his 210 pounds.

"Hey, would you sign me an autograph?" the grounds-keeper asked, patting his shirt and trousers for a pencil.

"Not now, man. I'm going to be inside this stadium for four-teen weeks—I'll be around. You'll get me, don't worry, you'll get me, man."

Taylor and I were sitting in the Senator's dugout talking about one of the Redskin's favorite subjects—the difference between the 1968 and the 1969 squads.

"Last year we were just trying to fool everybody," Taylor said. "We go into a ballgame, and people were actually fooling us. The coaches say to me, "Taylor, they going to put you in double coverage, and we're going to fool their asses and not throw to you. Well, sure enough, the other team'd have two guys on me for a few plays and then they'd drop off. But Sonny'd be watching me those first few plays and figure they were going to be on me all day. And they weren't. Hell, man, it's kind of hard to go out there all day and not get a ball, you know what I mean? Like midway through the season, man, the player's mind just wasn't there."

"So what happened?" I asked, hungering for the explanation

of the Redskins' annual collapse.

"I'll just put it like this: the quarterback could get to Coach Graham more than to Coach Lombardi. Sonny took advantage of Coach Graham. Hell, Coach Graham would come up with a game plan, and before the practice week is over, Sonny'd throw half the game plan out, and we'd do what Sonny wanted to do. Not that I'm knocking Sonny, 'cause he felt like he knew what would work. Now, anybody can make a suggestion, but this wasn't any suggestion that Sonny was throwing out. Like, that was it, that's what we did."

Taylor spoke with some flippancy, and there was in his tone less a criticism of Jurgensen than a regret that Sonny's own game plan did not include more tosses to the Redskin split end, the Grand Prairie flash himself. His talent had always been exceptional, the kind that quarterbacks turned to when a game-saving play was needed.

Once he told me that the high school kids used to abduct him when he was ten or eleven for the pleasure of his company in sandlot tackle. "It was tough, man. The only way to escape them cats was to play hard for an hour or so, and when they called me to go deep for a pass, I'd just keep going, all the way home. I'd just run and never look back, all the way home."

I asked him, as you might ask Mozart, when it was he realized he was someone out of the ordinary.

"Well, when I was eight or nine, I had this energy built up and I just had to find some way to get it let off. And I did like to move that football, no doubt about that. Now, when I was in high school, the thing that motivated me most was all the girls went out with football players. It was kind of a drag to be without a date, so I figured the best way to get a date was to be a football player, so I took it up. And the more I played, the more I liked it. The challenge of football was one to one—you either take me or I take you."

"Like girls, eh?" I said.

"Hell, man, after a while I got so I don't need any football to get along with the girls. Not by the time I got to college at Arizona State, anyway. Man, let me tell you that college ball is rougher than you think. People figure that's just a bunch of kids running around out there. It's rough, man. At the college stage in a boy's life, he's at his physical peak, he's able to rebound from those bumps and bruises and he's able to put out. In the pros you get buffeted around, but, man, it's nothing like what those college boys do to you. They go banging in there, 'Whop!' and piling on and roaring here and there like a bat out of hell. They out of their skulls. Those cats'll kill you. I know what I'm talking about."

"In spring training my sophomore year I broke my neck—four vertebrae. 'Hey, Coach,' I said, 'my neck don't feel good.' 'There's nothing wrong with your neck, you jackass,' he said. So the numb went away a little, and I made a tackle and when I went to get up, my body got up, but my head just stayed there right on the ground. And the coach says, 'Hey, get this jackass off the field.' So the trainer put some ice on my neck and after practice they took me up to the infirmary for an X ray and the doctor said, 'Son, your neck is broken. You got here ten minutes later, you'd be dead.' Dead! Man, that scared me. I mean those colleges let you lie right out there on the field and die. That's something to think about. Well, they put a cast on me and for six months I was walking around like a mummy."

"I guess that cast must have cramped your style with the girls," I said.

"Man," he said in a tone of jovial reproof, "that wasn't girls, that was business, that cast on my neck. 'Cause I knew football was paying for my education. Man, you know how it is, at that particular time you got a reputation. I'm not a great lover, but I could walk with the rest of them. But my parents didn't have any $1800 like Arizona State was paying for me to play football. You ever met an $1800 girl in college, you understand me? My junior year I went back to play again, and I tell you cold chills went all over me, but I had my scholarship, and they don't give those scholarships for nothing. I mean you got to carry water or something."

"How did it go?" I asked.

"I did as well as expected. I mean you can only score, right? You can only run for a touchdown, you read me?"

Taylor had been a running back his Redskin rookie year under Coach Bill McPeake, who had been fired at the end of the season. When Otto Graham came to Washington, Taylor was converted to a wide receiver.

"Nineteen sixty-six was the year they brought down the baby bulls from New York, Steve Thurlow, and Joe Don Looney, so they said, hell, we don't have room for Taylor here in the backfield, so let's make a flanker out of him. They wanted those cats to play, but there was no way those cats could outrun me or outblock me back there, but I got moved out. You read me? You see what I'm talking about?"

I did. Those rhetorical questions were codewords for the "Marshall jinx," Taylor's way of saying that Looney and Thurlow were given the backfield jobs with no credentials to speak of, while the NFL Rookie of the Year, with 755 yards on the ground and 805 yards in the air, was shunted to a new position.

"What Otto, McPeake, and the press used to say was that Taylor will overrun his guards and blockers. But that wasn't the case. You always going to run past your blockers if they're slowed down at the line. I mean, I'm no fool. I didn't run out there just for the hell of it. It was because there wasn't anybody around to run out there with me. They want me to go back to the line of scrimmage and sit with them guards till they get up off their asses where they been knocked? And then when we all ready we start running together? I mean, hell.

"You hear some strange things in this game. Like Otto. He had a way of disciplining players. Man, like one player would get fined for something, another do the same thing and no fine. Hell, we were playing the Vikings in Minnesota last year; I got fined $200 when Paul Krause intercepted a pass on me. Me? Two hundred dollars? I said, 'Coach, why you fine me for, I didn't throw the damn thing.' He said, 'You didn't show any hustle out there after the interception.' Well, hell, it's impossible for me to do anything about it. I'm running full steam down the field. The ball is coming, and I'm running to stay in stride with the ball. Krause intercepts going full speed the other way; now, how the hell can I catch up with him? It's impossible. I'm twenty yards downfield before I can slow down and turn around, and he's twenty more yards the other way already. Why, hell, that's forty yards away. I ain't that fast. I ain't going to catch any defensive back with any forty-yard head start.

"Course, Coach Otto didn't blow in your ear like Coach Vince. Man, Coach Vince is something at those movies."

"Different from Otto?"

"Is he? Oh, ho, ho. Jesus Christ, is he! Lombardi looks at everybody where Otto would just look at the point of attack. Coach Vince breaks down the whole play, man for man. 'Cause our plays are designed not to go to one spot, like the eight hole outside; they can also go inside, so everybody has got to block, 'cause you don't know where that damn ball is going. As far as Coach Vince is concerned, a receiver is *supposed* to catch the ball. If he can't do that, he can't do shit. Hell, catching is nothing. It's the rest that counts, like an extra block, like getting across the field to help the guy with the ball. He can yell at you right in your goddam ear, but maybe he's right. I mean, man, it's good to catch that ball and see Jerry Smith or Bob Long there or coming up fast with that help."

As Taylor and I left the dugout and wandered down the tunnel to the clubhouse, the grounds-keeper approached again, pencil and paper ready. Taylor obliged with an autograph, and the man said, "Hey, you guys going to be better this year?" "No doubt about it, man," Taylor said. "We got the coach, and we got the system, and we got the players."

One of the truisms of football is that a fired coach has no friends on his old team. Words of praise for Otto Graham were not easily ferreted out. Like all losing coaches, he was a handy scapegoat, and the Redskins made appropriate use of their deposed leader.

Practice after practice, game after game, and season after season the proof piled up that the Redskins could not discipline themselves, that human nature was flawed. Graham had overlooked the evidence, for to admit to it meant that he would have had to discipline himself. At the 1968 training camp, for instance, he set the rule that all players would arrive for breakfast at 7:30 A.M., and then seldom got up for early breakfast himself. (That year the Dickinson cafeteria served three thousand dinners to one thousand breakfasts.) Consequently, there was a tendency to dismiss Otto's regulations as so much hot air. Lombardi, on the other hand, never missed a breakfast at Carlisle. (The Cafeteria served three thousand breakfasts and three thousand dinners.) A pessimist, Lombardi figured that the players wouldn't do their duty unless he was there to see that they did and to mark down the names of those that didn't. Graham, the perpetual optimist, began each day with the conviction that the players would take a turn for the better, would finally make breakfast.

Joe Don Looney was perhaps the symbol of Graham's trusting nature, his cock-eyed notion that men would reform their own shortcomings. By all accounts Looney more than lived up to his name.

In his senior year Oklahoma played the University of Southern California in Los Angeles, and Sooner Coach Bud Wilkenson gave an inspiring pep-talk in the dressing room before the game to whip his team into a fervor of determination. Before the Sooners were introduced at the beginning of the game, Wilkenson was standing at the end of the Los Angeles Coliseum tunnel waiting to lead the team on the field. Suddenly the chant of "We're here because we're here because we're here because we're here ... " sounded from the tunnel. "Knock that noise off back there. We're playing USC, men," Wilkenson said in a scandalized voice. "We're here because we're here, because. ... " "Is that you, Joe Don?" Wilkenson asked. "Not me, Coach," Looney answered, and then "We're here because we're here, because ... " Looney began to chant again as the team sniggered.

Joe Don was the New York Giants' number one pick in the 1964 college draft and at the All-Star game training camp in Chicago that summer. He was rumored to have thrown a piano out of his hotel balcony window on a bet. The Giants unloaded him to Baltimore before the season started. The Colts traded him to the Detroit Lions for middle linebacker Dennis Gaubatz at the end of the 1965 season. Looney walked out of the Lions training camp one year because a friend of his got cut. At length, early in the 1966 season Looney was traded to the Redskins, where he become a favorite of the press. Every third or fourth game he'd have a good day and the reporters would crowd around his locker. "Well, Joe Don," they'd say, "have you straightened out now?" "Yes, I've straightened out now," Joe Don would say. "Otto and I have talked it over and I have definitely straightened out." Like the full moon with a werewolf, this line portended a sudden change in Joe Don. He would either be picked up by the police that night, or would miss practice that week with one of his "headache seizures." He was a man who could not bear esteem or approbation, who would not throw his jock or bandages in the trash cans so marked because he refused to "take orders from a trash can."

Like Wilkenson and dozens of other coaches, Graham bore up with Joe Don because of his obvious talent, always hoping that Looney would finally "shape up." The climax to his Redskin career finally came in the 1967 Rams game in Los Angeles. The score was tied 28–28, and the Redskins got the ball in their own territory with a minute and a half left to play-time to get within field-goal range. The Redskins began to move downfield and with their drive stalled on third down and long yardage; Looney ran a draw for 15 yards up the middle and a first down. In the closing seconds of the game Washington pushed inside the Ram 30-yard line, and Dick Absher missed a 34 field goal that would have beaten a team that many regarded as the best in football that year.

Down in the dressing room after the game Graham called the team together. A witness recalled, "Otto said he was really proud of them, that they had played a great game, that they deserved to win. Then he said, 'Where's Joe Don?' And he shook Joe Don's hand and said, 'I was really proud of you today, Joe Don. I don't mind saying it in front of the team. I wondered whether you had the heart to play football and today you proved you did. Way to go, Joe Don.' And the team was all fired up and they were yelling, 'Way to go, Joe Don.

Way to have heart.' Well, come practice that next Tuesday Joe Don was criticized for missing a block in the films and wouldn't practice because he said he had a headache. On Wednesday there was an item in the Washington papers that Joe Don had been released by the Redskins."

Oddly enough, the 1969 NFL season was beginning with Joe Don Looney on the comeback trail once again, this time with the New Orleans Saints, the Redskins' first opponent of the year. The Saints has signed Looney after he had completed a military hitch that included a year in Vietnam. As usual, Joe Don was reported to have "straightened out," to have seen the light at last and settled down to a life of hard-nosed second effort and good team spirit.

Even Otto Graham would have known better. But to my surprise Lombardi had either bought the story of Joe Don's reclamation or pretended to. "The Saints are going to be tougher than you think," he announced. "Forget their exhibition season record. They've got those good big runners—Tony Baker, Wheelright, Andy Livingston, Joe Don Looney; those guys go 230 pounds and up. They can pound us to pieces. You can never tell about a guy like Looney. He could have a hell of a day." He squinted a bit, considering Looney, I supposed.

Looked at from Lombardi's standpoint, the fact that so many coaches had tolerated Looney's antics for weeks, even seasons at time, was irrefutable testimony to Joe Don's prowess as a runner. After all, it would be inconceivable to put up Joe Don unless he were something really out of the ordinary. It was a long shot, but a crazy bastard like Looney might just have himself a day, might just have gotten a grip on himself out there in some Vietnam fox-hole. Insofar as Lombardi was superstitious, even somewhat unnerved, it was over the unorthodox and unpredictable—the Joe Don Looneys and the Fran Tarkentons who could be great one play and god-awful the next.

And the Saints worried Lombardi. They an expansion team coached by his former Green Bay assistant, Tom Fears, who would be looking to draw first blood against a Lombardi team in regular season play. And it was always tough for the away-team in New Orleans' Sugar Bowl, filled with blood-lusting rebel fans. "That New Orleans, they're something else," Lombardi told me. "Al Hirt blowing that damn trumpet on the side lines, and they put up two big speakers on either end of the visiting bench, blaring right into your ears. Eighty thousand people screaming every time you've got the ball so you can't even hear your own signals, and when they've got the ball you can hear a pin drop. You know what I'm going to do? I'm going to take a pair of wire-clippers down on the side lines, and the first time I hear Al Hirt blowing that damn trumpet in my ear, I'm going to cut the speaker cords. No, on second thought, maybe I'll have someone from the cabsquad cut them," he grinned.

The Friday before the season began with the Saints game, Lombardi called an early halt to practice and drove his golf cart out to the midfield stripe where the kicking specialists were taking turns booting balls over a volleyball net a few feet in front of them. The net was erected to simulate the loft necessary to get the ball over the defender's raised arms. Curt Knight punched one up that cleared the net and goalpost bars 40 yards away. Then punter Mike Bragg took his placekicking turn; his first boot went under the net and wobbled strangely in flight. Lombardi shook his head dismally and glanced over at the press corps on the side lines.

"Look at him," a reporter said, nudging me, "he wants to come over here and tell us something, only he doesn't know how to without losing face."

Lombardi turned the golf cart around and started to putt back toward RFK Stadium, but suddenly changed his mind, made a U turn, and headed toward the writers. "Look at him come. What'd I tell you," the reporter laughed. "You know who he looks like? General Patton. All he needs is a set of pearl-handled six-shooters. Honest to God, look at him."

Lombardi pulled up, and someone wondered about the short practice session.

"Season opener's two days away. I have to save their legs. You can't leave their legs lying on the practice field."

He was asked about the prospects for Sunday.

"I have got to win." That imperial pronoun came as something of a jolt, an admission a shade too frank, a single capital letter that summed up the stakes of the Saints game. The Redskin team was his now; he had had it long enough to put his stamp on it. From here on, the victories were his, and so were the defeats. Lombardi was not ignorant of the way of the world—he knew who had gotten the praise when things went right in Green Bay and who would get the blame if things went wrong in Washington.

Then, he thought better of the blunt personal pronoun and amended his remark. "I mean, I hope we can win," he corrected. We all knew he had meant it the first way. Nonetheless, he was in an apologetic mood. He had made the final squad cut earlier in the week, at last paring the team down to the legal forty-man limit. The last four to go had been Jim Boeke, a nine-year-veteran tackle acquired on waivers from the Lions; Sonny Randle, the aging but once great receiver for the St. Louis Cardinals; and running backs Dick Smith and A. D. Whitfield.

The first three on the list had been new in Washington and had had no supporters to lobby on their behalf, but Whitfield had been a four-year veteran, a great favorite of the fans. One of the Washington reporters had already written a "Dear Vince" open letter in his newspaper column, which read in part, "There was nothing wrong with waiving A. D. Whitfield. So what if he was your best runner? So what if he did hit the holes quicker than anybody you've got and ran like the cops were after him in the open? If anybody mentions this to you, just shrug it off. You know, give it the so-what treatment. I know A. D. didn't block as well as you hoped he would, but if you just keep quiet maybe the fans will forget there are twenty-three other guys not blocking the way you want them to block."

If Whitfield's removal had stuck in the craw of the Washington faithful, so too did the departure of Harry Theofilides. All football fans love a scrambler, the gutsy little guy who skips out of the reach of those snorting, clutching linemen, who zig-zags across the backfield to unload a dramatic pass, to scurry for a handsome gain, or even to be finally caught and crushed. Theofilides had that sort of dash, and he was, as they say, a winner.

But there were winners and winners. To Lombardi's mind, the consistent winners were taller than 5'10" and didn't scamper around the backfield, hoping that some receiver would miraculously bob free in the chaos downfield.

In late September, then, when the Cleveland Browns put Frank Ryan, a 6'3" dropback quarterback, on waivers, Lombardi pounced. At thirty-three, Ryan had led Cleveland to one NFL championship in 1964 and to the finals in 1965. He had played in the Pro Bowl for three straight years, had a history of playing hurt when he had to, and held a Ph.D. in mathematics. He was, in short, a smart, experienced leader, a Zeke Bratkowski who could come off the bench and win if anything happened to Jurgensen. So Lombardi axed Theofilides and signed Ryan three days before the Saints game.

Part of that "Dear Vince" letter also addressed itself to Theofilides: "For heaven's sake, stop saying Harry was too short to be a quarterback. Remember Eddie LeBaron? Don't forget Theo's 5'10", and you're only 5' 9", Vince, and we don't want the fans knocking you, do we? If anybody mentions it, and one of those smart-apple reporters is sure to bring it up, just say you were overloaded with quarterbacks and Harry had a business opportunity he couldn't afford to turn down, or something like that. Don't let it bother you that he was a great favorite with the fans."

The Green Bay Press Gazette had not run letters like that to Coach on the sports page. Far from it. Lombardi was at once outraged and amazed at the gall of a mere reporter questioning his judgments. After all, he was the one who saw the game films, he was the man who would be held to account in the end. But while he resented having his decisions questioned, he was also a man who knew how to protect his flanks, and that was why he had driven his golf cart over to the side lines for a friendly chat with the press. As usual, when he had something on his mind, he left it for the last. And since no one brought up the acquisition of Ryan and the removal of Theofilides, he cleared his throat.

"Did you see Ryan throw today?" he asked, with a small marveling shake of his head. "He really threw the ball out there. It was gratifying to see it."

It was an extraordinary claim. No one who had watched Ryan throw the ball that week could square his floating, off-target heaves with gratification. Ryan had been in the doghouse in Cleveland, his arm was rusty, and he was unused to the Redskin patterns and unfamiliar with the team's receivers. He had not been overly impressive the first few days in Washington, and it was absurd to expect that he would be. In time he would prove that he could throw the ball even farther than Jurgensen, and toward the middle of the season his practice passes were as accurate and sharp as Sonny's.

"Ryan is intelligent and a good athlete," Lombardi reminded us. "You have to have them." Well, the same could be said of Theofilides. He threw well, ran well, was twenty-five, and, like Ryan, a mathematician.

"What happens to Theo now?" someone wanted to know.

"I hope somebody picks him up. I'll do what I can for him. I owe it to him." He frowned, his face taking on a doleful and reflective look, perhaps considering whether he had done right by Theofilides, contemplating the fine line that separated injustice from necessity. Football was a ruthless profession. There were only forty jobs on the team; it was not like a bureaucracy where employees who outlived their usefulness could be squirreled away in remote corners and still draw their pay. Forty was the NFL limit, and to keep both Ryan and Theofilides made forty-one. So Theo had to go. That was the code. To Lombardi's mind it was fair.

Theofilides, naturally enough, took a different view. He was an intense and tenacious man, who believed he was a starting big-league quarterback. He had landed with the Bridgeport Jets after being let go by the Redskins, and his mood had not mellowed when I had breakfast with him one November morning at the Shoreham Hotel. In sporting circles Theo was known as The Galloping Greek, and he looked like some bronze cast from antiquity, Pan perhaps, with his curly hair, darting eyes, and a restless, willful look.

"You think I'm not bitter?" Theophilides said. "To keep me on the team until after the forty-man cut and then let me go? What kind of a chance did I have to land somewhere else? I knew what the score was when he came here. He don't like short quarterbacks and he don't like scramblers. That's two strikes on me right there. So I wanted to find out where I stood. I went up to the Redskin office last February to talk to him. Everybody in the office was, like, astonished. You? You want to talk to Vince Lombardi? Well, hell, he's just another person, another guy. So I told them, 'I want to see the coach, man, I want to talk to the guy.' They called back and said I was outside and wanted to see him, and he said send him in. 'Well, Harry, what do you want?' he said in a real nice way. I said, 'I just want to ask you one thing. Am I going to get a shot at the job this season, a fair chance? I know I'm small, so if you're not going to give me a fair shot, then release me and I can try someplace else.' He said, 'I'll give you every chance I give the others. No more. No less.'

"Lombardi was going with Sonny almost all the time in the exhibition games, and that made sense because he wanted Sonny to know his system. But what if something happened to Sonny? He'd need a backup man who knew his system too. So I wanted to know how I stood and I went up to him and asked him directly. He said, 'As of now, you're my number-two man.' And the exhibition season went on and on, and I still wasn't playing, so I was going to talk to him again, when he tells me he's going to let me play the whole second half against the Eagles. I went in there and moved the club, but I had three balls intercepted—one of them, I got tackled in the arm just as I was releasing, and another bounced out of a receiver's hands and got caught by an Eagle. But I drove the team down for a score and I was taking them down for another one when Dyer fumbled. Hell, I didn't do that bad. I was reading my keys pretty good.

"So I made the final squad cut. It was announced on Tuesday, and that same day I hear that Frank Ryan is coming. There are all those rookies relieved at making it, and I was down as hell. I went over to cheer up A. D., who got cut, and he ended up cheering me up. I went out to practice on Tuesday and Wednesday, and Ryan showed up on Thursday. After practice Tim Temerario comes up, he's the ax man, and says, 'Harry, the Coach wants to see you.' I knew it was all over. So I walked in there and Lombardi got up and said, 'Well, Harry, I put you on waivers.' I said, 'Why? Why did you wait so long to do it? Why? Why didn't you release me earlier so I could have had a chance somewhere else?' He looked at me and said, 'I thought you could do the job.' I tell you, I had mixed emotions. I was hopping mad and I was down, real down. Lombardi said, 'If you make it through waivers I'd like to keep you on the cab squad.' But I said no. I thought if he doesn't have confidence in me now, I know he's not going to show it later. I was tired of this rejection. Four years in a row, listening to that; 'Harry, if you were only a little taller.' Well, hell, I told Lombardi I was short that first time I saw him in February. He said he'd give me my chance, and what kind of a chance did I get? A half in Philadelphia. He said I was his number-two man, but so what? I was still leery. I got in there and I was afraid of making a mistake, and I played too cautiously. I knew I should throw the ball, but I'd call running plays so I wouldn't make a mistake on the pass.

"He talks about love all the time. I love this game. A. D. Whitfield loves this game. What kind of chances did we get? If I didn't feel bitter I'd be stupid. You know what I was tempted to tell him the day I got cut? I wanted to say, 'Don't ever give me the chance to come back and play against you. Because I'll beat you. And I will too. I would beat him on my own.

"You know, it's funny about me. I was a free agent out of Waynesburg College who got a break, got a chance to try out with the Redskins. I was lucky to come to Washington in the first place, but after that the luck ran out. Now I know what I'm doing as a quarterback, I'm at my physical peak, and I got no place to play. Some day, some day I'm going to get a chance to beat Lombardi. I'm going to go all out for that. Not because of his reputation, what he did in Green Bay, but because of what he did to me."

As Theofilides talked, it was impossible not to be swept along by the force of his intensity, his indomitable, Lombardi-like faith in himself. He had played that game against a Lombardi team a thousand times in his mind's eye, and it was safe to say that the game had been salted away every time on a breathtaking Theofilides scramble.

Chapter 10

It was a muggy overcast day at the Sugar Bowl. The Redskins won the coin flip and elected to receive. On the Saints' side lines Al Hirt lowered his brass trumpet and the public address system introduced the 1969 Redskins. "At wide receiver Charley Taylor, at left tackle Jim Snowden, at left guard Vince Promuto, at center Len Hauss, at right guard Willie Banks, at right tackle Walt Rock, at tight end Jerry Smith, at flanker Bob Long, at quarterback Sonny Jurgensen, at halfback Gerry Allen, at fullback Henry Dyer, and introducing Vince Lombardi and the rest of *his* Washington Redskins."

Lombardi strode onto the field wearing a flaming red golf visor, a blue shirt, and a red-striped regimental tie loosened at the neck. I was sitting in the stands with Marie Lombardi, Ed Williams, and his law partner Paul Connolly. Mrs. Lombardi asked if she could borrow my field glasses for a moment. "I want to see if Tom Fears looks any older," she said with *sang-froid.* She passed back the binoculars a few minutes later. "He looks the same as ever," she said. I then peered at Fears through the glasses. He looked haggard and dispirited.

The Saints' kicker, Tom Dempsey, a huge man with a de-formed toeless foot, teed up the ball. This was it. The season had begun. Dempsey's kickoff came down at the 3-yard line, where Flea Roberts fielded it and ran the ball back to the Redskin 36-yard line. Gerry Allen carried for 3 yards off the right side, and then everything came unstuck. Dyer ran a draw play over the middle and was hit for a 4-yard loss by defensive end Doug Atkins, playing in his eighteenth NFL season. Jurgensen took too long at the line of scrimmage, and the Redskins were penalized 5 yards. The team rehuddled but the same thing happened again. It was third and twenty-one and Jurgensen's pass for Gerry Allen was badly overthrown. The Saints got the ball at midfield with two and one-half minutes elapsed in the first quarter.

After a missed Saints field goal, Jurgensen took over and hit Charley Taylor on a 7-yard pass. His next two throws were miserably off target and the Saints got the ball back on their own 37-yard line after a short punt by Mike Bragg.

The Redskins' offense had fallen apart on the first two series and now it was the defense's turn. Andy Livingston swept left end for 8 yards, swept the right side for 7, bucked over the middle for 4. Then Tony Baker tried the right side for 5. Quarterback Billy Kilmer hit tight end Ray Poage on the Redskin 35, and Poage carried the ball down to the 15-yard line. Livingston swept the right end for another 5, but a penalty brought the ball back to the 15 once again. Livingston, who looked as if he could have kept running all the way to Dallas in pelting 5-yard bursts, came right back for 6 yards to the 9, then 4 more to the 5 for the first down. Kilmer passed for a touchdown the next play, and the Saints took a 7–0 lead.

The Redskins got the ball for the first time in the second quarter at their own 12-yard line. Henry Dyer promptly fumbled, and the ball was recovered by Doug Atkins, winner of the Wisconsin Chapter of the Pro-Football Writers of America Association's 1968 Vince Lombardi Dedication Award. Under the circumstances, I did not see fit to remind Marie of that delicious irony. The redoubtable Livingston carried around end to the Redskin 5. Two Kilmer passes failed, and Dempsey booted a 13-yard field goal, making it Saints 10, Redskins 0.

Ed Williams swiveled around on the bench in front of me. "We were lucky to get out of that one with a field goal," he said lugubriously.

Suddenly in the next series, Jurgensen came alive. He was said to have looked up from his kneeling position and told the huddle they were all too nervous. On third and one, he dropped back and hit flanker Bob Long on a side-line fly pattern for 52 yards. Four plays later Taylor twisted and jumped high in the end zone for a 10-yard Jurgensen pass, and the Redskins were on the scoreboard, trailing 10–7.

Curt Knight's kickoff went 8 yards deep into the end zone. Carl Ward caught the ball, hesitated a moment, and decided to run it out. Hit at the 13-yard line, he fumbled, and Mike Bass recovered for the Redskins. Jurgensen pumped the ball to Jerry Smith in the end zone on the first play, and it was suddenly Redskins 14 to Saints 10.

"Oh, oh," Ed Williams said a few minutes later, "here comes Joe Don into the game." Livingston had already run for 74 yards against the Redskin line. It remained to be seen what feats the legendary Looney had in store for his former teammates. "Did you see in the paper where Joe Don's dog, T-bone, went berserk the other day and got in someone's henhouse?" Williams asked. "No sooner than they straighten Joe Don out, T-bone goes around the bend." Looney skirted left end, where Carl Kammerer plugged him for a 1-yard gain. That yard turned out to be Joe Don's rushing total for the day.

The Saints fought back during the rest of the game, trailing by a point at 14–13, and then at 21–20. The Redskins added a field goal late in the fourth quarter to go ahead 24–20. With two minutes left to play, defensive tackle Frank Bosch dumped Kilmer for a 10-yard loss on his own 2 on third down. Since the Saints needed more than a field goal to tie, they went back to punt and intentionally stepped out of the end-zone for the safety, hoping to get the ball back with better field position. That made the score 26–20. The Las Vegas odds-makers had installed the Redskins as five-point favorites, and that deliberate safety was going to cost the gamblers some money. "Well," Williams laughed, contemplating the six-point spread, "nobody can say the Saints are in the pay of the Mafia."

The Saints punted from their own 20, and Flea Roberts brought the ball back to the Redskin 38-yard line with 1:48 left on the clock. "I think," Williams said, "I'll light up my victory cigar. Would you like one?"

Down in the dressing room, having vindicated Williams's premature celebration, the team was in high spirits. Players strutted, almost swaggered to the shower room. Sam Huff, who was to be voted Defensive Player of the Week by the AP, was flexing his muscles and telling the reporters, "Not bad for an old man, huh?" On the ride to the airport, Lombardi was pumping that arthritic knee, smiling hugely.

But all of us knew the truth: the team had looked bad. A few big plays had saved the day. "Hey, Vince, you want to see the stats?" Bill Austin asked Lombardi. Coach frowned and brushed the mimeographed statistics away with his hand.

The first-class section of the Redskins' chartered jet was reserved for the coaches, staff, owners, and the behemoth defensive lineman too large for the tourist-class seats. I plopped down next to John Hoffman, a giant twenty-six-year-old rookie from the University of Hawaii. I told him I thought he had had a pretty good game, "Did I?" he asked anxiously. "You think so? Seemed like I got fooled a lot of the time." It was more than modesty with him. Like many rookies, he literally didn't know what constituted a good game. I said I thought his sacking Kilmer during the first Saints' series was one of the key defensive plays of the first half, coming as it did early in the game when the Redskin defense was in a state of nervous collapse as grave as the offense's. I got out my statistics sheet, which showed Hoffman credited with five tackles. Only Pat Fisher with six and Sam Huff with twelve had more. "Five tackles," Hoffman mused, "I guess that's not too bad." He glanced at me quickly to read my view of that matter. "Five looks prettty good to me," I said authoritatively. "Hell, Doug Atkins only got three."

Tommy Brown was credited with one tackle. He was across the aisle from us, stretched out across two seats, his face drained of color, wearing a hospital gown with one sleeve pinned to his side. He had pulled his shoulder out again on his one tackle, would need an operation, would be lost to the team for the rest of the season. This would not be his year to prove his Green Bay critics wrong.

The plane had not been airborne long when the two Cleveland castoffs, Frank Ryan and running back Charley Harraway, came up to the first-class section. Ryan sat with Harland

Svare, and Harraway with Bill Austin. For the rest of the flight, they diagrammed the Brown offense and defense on large pieces of paper. Svare and Austin would ask the questions and nod, as Ryan and Harraway drew out the answers. They worked nonstop all the way back to Washington.

On Wednesday I saw Hoffman in the dressing room after practice. "We saw the Saints films," he frowned; "I guess I didn't do so good after all. They're going to start Leo Carroll in my place this week."

After Wednesday's practice, I sat in the stadium press box talking to Jim Snowden. "I didn't have much of a game last week. Atkins did pretty well on me. Really, it seems like I haven't been able to put it all together this year."

Dave Slattery of the Redskin front office had been an assistant to Coach Joe Kuharich when Snowden showed up at Notre Dame as a freshman. "He was eighteen years old and had hips on him and a waist like a boy's," Slattery recalled. "He climbed on the scales at the field house and weighed 246 pounds. Looking at him, I couldn't believe he'd go that big. Best build I ever saw on a kid. We'd chased him all over Ohio trying to sign him, but we didn't even know we'd got that kind of athletic talent. Then Woody Hayes of Ohio State called us. 'You bastards,' he said. 'I fed and clothed that boy for four years, and you go and steal him on me. Of all the low down, dirty—.' We said, 'We want to thank you for your efforts, Woody. He was in wonderful shape when he got here from all that good food. And he was exceedingly well dressed.'" It was nine years ago that Snowden had stepped on the Notre Dame scales. He was ten pounds heavier now, but he still had a slender waist, boyish hips, and the graceful movements of the complete athlete. Indeed, his great physical gifts had always plagued him, had always excited the tinkerer in every coach. He had been an end in high school, but when he climbed on the scales at Notre Dame, the coaching staff read his weight, clocked his speed, and thought, "Jesus, this guy would make some fullback." So they made a fullback out of him, he got hurt, and they put him back in the line. Then Otto Graham arrived in Washington, checked his weight, looked up his speed, and thought, "Jesus, this guy would be some tight end." So they made a tight end out of him, his knees continued to hurt him, and they put him back in the line. Next Vince Lombardi came to Washington, looked at the films, checked off Snowden's size and speed, and thought, "Jesus, wouldn't this guy make some pulling guard? Couldn't he just lead those sweeps and knock those defenders ass over tea kettle?" It hadn't happened yet, but already there was talk of switching Snowden to guard in 1970.

It all added to the cumulative sense of insecurity that Snowden felt. Everyone was determined to make him something different than he was. And Snowden was too gentle, too obliging, to quarrel about it. At bottom, Snowden was that fairly frequent anomaly in the world of pro football: a great athlete who was not temperamentally suited for the profession.

"I don't know what it is," Snowden was telling me, staring out over the deserted baseball diamond, his face creased with worry. "I don't know why it's not coming out right for me— whether it's all these changes this year, what Coach Lombardi is looking for here, or something in me? Whatever it is, I just don't seem to know how to find it, how to get it all together. It comes from within, Coach Lombardi says. It bugs me that I'm not doing it. I know they're all depending on me. Down on that hot field, my legs are hurting me all the time. And everybody says I ought to be faster. I've got arthritis and bursitis in my knees, and I've got a growth in my left leg. I just haven't been able to move, and swat, and use my legs the way I used to. It seems I just can't find that inner thing Coach Lombardi is looking for, that special something. I don't even know what it is, although I've felt I had it sometimes. Not this year, but before."

Something else was clearly troubling him, and I asked what it was. He said, "I got switched again this year, from right tackle to the left side. That sort of bothers me. Because I know we're a strong right-side team. I know we're a right-handed team, and I enjoyed it the three years I was on the right side, and I did a pretty good job over there. You get used to the right side. I felt it had leadership, given the kind of team we are. And also, you get used to the guys you face over on that right side. Deacon Jones. Carl Eller. Willie Davis. You get a good game against them, you got a good chance of making All Pro. You dish out most of the punishment, say 60–40, to The Deacon, to Willie Davis, you feel you've done something. I miss the right side."

"Would you like to coach?" I asked.

"I used to think I would. I'd like to get my degree too. I think I'm nine hours short, and that's something that bothers me quite a bit too. I look back at my life and all the football players I ever knew—in high school and college, and I'm one of the few that made it, and everyone of them was trying to make it then—the high-school players in the colleges, the college players in the pros. And I did, and yet I look back and I see that I didn't get my degree, that I've been hurt so much. My son died when I was away at training camp one year, and I wonder what I've got from all this."

"How about black coaches?" I asked. "How would Lombardi work out as a coach, if he was the way he is and black?"

Snowden stared at me a moment, his breath taken clean away by that hypothesis, that sudden vision of Lombardi in black face. Then he gave a low, throaty chuckle. "That'd be something to see. Naw, naw hell, nobody'd play for him. Naw, I don't think anybody would play for a black Vince Lombardi for one minute. As far as a black coach ever getting a chance, I mean a head coach, I think you're going to have to come up with a black quarterback first, or a black center, or a black middle linebacker. These are the batteries of the offense and defense, the guys who give the commands. If black players get a shot at those jobs, then maybe you can get a Negro head coach. I could think of black guys qualified to coach right now. John Wooten, used to be with us, knows this game inside out, a leader, one of the nicest guys I met in football. If he couldn't coach, nobody could."

I had heard a lot about Wooten, from black and white players alike. Most admired him as Snowden did. A great pulling guard for the Cleveland Browns for many years, Wooten had

been given his outright release by Cleveland owner Art Modell following an imbroglio over a golf tournament, in which
a local country club had invited only the white players to
participate. Wooten had been branded a black militant, had
finally landed with the Redskins during the 1968 season, and
had been cut by Lombardi during the tail end of training
camp. I knew Wooten had gone back to Cleveland, where he
headed up the main office of the Black Economic Union, and
I asked Snowden if he would get me in touch with Wooten
when we went to Cleveland that Saturday. "Sure," Snowden
said, "you ought to meet John."

The practice week before the Browns game was like all the
other weeks of the season, the patterns of preparation falling
into a boring sameness—except that there was a certain feeling in the air, a 1–0 record, a touch of destiny that no one
dared to mention. One after another the team vowed they
would beat the Browns.

As if to celebrate the Redskins' flying start, the fans drifted
out to the RFK Stadium practice field to see their team. Lombardi instructed the security guards to clear the spectators
from the parking lot.

"Only use your gun if you have to," one of the reporters
advised the policeman in charge.

Unfortunately, Lombardi had no jurisdiction over the
grounds of Washington, D.C., General Hospital, above the
practice field; a group of fans lined up along the chain-link
fence. "Sock it to 'em, Sonny," they chanted as Jurgensen
faded back to pass. "Ah, ya big meat-head," someone bellowed, as Sonny's pass was underthrown.

Charlie Gogolak, only recently banished to the cab squad,
was booting some field goals at one end of the field. "Look at
the bum," a fan yelled for no reason. "He can't even pass his
bar exams." "Yeah," another fan responded. "We pay you
$50,000 a year, Gogolak; you better play some football or give
us our money back." Later, Gogolak gave a brave grin at his
locker. "My fan club. Aren't they wonderful? I think I'll invite
them all over to the house for dinner one of these nights. Yes,
I guess the membership of the Charlie Gogolak fan club has

fallen off a little this year. I did get a letter yesterday, though, from a kid wanting my autograph. He said he still thinks I'm the best quarterback in the NFL in spite of everything. . . . "

Vince Promuto showed me a fan letter he had received. The handwriting was the spidery work of a child, the language oddly stilted. After a flowery opening paragraph, the letter got down to brass tacks. What the writer wanted was for Promuto to get Sonny Jurgensen's autograph and send it along as soon as possible. The last paragraph said, "I am enclosing a small tip in reward for your kind services." A quarter was scotch-taped to the bottom of the letter.

"How about that! That's the damnedest fan letter I've got yet. This kid's something. He is really something, he is. A quarter tip!" Promuto suddenly exploded with laughter.

Chapter 11

As the team sat in the waiting room at Washington National Airport, listening for the Cleveland flight to be announced, Lombardi looked up and announced at large, "You know what they say. There are the great cities the of world—New York, San Francisco, Rome, and Paris, and all the others are just Cleveland."

It was cold and rainy in Cleveland. The plane circled over the huge bowl of Municipal Stadium and banked away from the gray water of Lake Erie to land.

John Wooten was in front of the hotel in his Cadillac. He had asked a half dozen of the black ballplayers out for dinner and had invited me to come along. We could talk later when he returned the players to the hotel for the 11 P.M. curfew. Wooten was a grave, soft-spoken man with deep-set eyes and a thin, sharp nose. We drove around town for a while, seeing the sights in the Hough area. The mayoralty campaign was in full swing, and Hough was Carl Stokes country: huge Stokes signs were staked in the front lawns of all the rowhouses, creating the eerie sense that all the houses had "For Sale" signs in front. Wooten said that if race relations were to have a chance in America, it was essential that Stokes win, for his defeat would mean that the gulf between black and white was unbridgeable. Race was the only issue that could defeat him, after all.

As the evening wore on, it became quite clear that Wooten commanded considerable respect from his former Redskin teammates. He was an articulate and earnest man and, like Lombardi, a man with the gift of intensity. On the ride back to the hotel Wooten happened to ask, "How many brothers on the squad now?" "Thirteen," someone said. "No, fourteen," Mike Bass said. It had been thirteen, but Bob Wade had just been activated to take Tommy Brown's place on the roster, so Wade made fourteen. I recalled that only a day earlier Bass had told me, "I don't know how many black players we've got on this club." I did not think this meant that Bass was untruthful. Lombardi always said he too had no idea who was black and who was white on the Redskins. They both meant by their faint exaggerations that color did not count on the Redskins, yet those fibs were also an admission by denial that color was a factor, on football teams as surely as in Cleveland elections.

It was about 10:00 P.M. when we arrived back at the hotel. Bill Austin was in the lobby, lurking at the magazine stand like a house dick. He apparently had the bed-check duty that night. Wooten and I rode the elevator up to my room.

"Did you see *The Great White Hope*?" he asked, "Did you see the play? There's a soliloquy in there by a white man. It goes something like, 'It's okay for *them* to become a top scientist, a political leader, but the champion of the world? Number one? One of *them* the best?' I think this is true, very much true. That's the real issue you're fighting in this country today. Race weighs very heavy on a black man's mind. No getting around that. Yet on the football field, not as much as you might imagine. That's why I love this game, why I say it is a beautiful game, really beautiful for a black man. For example, if I were going to present a case to the Board of General Motors, I would be very aware of the pressure of being black while I was arguing my case.

"But football doesn't allow that. I think in football you have a built-in trap door that sort of springs open and lets you fall away from that pressure and that fear when you're on the field. It comes to different guys at different times. When I lie down at night before a game all those things are shut out. I could have had the biggest argument in the world with my wife, a tragic death in the family, and I still could keep those things from me and go out and play. And on Saturday nights and Sundays for the ten years I was a pro, I was not aware of being black. That's why football is so beautiful to me, because you're a free man when you play it; you're all alone when you play that game.

"And football has created better race relations. It lets a man give something of himself and take something back without worrying about the outside pressures of life and race—to be able to sit down with Len Hauss from Georgia and Gene Hickerson from Mississippi and not care about what color you are. These are the kind of things, the relationships that I guard very jealously, these are the kind of things I would hate to see destroyed."

"Tell me something about the problems of being a black athlete," I said.

"Well, you got to understand I played nine years in Cleveland. Cleveland's something special for a black player. There's no place like playing in Cleveland. Those damn babes up there in the stand yelling!

"So I've experienced the best football has to offer. But there are towns that are not as good. There are clubs where black ballplayers don't feel they have much of a chance. Your black ballplayer knows when he reports to camp that he's going to be one of two things. He says to himself, 'Am I going to be a starter? Or will I have to be a sonofabitch on those special units?' He has to sit down and figure it out. Which one is he going to be? Because he knows he isn't going to ride the bench and be groomed for the future like a white ballplayer will. That's true. You look around the league and tell me how many black players are on rosters, and they're not a starter or a sonofabitch on those special teams?

"Okay, so when a black figures out he isn't good enough to start, he says to himself, 'I'm going to have to be a headhunter on the special units. It's the only way for me.' I mean hell, you take a guy like Joe Don Looney. If he'd been black, he would have been kicked out of this league years ago. Hell, he wouldn't even have gotten in the league. Had Joe Don been black and created the chaos he did at Oklahoma, he wouldn't have made it to his sophomore year. I could name you three blacks who weren't drafted by the pros this year cause they'd gotten involved in boycotts and demonstrations on their respective campuses. The scouts could tell you those guys were ranked pretty high. These three guys were blackballed. Now you tell me, was Joe Don Looney drafted?"

"I understand they tried to blackball Flea Roberts," I said.

"Tried?" Wooten's eyebrows raised.

"Well, they didn't succeed. He's on the roster."

"This year. Last year he was doing nothing. Sure, the Saints blackballed him. He was sitting out in our Los Angeles office working for us. That's where he was. Lombardi asked me about Flea. He said, 'Tell me about the Flea. I know he's a good football player, tell me about the rest.' So I ran down Flea's situation, and Lombardi said, 'Okay, that's good enough for me.' Lombardi's a fair man."

"How was it playing for him?"

"I came to camp with great enthusiasm. Then, when I'd been there a couple of weeks, I wasn't the same guy. My mind would be wandering. I enjoyed sitting there listening to Lombardi. I enjoyed listening to his screaming 'cause I knew what he was screaming about. He was screaming about minute details that separate winning from losing. He was even hollering about it on Monday and on Tuesday. So all of these things intrigued me. To me, this was what the game of football is about. Yet the will to play wasn't there. It was like shooting marbles, or riding a bike. You did it without thinking about it, and it was fine, but that's not football. And then one day one of the coaches, not Lombardi, told me he was going to 'kick me in the ass' if I missed another block. You don't talk to men like that.

"Like I say, Lombardi's a fair man, but you don't know whether he's being fed behind the door either. So I said to myself, 'Nobody's going to make me quit, make me get up and walk out of camp and have people say it was too hard for John Wooten. By the same token, I'm not going to play for anyone who puts down this kind of crap.' They could cut me, I didn't care, but I wasn't going to leave.

"So I had a hyper-extended knee, and I asked this assistant coach if I could cut scrimmage, and this guy goes over and whispers something to Lombardi. Apparently he thought I was loafing.

"Lombardi screams, 'Why aren't you scrimmaging?' So I told him it's my knee, and he yells, 'Get in there. Suppose you were the only guard I had in a game and your knee was hurt? What would you do then?'

"And I said, 'I'd suffer and I'd play. I played nine years starting guard at Cleveland and I played every damn game, injured and healthy.'

"And I stopped caring after that. I think he saw that. I think he did, as the close observer of football that he is. If he had come up to me and said, 'I know it's been tough for you. Hang in with me, help me out,' that probably would have changed my mind, because I had enough of just that kind of respect for him.

"I think I would say my respect for Lombardi, and you had to respect what he'd done in Green Bay, grew a little after playing for him. I think he respects class. The amount of pride he tries to instill into his players, he tries to build not only class football players, but class people.

"I think the Lombardi training camp was a bitch, tougher than anything I'd ever seen or dreamed about. The guys were so scared, so afraid of this man, so shaky—there were errors of omission and commission. But the ballplayers had one thing going for them. They *believed* in the man. Yes, they believed in the man, and what they really didn't realize was they believed in themselves. Because that's all he was believing in. His philosophy is built on the fact they had it in them. He was asking them to believe in themselves and believe in him, and he would put it all together. And that's why I think the Redskins are going to be the coming team, the champions. They may not win it this year, they may not win it next year, but they're going to win it."

His voice trailed away to a low, intense flatness of belief as he intoned that last phrase. "How about this year?" I asked. "Do they have a chance?"

"In order to win it this year, they can't afford to screw around with the ballclubs they can beat. No screwing around with Atlanta, Pittsburgh, Philadelphia, the Giants—those kind of clubs. Then they got to beat three clubs they're not supposed to beat—Cleveland, the Rams, the Colts, and Dallas. They got to take three of the five they got with those teams. They should beat Frisco. Hell, they got to beat Frisco. They're going to need to win twelve ballgames to win. Dallas may very well go 12–2. Dallas is that good.

"And for the Redskins to do it, Charley Taylor's got to stay healthy. You see, Charley suffers from number-one-itis. Charley has got to be the best or he's in pain. And Charley may very well be the best the NFL has ever seen. But he suffers, he's afraid not to be number one. If it gets to where Charley is not going to win that receiving title, Charley is going to be a sick boy, crippled with diseases and injuries you never heard of.

"Now, of course, you can't lose your quarterback and win. No matter how good that backup is, Sonny has got to stay healthy. When you get a chance to get a backup as good as Ryan, you got to be crazy not to. Getting Ryan and dumping Theo was just economics. You may not like to do it, but you got to. Now that line is very shaky, your offense and defense both, shaky as hell. Moving Snowden to the other side, that was stupid. They should have called him in the spring and worked with him then to see if he could switch from being a right-hander to a left-hander. Willie Banks is going to be a great guard. On the defense, Spain is young, inexperienced. Hoffman is going to be an outstanding player, but not this year. He's still in awe of being in the National Football League. Kammerer is steady, awfully steady. The linebacking corps is adequate. Sam is fine if he doesn't run out of gas before the year is out, and I'd guess he's too old not to. The secondary is in good shape. Mike is solid, Brig is solid, Pat Fisher is extremely solid. Rickie is good, but he's a hunch player and won't always go where the defense is called.

"But then you got Lombardi. You got to add something on for having him. But this year having him may hurt too. It's going to be hard on Sonny to learn his system. I'd guess it'll take the whole team half the year at least before they know the Lombardi system. You got to play it before you know it."

"Who are you going to be rooting for tomorrow?" I asked.

"I'll be pulling for individuals, not a team, I guess. I'll be pulling for guys like Brig, and Len Hauss, and Pat Richter, and Jerry Smith, and Snowden, and the Flea. And by the same token, I'll have to pull a little bit for Walter Johnson, and Dick Schafrath, and Gene Hickerson, and Leroy Kelly, if he plays. There are going to be some beautiful people out there tomorrow. It's a beautiful game. I enjoy it. I really do. Enjoyed it, I mean. It's one of the few jobs anywhere where a man is free. All alone out there and yet part of something, too."

Chapter 12

It was a gray day in Cleveland when I woke up Sunday morning. I told Leo Carroll I would drop by his room for a talk before the team breakfast. Carroll was a slender blond with a solid line of eyebrows and sideburns that got imperceptibly longer week by week as the season progressed. "Leo is the master of the Viet Cong growl," an offensive player had told me. "He sounds like he's tearing you to pieces in practice. In fact, he ain't doing shit except growling."

"I'm really a rookie, I guess," Carroll told me. "And then again, I'm not. This is my first real game, yet I've been in the League for three years. So I won't get knocked on my ass and someone will say, 'Welcome to the NFL, kid.' That kind of rookie treatment is over for me."

"What did you do last night?" I asked.

"I tried not to think. If I think a lot about today, starting and all, I get scared, real scared. About five o'clock I went out and had a couple of beers, some dinner with some of the guys, talking about everything and nothing. Then about eight we went to the show. I was asleep at eleven and I woke up around two, wide awake. I just lay there an hour or so, looking at the ceiling and then I drifted off again, dreamed about the guys I'll be playing. I don't even know their names, but I can see their faces, and how they block and how they move. It's all up to me. I can make it today. I can be first team. I've got the chance, and it's up to me."

"What's the figuring on Cleveland?"

"If we can force them to pass, we'll win. That means the pressure is on the defensive line. We got to get to Nelson. The whole deal is to stop those backs of theirs on first and second down, to force the pass. If we let them run on us that first and second down, they'll run us off the field. I'll tell you this, if we can beat them I really believe we'll be in the play-offs."

"If?" I asked.

"Yeah, you're right. There shouldn't be an 'if' in there. Lombardi doesn't go for 'ifs.' Like with the Packers—they are champions and they knew it. Even last year when they were losing, they didn't go out on the field and say, 'We have to beat *them*.' They'd say, '*They* have to beat us.'"

"The Redskins aren't ready to say that yet?"

"Well, I said 'if,' I guess. I suppose I don't really know about myself yet, or even know about the team. I am thinking, '*We* have to beat Cleveland,' and that has to mean something, has to show a state of mind. But I'll say this, if we beat them, it'll make a difference, a big one. We won't have to talk about 'ifs' then."

I could see what Wooten meant about the special quality of Municipal Stadium, the pleasures of playing there. It was a vast, dilapidated ballpark, the grime and the concrete buffed together, with great steel pillars supporting the upper deck. The outlines of the Cleveland Indian baseball diamond were still visible on the gridiron. But for all its age and its sorry physical decline, it seemed a stadium that still had the flush of its past, the sense that it had seen its share of great sporting events. The sky was wintry and dark over Lake Erie to the east, and the sea gulls dipped and floated above the choppy lake waters.

The Redskins took the kickoff and moved it downfield to the Cleveland 38, where Larry Brown's third-down buck in the middle fell short of the first down by a yard. Knight tried a 45-yard field goal that was wide to the left.

The ball changed hands a couple of times, both defenses holding well. Then, with two and a half minutes left in the first quarter, the Redskins took over on their own 20.

The first play from scrimmage, Larry Brown found daylight around right end and went 58 yards to the Cleveland 23, breaking tackles, lurching off balance, but somehow remaining upright. It was a breathtaking run, and three plays later Jurgensen capped it with a touchdown pass to Jerry Smith.

Cleveland came right back on a long drive to tie the score 7–7. The Browns added a field goal as the half ended and went to the dressing room, up 10–7.

It had been a solid, almost a physical half for the Redskins, but the question was what they would be like in the second half. Sam Huff, the man who held the defense together, had been knocked unconscious in a goal-line pileup during the Brown touchdown drive and had to be helped from the field, his face blank, his knees rubbery.

Bo Scott ran the second kickoff back to the Cleveland 44, and the Redskin defense trotted back on the field led by Huff. On third and five, Bill Nelson tried to hit Gary Collins, but Rickie Harris picked off the ball on the Redskin 38 and brought it back to the midfield stripe, Huff leading the blocking convoy. He crashed into Brown tackle Monty Clark and went down like a sack on the Cleveland side lines. He lay there for a while, completely still, the Cleveland doctor bending over him. At length he was helped to his feet, and he stumbled across the field to the Redskin bench, finished for the afternoon, his role in shoring up the Washington defense, calling the defensive audibles, and readjusting the line turned over to rookie John Didion.

The Redskins worked the turnover down to the Cleveland 25, failed to come through on a third-and-one situation, and took a 32-yard field goal, tying the game at 10–10.

Huff's presence was missed as the Browns went back, ahead 17–10 on an 80-yard drive, climaxed by a 17-yard draw right up the middle by Ron Johnson, untouched by Redskin hands. Early in the fourth quarter the Browns added another field goal to make it 20–10.

But with a little less than ten minutes to play, Jurgensen got the Redskins back into the game, mixing his runs with passes over the middle to drive 70 yards for the score in seven plays. Brig Owens juggled the snap from center on the extra point, there was no kick, and instead of drawing within range of a field-goal tie, the Redskins were now four points down at 20–16.

The Browns took over on their own 20 with six minutes to play.

Six minutes for the Redskins to get the ball back and score a touchdown. Reece Morrison, who had already run for more than 100 yards, carried for 4 more over right tackle. Nelson came back with the same play, and Frank Bosch stopped Morrison cold at the line of scrimmage, making it third and six. There was a little more than five minutes left, and Nelson dropped back to pass. Bosch broke through, knocked the ball loose, and Leo Carroll fell on it at the Brown 13-yard line.

Suddenly there was an urgent sense of upset in the air. Jurgensen and the offensive unit charged onto the field, and ten seconds later he faded back, pumped the ball a couple of times, and, bang, hit Bob Long in the end zone for a touchdown. It couldn't have looked simpler; it was as if Jurgensen had been doing this sort of thing his whole life. The conversion was good, and with four and a half minutes left to play, the Redskins led 23–20. That missed extra point suddenly took on a new dimension, meant the Browns could tie with a field goal.

The kickoff was short, and Bo Scott returned it 19 yards to the Cleveland 26-yard line. All that the Redskin defense had to do was hold for three downs and the offense would get the ball back and possibly run out the clock.

Reece Morrison carried around right end for 12 yards and the first down. There was 3:30 left on the clock, and all the Redskin defense had to do was dig in for three plays. Rookie Ron Johnson went for 2 yards off tackle. That was good; two more plays like that, and the game would be on ice. Nelson hit Warfield for 11 yards and the first down on the Redskin 49-yard line. There were two and a half minutes left, still time for the defense to stand firm and keep the Browns out of field-goal range. Ron Johnson ploughed 6 yards up the middle to the Washington 43. Reece Morrison turned left end for 10 yards and the first down on the Redskin 33, pretty reliable field-goal distance.

There were worse things than a tie, for it didn't count against you in the Division race; 1–1 was still 1.000 in the standings. Besides, 38-yard field goals had been missed; kicks even closer had been blocked. Maybe that "great big sonofabitch" Spain Musgrove would burst through there, putting his training-camp lessons to work. It was first and ten, with 1:30 left on the clock. Nelson dropped back to pass behind good protection. He scanned the situation downfield. Incredibly, the Redskin secondary had every receiver sewed up. Still Nelson peered downfield for a target. Carl Kammerer spun off his man on the Redskin right side, but was blocked to the ground about 3 feet from Nelson. Kammerer appeared to be rising to his knees to lunge. Nelson cocked his arm as if he had finally located a target, but Kammerer sunk back to his knees, and Nelson kept the ball. Kammerer started to crawl toward him, but it was too late. At last Nelson found Morrison open on his left side at the Redskin 15-yard line. The play took six seconds, but it seemed infinitely longer. On the next play, Gary Collins got behind Pat Fisher and hauled in his first pass of the day for the touchdown. It was Browns 27, Redskins 23. There was a little more than a minute on the clock. That missed extra point loomed even larger now: the Redskins needed a touchdown; nothing else would do.

Washington went to work on their 20, but a holding penalty put them back on their 10. A swing pass to Henry Dyer and a Dyer plunge got the first down. Another penalty made it first and fifteen at the Redskin 29, with nine seconds showing. Everyone in the stadium knew what Jurgensen had to do. It was the old days again. He had to send them out on the fly and put that ball up as far as he could get it. Jurgensen dropped back and waited for the receivers to break free. The Brown secondary was not without a hunch on the play, and no Redskin broke loose. The lines seemed to vanish; Jurgensen was back there all alone, with all the time in the world to pass, but not enough left on the scoreboard to wait indefinitely. He took off up the middle, running remarkably well, breaking tackles, faking defenders to the ground, looking frantically for somebody to lateral to. Charley Taylor was nowhere around, and there weren't even any lumbering linemen to be seen. Jurgensen puffed on, the gun sounded, and he was at last brought down in a heap at the Cleveland 38.

It was a splendid last-ditch effort, but the score was still 27–24, and it was still a blown game, one that had been won and thrown away. Up in the stands a cardboard placard was raised high. It said, "Vince Who?" The Redskins trudged off the field to the boarded-up baseball dugout that led to their dressing room, their shoulders stooped by circumstance and what they faced below in the clubhouse.

It was easy to say that Huff would have held the Redskin defense together, would have closed off the vulnerable Washington middle, would have come up with the big play. It was easy to say, and that was what Lombardi told the press afterwards. But before the Redskin dressing-room doors had been thrown open to admit the reporters, he had spoken words nearer to the mark. He had eyed the team with something like savage contempt and said, "You lost this one for me. They ran through you people like you were pure air. I needed this one for the title, and you threw it away."

The dressing room was still traumatized by the time I fought my way down from the press box. The players peered into their lockers, poking absently at their belongings, their heads bowed. Carl Kammerer sat on a stool in front of his locker, his shoulder pads on his bare torso, staring uncomprehendingly into his locker, like a flood victim confronting the ravages that had obliterated all his best hopes. His body was dotted with the red splotches of new bruises.

A few cubicles down the line Leo Carroll savagely ripped the tape bandaging off his hands. He wadded it up into a ball and hurled it toward the trash can in cold fury. "The defensive line lost this game. They ran around me at will, just at will. Over me, around me; Jesus, I was terrible. We just have the four of us up front to blame. We blew it."

Outside in the parking lot, there was no noticeable scramble to board the bus that housed Lombardi and the coaching staff. Just the opposite. Those who could, slunk aboard the other bus, and who could blame them? Lombardi looked stricken, defeated, gray with fatigue. God only knew what he had gone through in those closing four minutes of the game, watching defeat snatched from the jaws of victory, experiencing the elation of taking over again where he had left off in 1967, of commanding a team that had beaten the best in the Eastern Conference. It had ended in the squalid despair of commanding a team that had thrown it all away.

Every coach lost a heartbreaker or two, that was the way the ball bounced, that was the nature of the beast. But this one was *the* heartbreaker, and Lombardi was realist enough to know it, his face ingenuous enough to show it.

The Redskin buses crept through the heavy traffic for the freeway and the airport beyond. We stopped at a red light, and a yellow schoolbus with Maple Heights written across its side pulled abreast of us. For a while the kids in the bus peered at us idly, and then the recognition began to dawn on them that ours was a peculiar cargo—twenty large men and one woman in a mink coat. All at once the kids crowded up to the windows, huge twisted grins pressed to the glass. "There he is," someone squealed. "Hey, Vince," another yelled. "Can I have your autograph?" "Good luck," someone called. "You guys are losers," someone trilled. I assumed it was an outing of school children coming back from the game. There was a radiant-looking girl with a long foxy nose across the way from my window. Next to her was a boy, his face distended in a jeer against the windowpane. The kids began to clap in unison, and it was hard to know from the looks on their faces and the rhythm of their applause whether they were taunting Lombardi or paying him tribute. Marie smiled and waved timidly. Lombardi gave a large, sad smile, and lifted his hand in a wooden cigar-store Indian "How." The famous teeth were flashing, but there was no light in his upper face, just an ineffable deadness of spirit up there.

The bus whirred toward the airport, and Lombardi closed his eyes and began to doze off. He worked his arthritic knee back and forth a few times, his chin slumped on his chest, and he was asleep. Occasionally his head would jerk up, only to flop back down. Harland Svare, a man as cool and collected on the side lines as Lombardi was emotional and distraught, fell asleep too, his head bobbing up and down, a man as oppressed by the performance of his defensive troops as Lombardi. Bill Austin read the Sunday sports pages of a Cleveland newspaper. Sam Huff grinned and cracked jokes about getting his "bell rung." Victory made all men the same. Defeat etched the differences in their personalities.

On the flight back from New Orleans, the team had choked the aisles, kibitzing at card games, as jovial as two cans of beer and a winning afternoon permitted. On this flight, they stuck fast in their seats, slouched down as inconspicuously as possible. The Lombardis ate their filet mignons together at the back of the first-class section and, as we neared Washington, Marie changed seats with Paul Connolly's nine-or ten-year-old son. I could not envy Master Connolly his wide-eyed tête-à-tête with Coach. Lombardi appeared to appreciate young Connolly's discomfort, his anxiety at the prospects of being exposed to some sudden temper tantrum. Lombardi smiled, calling on the last reserve of "second effort" to muster some charm for his seatmate. Under the circumstances, it was probably the day's highwater mark in self-discipline. Master Connolly looked almost chipper by the time we touched down at Washington National.

I walked to the parking lot with one of the assistant coaches. "Tough one to lose," I allowed. "Be a long night for you, I guess."

"Yeah, you suffer," he said. "But you been through this damn crap as long as I have, you get over it okay." Some barefooted youths in love beads, psychedelic shirts, and levis were coming toward us. "Jesus," he said, the disgust of the day rising up in him with alarming vehemence. "There are some beauties. These are the guys going to save us from the Russians. I'd like to get a hold. . . . " His voice trailed away in an impotent grunt of frustration.

On Monday, before lunch, the press trekked to the Redskin offices to hear Lombardi's official post-mortem on the Cleveland game.

"Did you think you were going to upset them?" a reporter asked.

"I thought we were going to *beat* them, not upset them," Lombardi corrected with some pugnacity. "We just didn't stop them. The defensive line broke down, particularly on that last drive. Sam's going out hurt us. He holds the defense together, no doubt about that. God knows how long they gave Nelson to get off that Morrison pass. We would have been all right if they'd played the defenses we gave them, but they decided to play their own game. When Sam went out, they adjusted to help Didion, and you can't do that."

"How about that last touchdown throw?" someone asked.

"No complaints on that. Pat Fisher had Collins covered like a glove the whole game. It was a perfect throw, and Collins has five inches on Fisher. A perfectly executed play."

There were a few desultory queries, and then Lombardi said, "The big thing is not to let the team get down. If everyone knocks them, they'll be down, and God knows how or when they'll get back up."

It was an awkwardly put entreaty for the writers to play ball, one that might have slipped by in Green Bay, but one that quite naturally ruffled the Washington writers.

"Does that include the press, that 'knocking' stuff?" a reporter challenged.

Lombardi clearly sensed that he had given offense, had gone beyond the bounds of propriety. He wanted, I suspected, to backtrack, to make amends, even to apologize, but he was a man who had had such limited experience in owning up to errror that he did not know how to do it.

There was a certain sense of tension in the air, and Lombardi chose to dispel it by saying, "If you want to knock somebody, knock me, not the team. I don't have to prove anything. I'm big enough to take it. I don't give a damn."

"I thought you didn't want publicity," a reporter said with sarcasm.

"I meant praise, not knocking," Lombardi said, and wandered out of the room.

That Monday night, my wife and I went to the theater. There was a sprinkling of Redskins in the audience, and we sat next to Vince Promuto and his wife. We were talking about the Cleveland game and Promuto said, "I've been with this team ten years, and that flaying Lombardi gave us in the dressing room afterwards was the first time I've ever heard anything like that. It's usually, 'Well, men, you played hard, the other team harder. You made the big effort, but the breaks didn't go our way. Way to go anyway, men.' Lombardi's a little different. He really tore into us, and we deserved it. We blew the game. I tell you, the guys were scared. Now they know what it's like losing under Lombardi. It's no fun. Losing a real game is one different thing from losing an exhibition, I'll tell you that. You know, it's nice if football builds character and all that stuff, but that's not what it's really about. It's about winning. If you're not winning, you're not doing nothing. You're not doing what they pay you to do."

At intermission there was a group of business men in the row behind us, talking in loud voices. Promuto turned around in his seat and said, "Where you guys from?"

"Out of town," one of them grinned.

"Whereabouts?" Promuto asked.

"Cleveland. I guess you heard of that town, huh?"

Promuto laughed. My wife was amazed at the good humor with which Promuto accepted that barb. And for me too, it was hard to accept that the tragedy of Cleveland could fade away. But the season had to go on. The 49'ers were next, and the Browns were best forgotten.

But not quite. There were still some movies to be seen.

Chapter 13

Yes, out at RFK Stadium Tuesday morning, the films of the Browns game elicited a note or two of acrimony from the coaching staff, a caustic comment or so from Coach. As one player told me afterwards, "I was shaking and I didn't even get in the game." I had arranged to talk with Carl Kammerer after practice and I assumed the morning séance had not left him joyful.

Many professional football players, no matter where they come from—the swamps of Florida or the coastal islands of Maine—regard themselves as westerners, as Dodge City marshals, in fact. There was always a fair number of hand-tooled leather cowboy boots standing tall in the Redskin locker stalls, even an occasional broad-billed Stetson or a leather vest on which to pin the marshal's star. It was not a farfetched conceit for a pro football player, for the game embodied the harsh life-and-death code of the West, gave the player the sense of being a man tall in the saddle, handy with his fists, alone against the primordial frontier vastness and loneliness.

Carl Kammerer wore his cowboy boots with the stamp of authority. He was a Californian, with the big and breezy manner, the sun-bleached hair, a handsome weather-beaten look, and most of all the carriage—the erect back, the loose, dangling arms at the ready, the swaggering walk full of menace and purpose.

"Well," Kammerer began out in the Senators' dugout, "I played for the 49'ers two years as a middle linebacker when I came out of the College of the Pacific in 1961. Went to the All-Star game, and there were four of us middle linebackers there who're still playing pro ball, Marlin McKeever, E. J. Holub, Myron Pottios, and myself. Then I got traded to the Redskins in '63, and in '64 Sam Huff came along, so they moved me out to defensive end."

His voice was flat, devoid of interest, his mind engaged elsewhere.

"Listen," he said abruptly, "my mental attitude isn't too hot today."

"You're down," I said; "that's part of football. Let's talk while you're down, We'll have plenty of chances to talk again when you're high." As I spoke I had in mind that ghastly moment, forever frozen in time, when he had failed to get up to nail Nelson. And no doubt that moment had been frozen still on the projection screen that morning as well.

"Tell me about Cleveland," I said.

"Football is just this," he began. "On the big plays where it really counts, where something has to happen, somebody then must make that play. On that next-to-last play, that Nelson pass to Morrison, what can I say? I spun around, fell to the ground, got up again, was ready to tackle the quarterback, and he threw the ball. It happens a thousand times in a career. This time it happened, and we lost the ballgame.

"I try to leave the Sunday game alone after the Tuesday films, but that one on Sunday is hard to let alone. If it ever happened again I would know I had to play it differently. I tried to make an inside move. I realize now I should have moved to the outside. There was no way I could have been cut down to the outside; I could have got in to him if I'd come from the outside. I know it was their running, the ability of the Browns to run against us for the yards they did that won the game for them. Hell, they ran for 5 yards, 4.6 or so, per carry. It's very academic. You run 4.6, you always get a first down in three plays.

"No, if anything good could come from this, it would be that each man on the club would take an inward look at himself, particularly the defensive people like myself. If the whole group of us can do this kind of thing and learn from it and never break apart like that again, then the game will have served some purpose. But if we don't, then it could be a long season." He weighed that possibility, his eyes narrowing in bleak concentration, not ruling it out. Not by a long shot.

"It's just like Lombardi said in the dressing room afterwards. When a team takes the ball with four and a half minutes to go, they're telling the whole world they have to have a touchdown to win. We go into a defense that's designed to stop them, and we're telling the whole world we've *got* to stop them. And we don't do it. That's telling the whole world we don't have it. We get a penalty and jump around, instead of coming right back and defying them, defying them to do it against us. That defiance is what you need. Your good people, your experienced people, come to life in a situation like that. They defy the Browns to get the yards they need, they defy them. It's not a killer-type thing, it's defiance."

"Did Sam being out of there hurt?" I asked.

"Sure, it did. But when something happens to one of your key players, you've got to pick up the slack, the whole team does. I was the most veteran guy in there and I had some things to say in the huddle during that last drive, told the guys we had to rise up together. It didn't seem to take a strong hold on them, like I hoped it would. Maybe they were still thinking about Sam. But hell, you've got to forget about Sam. There's something that's being asked of you right now, and you've got to forget about Sam.

"Though, to tell you the truth, I'll remember what Sam looked like for a long time, a long, long time. Boy, I've only seen one other guy rocked like that in my nine years of pro ball, and that was Clyde Conner in San Francisco. He actually arched his back and his whole body was quivering, just so reminiscent of death you can't forget it—like in an old Greek play where they carry on in ritual moves and everything all exaggerated. In Sam's case, his eyes were a gray death stare, looking into the air, looking nowhere, and then his eyes started to open and close rapidly and his lips were quivering. That was the first time. The second time he turned blue, just like in a cartoon where a guy falls in a frozen lake. I thought Sam was goners that second time.

"It only happened to me once, getting cold-cocked like that. That was in training camp, and somebody kicked me in the head. When I came to, everything had movement to it. You'd look at a straight line and it was crooked, had gaps in it, jagged, broken, and not only that, the damn line was vibrating and there were circles in the air moving around. I never have seen anything like that before, and I don't care to see it again."

"Go back to what it was like for the rest of that final drive," I asked.

"As the Browns kept coming, there was more excitement, more mix-ups, with Harland calling the defense from the side lines. A couple of times nobody could read the signals. Didion was doing as well as a rookie can in a spot like that; he was interpreting most of Svare's calls and then calling the defenses. A couple of times in the huddle he had to ask what different things meant. I didn't know what they meant either. The other linebackers? Chris Hanburger knew some of them, but not all of them. One came on us real quick, and no one knew what in hell it was supposed to be. Didion said to play the special defenses we put in, and whether that was the signal Svare had in mind, I just don't know. I just kept thinking, everything would settle down and we'd play football. I just kept thinking this was *our* defense out there; we had to show we could hold them.

"God, if we had won in Cleveland, and we almost did. WE ALMOST DID. If our defense could have held, we would be going into San Francisco this week and we would be flying high. We would go into San Francisco as a forty-man team and not a single foot would be touching the ground. Now we are 1–1, but if we had two victories going into the third week of the season, we'd be on top of our division. We can still be on top of our division, but it now takes another win. We must win in Frisco. WE MUST. The quickness of it all. There are fourteen games. That's all. You've got to demonstrate you're going to be a winner, that you're going to build from 2–0 up. If we'd come out with a win, then we could build. With that loss, all of that has changed. It's all different now."

For Lombardi, Tuesday was the day he began stoking up the pressure for next Sunday. He showed the films of the Sunday disaster, ripped the culprits to pieces, took the field for a workout, and changed gears. From Tuesday afternoon on he was a devotee of the "power of positive thinking," persuading, guying, shouting, driving, but always pointing toward Sunday, always seeking to build rather than to tear down.

Defensive back Pat Fisher summed up the Lombardi technique for me as well as anyone. "Lombardi is a salesman. He has to sell us on winning. Each day he sells the team and sells us. He's leading up to the right moment to clinch the sale, and that's supposed to be on Sunday. That's the day we buy. He always tries to close the sale on Sunday. Sometimes he does and sometimes he doesn't. It's hard to sell forty men week after week. Damn hard. Probably impossible to get to all forty. Maybe thirty's all you need, maybe thirty-five. You just can't be sure, so you have to shoot for forty. I have the feeling that each day Lombardi tries to think of some little story or parable he might tell that will stick in your mind all week, make you susceptible for the Sunday sale, sort of like a car salesman pointing out a new accessory every day. Lombardi's all design.

"Lombardi is clever and he always couches his words positively. He never speaks in negative terms during the week, like most coaches do. Where they might say, we can't have any more interceptions, we can't have any more of this damn fumbling, we can't have these breakdowns in the line, Lombardi will go at it the other way. He'll say, we've got to throw the ball just as accurately as we did in the second quarter, we've got to continue opening up those big holes like we did in the third quarter. After Tuesday he doesn't remind you of the mistakes you've made."

There was, then, a fine line that separated success from failure, pressure from mere abuse, and Lombardi endeavored that week to remain on the clement, if not the acclamatory side of the line. The atmosphere in the clubhouse on Tuesday had been morose. Kammerer was not the only downcast veteran. Another Redskin old hand reflected on the Sunday tongue-lashing in the dressing room at Cleveland after the

"Coach"   (Photo by Paul Fine)

Redskin President Edward Bennett Williams announces "the second coming" on February 7, 1969. (Washington Daily News photo.)

The last pressure putt, three days before the opening of training camp at Carlisle, Pennsylvania. (Photo by Nate Fine)

"What the hell is going on here?" or "You guys are really something, you are." (Photo by Nate Fine)

The apt pupil. Sonny Jurgensen is all mouth as the master imparts his training camp lessons. (Photo by Nate Fine)

The rains come to Washington as Harland Svare and Lombardi watch
the Redskins beat the Bears in the exhibition season opener. (Photo by
Paul Fine)

Out on the gridiron, the '69 Redskins are enduring their first defeat of the year. Against the Buffalo Bills, of all people.
(Photo by Paul Fine)

"Our kicking game is the laughing-stock of the league," Lombardi announced during the exhibition season. Here in Atlanta he shows Charlie Gogolak the right way to put that old pigskin through the uprights. Bill Austin in the foreground. Harland Svare and Mike McCormack behind Lombardi. (Photo by Paul Fine)

Lombardi passes on some avuncular advice to his bench in the Atlanta game. (Photo by Paul Fine)

Lombardi scores a mild point with the press corps after Washington's 20–10 exhibition loss to the Cleveland Browns. The author is the writer to the extreme left who appears to be awake. (Photo by Paul Fine)

The Redskins win their season opener against the Saints—but in less convincing fashion than the Packers used to win their first game of the season. (Photo by Paul Fine)

A "defiant" 1–0 Redskin team takes the field at Cleveland's Municipal Stadium. Three hours later they are to trudge off in the opposite direction, 1–1 and minus some defiance. (Photo by Paul Fine)

Rickie Harris disposes of a $27-football, heaving it up into the stands in the general direction of his wife, after breaking off an 86-yard punt return for a touchdown to beat the Giants.

(Photo by Paul Fine)

Jurgensen takes to the ground against the Steelers. Pittsburgh defensive tackle Mean Joe Greene gapes from kneeling position as Ray Schoenke, Vince Promuto, and Willie Banks lead the way. (Photo by Paul Fine)

Seven–seven against the Eagles at halftime in the Redskins' dressing room. From left to right: Sonny Jurgensen, Frank Ryan, Dave Kopay, Flea Roberts, Vince Lombardi, and Charley Harraway. (Photo by Paul Fine)

Unbloody but bowed in Baltimore after Jurgensen's last intercepted pass puts the game on ice for the Colts and breaks the Redskins' three-game winning streak. (Photo by Paul Fine)

The chief executive celebrates the November Moratorium weekend out at RFK Stadium, watching the Cowboys beat the Redskins. To the president's left is his chief football counselor, Bud Wilkinson. (Photo by Paul Fine)

Leading the Eagles 28–14 in the fourth period, the Redskin bench watches the game and perhaps the season slip away. (Photo by Paul Fine)

Yin vs. Yang. The fragile quarterback vs. the charging lineman—in this case Bob Lilly of the Cowboys. (Washington Daily News photo.)

Vince Lombardi and Tom Dowling aboard the Redskin bus.
(Photo by Paul Fine)

Bob Lilly and Larry Cole converge on number nine. (Photo by Paul Fine

The spoils of defeat. Jurgensen on the sidelines after knocking Cowboy linebacker Chuck Howley out of bounds in the first Dallas game. Howley had just picked off a Jurgy pass to kill the Redskins' final drive of the game. (Washington Daily News photo.)

The legendary Philly fans do their thing. (Photo by Paul Fine)

Larry Brown

Charley Harraway

Jerry Smith

Brig Owens

Vince Promuto

Ray Schoenke

Joe Rutgens

Sam Huff

Bob Long

Carl Kammerer

Jim Snowden

Chris Hanburger

Flea Roberts

Charley Taylor

Pat Fischer

Len Hauss

Redskin linemen get the word at halftime. From left to right: Vince Promuto, Dave Crossan, and Dennis Crane. (Photo by Paul Fine)

This is the ring the Redskins might have worn, stuffed into the hip pocket of the man who had a collection of them.
(Photo by Paul Fine)

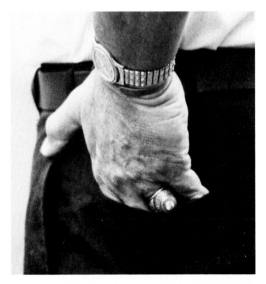

film sessions of the Browns game that morning. He told me, "Otto's first year here in '66, a lot of the guys were saying, 'What we need is a tough guy, a Vince Lombardi.' Hell, I'd read the sports pages. I knew about Lombardi. And I told them, 'You guys are just stupid if you don't go out there and win for Otto. You'll never have it so good again. Otto'll let us do anything we want, and if we win for the guy, he's going to be around for a long time. We can play this game for ten years on easy street, if you guys put out for Otto.' But, nah, they wouldn't listen to me. Had to have their tough guy. Well, by God, now they knew what I meant."

But by Wednesday the atmosphere was looser, and there was a certain amount of badinage to be seen.

In retrospect, the two most notable events of the Cleveland game were Sam Huff's two concussions and Jurgensen's desperation jog for 33 yards on the last play of the game. Although they were not in themselves events of any humor, they became such. Perhaps Huff and Jurgensen were the only players on the squad secure enough to endure ridicule in a situation so inherently mirthless as the Cleveland game. The players paid tribute to Huff's woozy spells by calling him "paperhead" and "snowflake," and Sam, who had no adversity to the limelight, reveled in the attention.

Huff and Jurgensen used adjacent lockers—the two widest ones in the dressing room—to accommodate the inquiring press corps.

Huff said to Jurgensen, "Sonny, if you're going to run with the ball, go for a TD, and, Christ, if it's the last play of the game, for God sakes, call a time-out. We had some time-outs left."

"The hell we did," Jurgensen countered. "We used up all our time-outs getting you off the field."

"The hell you say," Huff beamed. "The first half was the only time-out we used on me. The second half I was on the side lines when I got the old bell rung. That didn't cost us nothing."

"How was it in Cleveland?" I asked Charley Taylor, who had caught a mere two balls for 19 yards.

"I went, I looked around, and I come back," he intoned in a passable imitation of Caesar. "Man, we got down to the end of the game and we need a touchdown, and they're saying in the huddle, 'Hey, Charley, why don't you take off on a fly pattern?' Well, now, hell, I like to run that fly pattern as well as anyone. But, man, the player's got to wonder why he don't get a chance to run that fly sometime when nobody's looking for it. You see what I'm saying? I mean, like nine seconds left to go, you could say they might be looking for it, might have them eyes peeled for the long one." He shook his head in something like sorrow.

"Hey," he suddenly yelled, happy again. "Look at that damned Flea. Wait till Coach sees you in those controversial clothes. Man, he's going to ship you right out of here."

"Ssssshhh," Flea Roberts whispered, putting a finger to his lips. He ambled off in his leather vest, silk shirt with ten-inch collar wings, and brightly printed bell-bottoms.

John Didion padded around the clubhouse, a shy rookie under the best of circumstances, but now understandably shell-shocked from his Sunday introduction to big-league linebacking. "What did you learn from the Sunday game films?" I asked.

He gave me a wan smile and said, "Well, I finally learned who was hitting me all those times when I wasn't looking."

Yet for all the restoration of good humor, there were portentous signs to be seen, rumblings of doubt over what Kammerer had said could very well be a long season. It was possible to set aside the memory of that Cleveland collapse, but not so easy to dispel the nagging suspicion that it could happen again. One Redskin newcomer told me, "This is the first time in my football career I've been on a team that wasn't sure it could win in the last three minutes. Most ballclubs I've been on felt they could pull it out in the last few minutes. All of them knew they could hold onto a lead. I've always heard it said about the Redskins that they don't have what it takes when the going gets rough. It looks like that could be true. I don't like to be superstitious, but you got to look at the pattern, got to wonder whether that breakdown in Cleveland was the rule or the exception."

An extension of the Marshall jinx perhaps? A retribution the

Redskins were doomed to pay, whoever the coach? The wages of the past still fascinated me, and the memory of that evening with Wooten in Cleveland still lingered.

I went over to Brig Owens's house after Wednesday practice, and we sat in his recreation room. He leaned back on an easy chair, sipping a cream soda. Brig was a quiet man, not much of a talker, but with an air of solidity and reliability, the two arch qualities of a strong side safety. He had been a quarterback at the University of Cincinnati, a college with a professional type of offense, where one of his successors at quarterback, Greg Cook, had stepped in as first-string quarterback with the Cincinnati Bengals his rookie year. Nonetheless, Owens had been moved to the defensive secondary when he turned pro. Five out of the six Redskin defensive backs were black; all five had been offensive backs in college. In both pro leagues the story was the same: the defensive secondary was predominantly black.

Interestingly enough, a survey conducted for the NFL Player's Association by the Arthur D. Little Company revealed that the mean salaries paid to defensive backs were the lowest in football. The Little survey said that the over-all NFL mean salary was $22,068. Well above the mean, at $29,000 or more, were the quarterback and running backs. Just a shade below the mean, at $21,000 or more, were the receivers and linemen. The mean salary for linebackers was $19,269 and for cornerbacks and safeties $18,845. These were mean, not average, salaries, and if they did not claim to be comprehensive, they certainly mirrored the situation prevailing among the Redskins, a team which the survey found to be below the mean in its over-all club payroll. The St. Louis Cardinals had the highest mean salary at $31,970, and the Pittsburgh Steelers the lowest at $16,758. The Redskins were in eighth place at $20,640, some $1500 below the over-all League mean.

I asked Owens, "Do you think the secondary gets paid less than other positions?"

"Think? They do. You know the story. I think it was supposed to have taken place at Baltimore. The coach was showing the game movie, and someone caught a long pass and the coach shut the projector off and said to his cornerback, 'You get paid $20,000 a year to see that end doesn't catch that ball, buster.' And the cornerback said, 'Yeah, coach, only that end gets paid $80,000 to see he does catch it.'

"In my own case, when I was drafted by Dallas, they said they'd give me a real shot at the quarterback job. They had five rookie quarterbacks that year: Craig Morton, Jerry Rhome, John Roach, Ernie Kellerman, and myself. My shot at the job lasted one and one half days. Kellerman, who was also black, didn't get a much longer look. We were small, it's true, but Jerry Rhome isn't any giant.

"Dallas left a very bitter taste in my mouth. But I learned a lot there, I'll say that. Dick Nolan was a great defensive teacher. He had you back-pedaling so much that running forward seemed sort of funny. The first ball I intercepted in Dallas, I didn't know what to do. I just couldn't believe I was supposed to run forward with the damn thing, so I just carried it right out of bounds as quick as I could. Nolan said, 'Man alive, where are you going, Brig?'

"I can still remember that first scrimmage. I was playing free safety. The first tackle I made, I got a big lump on my eye and I thought, 'My God, this can't be like this all the time.' I came back to the defensive huddle, and Ernie Kellerman was back there too, playing strong safety for the first time. He looked at me and said, 'Brig, you okay?', a worried sound in his voice. He made the next tackle, and we came back in the huddle, the two converted quarterbacks out there scared to death, and he whispers, 'Hey, this is no damn fun, they better pay us for this kind of job.'

"Still," he reflected, "I regret I never had that shot at quarterback. At Cincinnati I always thought I'd become a dentist; wish I had at times. My college roommate just got out of dental school this year. And I have to say I think about $20,000 ballplayers having to cover $80,000 ballplayers. The difference doesn't mean that you're not trying to get that ball away from the receiver. But why the difference? What is the reasoning behind the lower salaries for defensive backs? Saying it's because defensive backs are black is probably too easy. But what is it, then?"

The team left to fly to San Francisco Thursday afternoon after practice. The Pentagon, Lombardi said, had run a survey and discovered that it took twenty-four hours to recuperate from the loss of each hour gained when flying east to west. Thursday noon to Sunday noon equaled the three hours lost flying to the West Coast.

On the plane ride out to San Francisco I sat with Bob Long, a lanky man with a wide-eyed look of boyish eagerness. He had been a fourth-round Green Bay draft choice in 1964 and had been with the Packers for four years as a backup receiver to Carroll Dale, before being traded to the Falcons for Leo Carroll in 1968.

Long broke onto the 1968 Falcon first string, and after eight games was having a pretty good year with twenty-two catches for almost 500 yards. After the eighth game of the season, a 41–21 loss to the Steelers in Atlanta, Long was driving home, feeling pretty sportive. He'd caught the last touchdown pass of the game and was humming along at 60. Another car coming the other way was doing 80, lost control, jumped the medial strip, and hit Long head on. When Long came to in the wreckage he heard a cop saying, "Hey, we got another stiff over here." It wasn't that bad, just a broken foot, four broken vertebrae, and two hundred stitches. Still, it was close enough, the sort of experience that makes a man philosophize about football and immortality. Long missed the rest of the season and came back to the Falcon 1969 training camp. Playing for Norm Van Brocklin made a man even more philosophical, if not downright skeptical. And in August, Long walked out, tired of abuse and finished with football, he thought.

"After I left Atlanta's training camp, I went back to Green Bay to look after my business interests," Long said. "I decided that I was finished. My body hurt too much, and the things Van Brocklin had said still stung. Other NFL clubs called me, and then HE called and left messages for me at different points. He knows the Green Bay scene pretty well, you know. Everywhere I went, it was 'Call Austin, call Carpenter, call Coach Lombardi.' I decided not to, 'cause I knew what would happen if I did. I knew once I talked to him I wouldn't be able to turn him down.

"Anyway, I was staying with the general manager of my pizza hut, and 7:30 on Tuesday morning I got this long-distance phone call and I knew he'd nailed me. My pizza-hut manager's phone number! Can you beat that! Well, it was Bill Austin, and he asked me where I'd been, and I said I was finished with ball. And he said, 'Wait a second, the Old Man wants to talk to you.' I knew he had me. It was funny because in all the years I was at Green Bay I don't think he talked to me longer than ten minutes, and nine of them weren't any fun. He was at me for a half hour. I was down mentally, my wife had just left me, I was still hurting from my car wreck, and after a half hour I felt I could play ball again. It was Vince Lombardi asking me, asking *me* to come back and play.

"What could I do? Playing for Vince Lombardi and the Green Bay Packers was the greatest thing that ever happened to me. Even the injuries and the pain were great when you think back on it. Like I had a bad knee up there, a torn cartilage, and I played on that bum knee for six weeks and one day I made a cut and the leg gave way, just dropped away, and down I went. He came running out there screaming and hollering, and he says, 'Long, get up, run on that leg, there's no pain in that leg.' Two days later they operate, and the doctor says it's one of the worst torn cartilages he's ever seen. I was supposed to be out for the season, but two weeks later I'm back out there running around. They call a zig-out, a tough pattern with a bum leg, and the leg gave way again, and down I went, and here he comes again. You know that voice of his. He says, 'Get up! Run on that leg! There's *nothing* left in that Goddam leg to hurt!'"

Long had a chuckle over that one, savoring those joyous moments back with the Pack, the bellylaughs, the camaraderie, the comic relief of writhing on the turf with an inoperative knee. What could you say? Football humor was a peculiar commodity.

I said, "There doesn't seem to be much laughter on the Redskins' squad this year."

"It's missing a little bit on this team," Long admitted. "We don't have anyone to break the tension. No Max McGee. I

remember once in Green Bay we'd won a ballgame on Sunday, and come the Tuesday films Lombardi was hopping mad.
We got to the meeting, and he slammed his fists on the table
and he said, 'Gentlemen, there's something wrong with this
team.' Christ, we'd just won seven in a row, I think. He said,
'I know what's wrong with this team. It's a lack of basic fundamentals. We're going to start all over again, we're going back
to the basics. Blocking and tackling.' The room was tense,
puzzled. These are guys up to thirty-five years old, hiding
behind each other, not looking directly at him. He reached out
and picked up a football on the table, and said, 'Gentlemen,
this is a football.' And here comes the voice of Max McGee
from the back of the room. 'Hold it, Coach,' he says. 'You're
going too fast.' Max could do that. Hell, Lombardi wanted him
to. The day I left Green Bay for Carlisle, I saw Max and he
said, 'Tell Vince to hold on. Everything's going to be all right
once *we all* get back there.' "

"Any Max McGees you see on this team yet?" I asked.

"Well, not exactly. We had a meeting a while back where
we were projecting a diagram on the screen, and there was a
fly on the plate crawling across the screen, and Lombardi
watched it creep along and said, 'Look at that damn fly,' and
here came Charley Taylor's voice out of the back. 'Hey,
Coach, what's that, a fly pattern?' Lombardi got a big kick out
of that."

Well, it was a start, not a classic knee-slapper by any stretch
of the imagination, but a tentative beginning. Already, I
sensed that the Redskins could use a little humor. Perhaps
Lombardi sensed it too and purposely strained to bust a gut at
Charley's tepid offering. On the other hand, perhaps he found
Charley's sally funny. Certainly, his sense of humor ranged
into mysterious areas.

"The thing is," Long said, "there may be guys on this team
who have that talent for making us laugh, but they're too
scared this year; maybe next year."

Chapter 14

I saw Kammerer before the 49'er game, and he said, "This is homecoming for me. I grew up out here, went to school here, used to be in business here. I've ordered ninety tickets for the game. When I was a rookie with the 49'ers I used to get fleeced on tickets. I learned you don't give a guy a ticket and ask him to pay later. You'll never see a nickel. I've split up my ninety tickets into three blocks and assigned captains to collect the money. My mother will get it from the family, a fraternity brother is handling old college pals, and an old business associate is servicing the others. I got the game to worry about, without running around collecting money."

Down on the side lines Kammerer had a pre-game ritual of seating the shoulder pads for a group of Redskin veterans. Ray Schoenke, Vince Promuto, Jerry Smith, Sam Huff, Pat Richter, Jim Snowden, and Chris Hanburger would form a line in front of Kammerer, and he would raise his palms over his head, like Atlas, and bring them crashing down on their shoulder pads. Then he would cuff each man on the side of the head, first one ear, then the other, and the man would trot off, and another would step in to take his place.

Those ninety friends and relatives up in the stands lent an extra measure of zest to the ritual, made it something of a command performance for the hometown gang. But if they all had paid their money for the pleasure of watching Kammerer play, they were to be disappointed. He was yanked early in the second quarter, and John Hoffman joined Leo Carroll at the defensive ends.

As the ball changed hands repeatedly throughout the first

and second periods, the kindest thing that could be said was that the 49'ers moved it a great deal better than the Redskins, but somehow failed to move it far enough to score. John Brodie was mixing his plays fairly well and had established a running game, just as the Saints and Browns had. Although he was completing most of his passes, Jurgensen did not seem sharp. The Redskin running game was punchless, inept, and gained a mere 13 yards in the first half.

Toward the end of the second period, the Redskins finally drove to the 49'er 25-yard line. The pass for the first down failed, and Curt Knight came on to try a field goal from the 31 that would have put Washington ahead 3–0. John Didion, who was establishing a reputation for turning even a point-after-touchdown into a moment of high drama, snapped low. The ball rolled along the ground, evaded holder Brig Owens, skipped past the astonished Knight, and bounced crazily toward midfield. Owens got up, but Knight had a head start, retrieved the ball, and faded back to consider the situation. He made the right decision, which was to heave the damn thing out of bounds. Unfortunately, he underthrew it, and 49'er tackle Charley Kreuger intercepted on the San Francisco 47-yard line. With the help of a face-masking penalty, Brodie drove the 53 yards for the score in six plays, putting San Francisco ahead at the half, 7–0.

Flea Roberts fumbled the second-half kickoff in the end zone, snatched it back up again, and carried it out to the Washington 36. A swing pass to Charley Harraway, two more longer throws to Charley Taylor, and the Redskins had a first and goal at the San Francisco 9. The drive finally petered out at the 2, and Knight kicked the field goal to make it San Francisco 7, the Redskins 3.

The 49'ers added a field goal of their own, and toward the end of the third period, the Redskins, with the help of two penalties, drove 70 yards to knot the score at 10–10.

San Francisco came back with an eight-minute drive, covering 80 yards to pull ahead 17–10.

There were six and a half minutes in the game, and the Redskins revived at last and began to play Lombardi ball-control football. Jurgensen hit on nine of eleven passes, and Larry Brown and Charley Harraway ground out 26 yards on four carries. A 49'er pass interference call gave the Redskins a first and goal at the San Francisco 1 with thirty-eight seconds left in the game. Harraway tripped going into the line, lost 2 yards, and the Redskins called time out with thirty-four seconds left. Jurgensen threw high for Charley Taylor in the end zone, and then on third and three, with twenty-six seconds to go, he hit Jerry Smith for the score. Knight's kick was good, and the game was tied again at 17–17.

The 49'ers took control on their own 20 with a little over twenty seconds showing on the clock, time for Brodie to set up the bomb. On first and ten, Frank Bosch socked Brodie for a 5-yard loss, and the 49'ers called a time-out. Brodie threw to tight end Wayne Moore in the left flat for 4 yards before he stepped out of bounds to kill the clock with fifteen seconds showing. Now it was third and eleven, and the Redskins, like the Browns the week before, had a premonition that it might be wise to drop into a prevent-deep-defense, that it might be smart to keep an eye out for that long ball. Brodie threw deep and off target to flanker Clifton McNeil. San Francisco had to punt, having consumed less than twenty seconds on the series.

Flea Roberts signaled for a fair catch on the Redskin 44, bobbled the ball, but fell on it, and Washington called time out with two seconds showing. Lombardi was going for a free kick, a 56-yard field-goal attempt that, if good, would tie the NFL distance record. The free-kick option meant that the ball was spotted at the line of scrimmage and the defenders had to remain 10 yards distant. No rush, no snap from center, no quick hands to spot the ball—the pressure was compressed into the isolated act of kicking that pigskin. Ironically, the free-kick rule did not apply when the ball was dropped on a fair catch. The referee had overlooked that fact, and the 49'ers had neglected to protest it. The kicking team came onto the field, Knight shooting for a game winner that was illegal. But illegalities were not reversible in football. They stood, once the play was over. The Redskin bench was on its feet, a single optic screwed into that teed-up football. Brig Owens bent over it, his index finger pressed against the seam at the top of the ball. Knight eyed it, bent low, and swooped forward, his right foot cocked like a pistol hammer. The kick was at an angle, there was a slight tail wind, and you could almost hear the smack of the square-toed boot on the football. The ball rose in a soaring arc. Enough height and enough distance. Everyone on the field—the Redskin bench and the 49'er defenders—raised his face to the sky, watching the ball's flight path. From the press box it looked true, but then, as the ball neared the uprights, it began to fade, to drift off course, and to pass to the left of the goalposts. It couldn't have been more than a yard off target. In the end zone the referee bent low to the ground and made a scissors motion with his arms. No good, no ballgame.

So it was 17–17. The Redskins were going home to open in Washington with a 1–1–1 record. A team that was neither here nor there, a team that had tasted all of the outcomes that football provided. They had trailed in all three games—had come from behind to win one, to tie one, to pull one out and then throw it away.

At least the familiar Redskin pattern of collapsing in the second half had been broken. They had not played well in Frisco, but they had driven the length of the field when they had to salvage the tie, they had shown they could hang in there, could play some Lombardi-style fourth-quarter football.

"Only four points separate us from an unbeaten season," Lombardi droned in the week to come. I was surprised that he conceptualized it like that. I would have thought he would have phrased it, "Only six points separate us from a perfect, victorious season." Winning, not tying, was the name of the game, as he had so starkly defined it in the past. It was odd to think that the man who said that second place was meaningless appeared ready to settle for a 1–0–2 record, good for second place in the Capitol Division where Dallas now stood 3–0.

On the plane ride back to Washington, Lombardi looked wrung out, but at peace with himself. He smiled amiably at the people wandering up and down the aisle. That look of desolation that had marked his face after the Cleveland game was gone; that revelation in the Municipal Stadium dressing room that "he" had wanted to win at all, but that "they" had let him down had been supplanted by an admission in San Francisco's Kezar Stadium locker room that "they" had done as well as they could, had fought from behind, and that "he" was satisfied. Also missing from his face was that deep, bone-aching exhaustion and frustration that could only be slaked by sleep, could not be resisted, was beyond the control of will. Now he looked sleepy and content—a man whose tranquility was worth staying awake to enjoy.

I squatted down beside him in the aisle. Marie was crocheting in the seat next to him. "Madam LaFarge," he laughed with a nod in her direction, pleased with this Dickensian allusion.

"You seem at ease," I said.

He gave a friendly smile. "We did our best. Came from behind and controlled the football when we had to. You can't ask more than that. There are a lot of castoffs on this team. We're a bunch of rag-tags really. Only a handful of great athletes here, and I don't know yet how many of them have that spark, that sense of personal greatness that winners have. There are a few, a very few people here who are near-great athletes, and of those only one, one player, has shown me the spark so far."

I said, "I get the impression you're in a state of ambiguity. You don't really know what you want. Whether to go all out, go with your veteran players, and gamble on winning it all, or whether you ought to hedge and build for the future."

"That's very astute of you," he said.

"Would you go for it if you knew you had the horses or knew you were very close to having them?"

"Yes."

I thought that was probably true. Lombardi was wary of such football words as "meanness," "viciousness," the "killer instinct"—reasoning, no doubt, that it was foolish to bandy such terms about, that it might anger overly fastidious football fans.

I asked how important it was to have people with the "killer instinct."

He made a face at that "killer" and frowned. "I would say on Green Bay we had maybe 50 percent who gave 100 percent. One hundred percent? What is that? It's all there is. There isn't anything else more. But what is it exactly? Who can say? You use some words for it, I use some others."

I said 100 percent was an impossibility, a non-attainable goal in football. "You don't ever rate your blockers at 100 percent. If you got 70 percent out of them on the run and 85 percent on the pass, you'd have a hell of a line."

He laughed. "You still need the guys who give 100 percent to be champions. You define it your way, I'll define it mine. I know it when I see it, I'll tell you that."

Baseball season was over when we returned to Washington, and the Redskins took over the Senators' locker room. Lombardi, frustrated in his attempt to get the Senators to divide the cost of a stadium-sized carpet of astroturf, now made overtures to split the cost of wall-to-wall carpeting for the dressing room. Even there he misjudged the dogged stinginess of Bob Short. So Lombardi did it alone, installing a wall-to-wall light green acrylon carpet (he took it up again after the football season) and stereo speakers to pipe in rock-and-roll tunes for the team.

Short's attitude, I suspected, was little short of incredible to Lombardi. Professional sports was, after all, a profession, he reasoned. Doctors, lawyers, and accountants did not labor on a concrete floor. That baseball players would do so put them in a league with disbarred attorneys, crooked bookkeepers, and tipsy chiropractors. An unseemly situation altogether. But then, what could you expect of a man who failed to grasp the tonyness of astroturf?

The opening of the new locker room marked the physical breaking up of the team into regulars and cab squad. The forty-man roster moved to their new surroundings with exactly forty locker stalls and left their taxi-squad brethren behind in the temporary locker room, with its jerry-built lockers, tiled walls, no speakers, and concrete floor. "The Ghetto," the cab squad called their dressing room.

And the taxi squad had the downtrodden look of a persecuted minority. The regular team could hardly be expected to feel too solicitous of their fate, since the cab squad's function was either to beat out a regular player at practice or to be available if a regular were rendered useless by injury.

Yet, there were exceptions to every rule. A. D. Whitfield was on the cab squad, and he was a player for whom the regulars, by and large, wished the best. In so far as it was possible to know what 100 percent meant, Whitfield seemed to give it. He was a likeable man, who ran well, played hard, and gave his best, but at 5'10" and 200 pounds he was not the "Big Back" Lombardi yearned for. He had been put down on the cab squad because he did not block "crisply" enough by Lombardi's lights.

Whitfield, Jerry Smith, and I were talking together the week after the 49'er game. They were friends who had been through three seasons together, and now their careers were veering in sharply different directions. Smith had had his usual clutch Sunday in San Francisco—six catches for 77 yards, two of them in that final, pressure drive. One had been for the touchdown, the other a 22-yard slider on his knees in a second-and-twelve situation. Whitfield had watched the game from the side lines, suffering no doubt from the knowledge that he could have moved the ball better than Harraway and Brown had, that day.

"I was born in Rosebud, Texas," Whitfield said in his piping rapid-fire voice, "which had a population of 1708 at that time." Smith beamed approvingly at this information, its precision, its small-town flavor of belonging somewhere. In spite of his resemblance to Joe Palooka, Smith had been the Redskin resident hippie in 1968, his reddish-blond hair visible at the base of his neck below his helmet. He wore it now in more severe, post-Lombardi trim, but he still preserved something of his California flamboyance, his surfer's independence.

"Down in Rosebud," Whitfield continued, "in my school years I used to work with my uncles hauling bunk hay and pick a little cotton, too. Always worked. And then, as I got older, I used to work the acetylene torch around my father's junk yard, cutting the bodies up. He had about four acres filled with wrecked, beat-up cars. My father always taught me to be independent and always taught me the value of a dollar. He didn't hold with fooling around, and when I got to high school, he wouldn't consent to my playing football, said it wouldn't do me any good later, said I'd be better off playing in the school band. I played the trombone for seven years. The spring of my freshman year I cut band practice to go out for spring football.

"Course the word got back to my parents. I should have known it would in a town as small as Rosebud. We finally worked out a compromise. I'd do both. At half-time I would take off running and change into my band uniform behind the stands. My cousin, he played the saxophone and quarterback. By my senior year I said, 'The hell with the band.'

"This was a segregated school down there, and my parents were real high on me getting an education because my father was the oldest of seventeen kids and had to drop out in the fifth grade, my mother in the eighth. And I think back to some of those guys who had great football talent and had to drop out, not play college ball or pro, and that's why I know the value of what football has done for me and the sacrifice my parents made for me to play it. Anyway, in those days you had to be versatile. Only two hundred kids in the school from first grade through twelfth grade, and some of 'em moving out of town to pick cotton. You had to play offense and defense and play in the band, and take part in the state spelling bee after the game. Those were tough days. The Negro schools weren't much down there as far as facilities went, and Rosebud was worse off than most.

"I remember going to a triangle track meet, and the other two schools had track uniforms, and we didn't. I still remember us trying to dye our pants green and white for the school colors in the gym sink. They came out looking a dirty red.

"Our school was so poor I've always been fascinated with equipment. Makes me feel important just to have it. Sometimes I look at those pads in my locker, and I say to myself, 'I wish those kids at Rosebud could see me now.'

"Rosebud is home, but I always knew I had to get out of there if I wanted to do something with my life. My uncle and I used to go out to the flashing red light, the only one we had in town, and it just flashed, never turned colors, just flashed red. And we used to sit and watch the cars go by and think, one day one of us is going to be in one of those cars. And whenever I go back to Rosebud, I go out and sit at that light and think how lucky I am.

"Well, when I was a senior, we had a track meet and I ran a 9.7 hundred, and a coach from North Texas State was there and gave me bus money to come up to the campus and see the school. My cousin drove me up, and when I got there the coach gave me a pair of cleats. I went out on the field, and they had a guy throwing passes to me, and I caught footballs with my suit coat on. Geez, I was nervous. The coach stuffed some money in my pocket, and when I pulled it out: $150. I thought, gee, I never seen that kind of money in my life and I got home and showed it to my father and he was amazed. He couldn't believe it.

"I played four years at North Texas State. All-conference my sophomore year, broke my arm my junior year, my senior year a real fine rushing year. I kept getting all these forms and questionnaires from the pro teams and I was floating. A few scouts came up to school and they took me aside and said, 'Now you stay tight around home, hear, because we're going to draft you and we'll be calling you soon as we do.' I waited by the phone, and waited, and finally I read in the paper where the draft was over. I couldn't believe it, after all the sweet-talking they'd done.

"I just couldn't accept that they didn't want me. So I called Pete Rozelle. I got on the phone and called the Commissioner. That was one surprised cat. I said, 'All these people been leading me on.' And he said, 'Okay, this is normal. This is what you got to expect. This is what happens all the time around here, but I guarantee somebody will contact you in the next three, four days.'

"And sure enough, the next day the Cowboys called me up. I don't know if they wanted to, or Rozelle told them they were the ones had to give me a look. I didn't care.

"I made the Cowboys team, then they waived me after the season started, and I went to Montreal as the answer to the Alouettes' problem. And then another big back comes on the scene, and it seems that every time I got somewhere, another big back came along, and they start experimenting with him. No reason at all, and I got pushed back and had to start all over again. In 1966 I went back to the Dallas camp and got waived to the Redskins. I was Washington's leading rusher in 1966 and 1967. Now, this year, it's the same thing again. The search for the big back. I mean, what do I have to do to prove I want to play this game, what more do I have to do to show that I have played it?"

"Listen to that sonofagun," Smith said. "Now you know why all the guys want A. D. back. You ask yourself, why? Because he'll bust a gut to play for this team. He'll go all out.

"It's funny, he came from a colored community and associated with black people most of his life. And I haven't associated with too many Negroes—we had one Negro girl in my high school, and I went to a Mormon junior college, and there weren't any there. Then all of a sudden, you meet Negroes for the first time. It happened to me at Arizona State, which everybody thinks of as a Negro school because of all the black athletes. Up until last year I was the only white pro ballplayer out of A State and, as a matter of fact, when I was drafted, the Redskins thought I was a Negro. They were going to make me into a defensive back."

I took a mental note of that off-handed admission of how pro defensive backs were made. Perhaps it also accounted for Smith being only a ninth-round draft choice in 1964. Defensive backs were not selected so high in those years.

"Then you come up here to the pros," Smith went on, "and all the players are sort of thrown together, like foster children, and no barriers exist, and you just make your friends. Like Theo, Brig, A. D., and I—we got as close as anybody on this team. And it's funny, I didn't think very much about the outside world, never bothered too much about things like civil rights. Then we had another friend, Tommy Walters, a white linebacker from Mississippi, and I guess it was after my second year, we were partners in a tree-cutting business and I went down to Petal, Mississippi, to cut some trees. And one of the guys working for us, a white guy, got hurt and I took him down to the doctor's office and walked in. Outside, the office was very attractive. Inside—wooden floors, dirty, stick furniture. I looked around and said, 'What the hell is this?' And the nurse came in and said, 'Oh, you're not supposed to be in here, this is the Negroes' waiting room,' and she took us to this other waiting room with plush carpets and stereo, and up on the wall on the entrance way, she points to these two signs: White and Colored. Well, that shook me, that started me thinking. I run with guys like A. D. and Brig, and we don't have experiences like that when we're together. But I got to thinking that they'd seen plenty of it on their own. And when I'm on my own, I see how hypocritical this society is. Maybe it's just immaturity, but my solution is to be an individual, to stick close to myself and the guys I like.

"Last year," Smith said, "the reason I had the long hair was I wanted to be an individual. I didn't want to be a hippie. I just wanted to feel free, I wanted to experience love, I wanted to travel, I wanted to be myself. But I found out you can't be an individual in our society.

"At the same time, I wanted more than anything else to be consistent. I want to be the guy who can always catch the ball when you need it, the guy you throw to on third down. I don't care what I catch, long or short, routine or spectacular—the real satisfaction is to catch one when it's really needed. Hell, of course I enjoy catching the hard ones, but it's the consistency that really satisfies me. And maybe one of the reasons I wanted to be a free spirit is I've been experimented with so much. I mean, every year since I came up to pro ball, I've been in the top ten receivers in the league, and like the year after I finish number two in the league, Otto changed me to flanker. It makes you wonder what consistency counts for. It's like you being a successful writer and then someone says to you, you can't do that work any more. We're going to put you in charge of the print shop, and somebody else is going to do the writing from now on."

"That's right," Whitfield said, "you see the thing about football is, it's not like life. In life you can make your own choices, you can say, 'Gee, this isn't right,' or 'Gee, this is.' Not in this game. There's but the one choice, and the coach makes it. So football makes a man mature late. You're twenty-five, thirty, sometimes thirty-five years of age before you go out in the world and be in charge of yourself and learn something. Now it's that way everywhere in football, and with Lombardi more so than most coaches. But it's good in a way because with him, you know he's going to make the choices and you have to accept that."

"Yeah," Smith said, "I got the feeling this team is going some place. If not all the way this year, then next year."

Whitfield nodded. "I can see the team improving week by week. Even though I'm on the side lines and it hurts there, it really hurts to be there."

It was, of course, hard to say whether the team was getting better week by week, hard to know even if it was a radically different team from the 1968 Redskins. The scores of the three games did not form any upward trend. Even so, there were patterns that were forming. The NFL statistics released in the middle of the week showed Jurgensen in second place among the passers, with a 64-percent completion average for better than 600 yards and six touchdown passes. Craig Morton of Dallas was in first place with a 69-percent average, but he had only thrown a third of the number of balls that Jurgensen had. Charley Taylor, who had had a big day in San Francisco with eight balls for 92 yards, was tied for second in the pass-receiving race, and Jerry Smith was tied for fifth place. It was a statistical rundown redolent of the Redskin past. Yet, there was this difference: Jurgensen was no longer throwing the long ball, partly because the other teams were defending against it, and partly because some of the zing had departed from that golden arm, but he was also playing a steadier, more conservative sort of game, throwing more shortstuff to his backs, working to establish a running game. That was the Lombardi offensive philosophy, and as a result, rookie running back Larry Brown was in tenth place in the rushing statistics with 157 yards and a 4.6 average. And there was still another difference. As Lombardi put it, "Our players have not quit for a minute this season. They have fought back." They had fallen apart in Cleveland, it was true, but they had not yet quit.

Chapter 15

Now the Redskins had come home to face their fans for the first time in the regular season. The St. Louis Cardinals were coming to town with a 2–1 season record, a team that year after year was widely picked to win the Century Division and year after year failed to do so. "Playing at home with our fans pulling for us ought to give us a big lift," Lombardi allowed, "but I got to say the Cardinals have the best running backs in the league."

I had already heard him say the Packers had the best backs in the league; that the New Orleans backs could "pound" a team into submission; that Cleveland's running game was so good that they could afford to keep Leroy Kelly, the defending League rushing titlist, on the bench and still run over you; that San Francisco had a whiz-bang balanced running attack with Doug Cunningham and Ken Willard. It was a *Leitmotif* that sounded unfailingly, an almost weekly lament for his own deprivation.

Lombardi was, after all, a football traditionalist. To him, the ground game was everything; not to have a great and acknowledged runner was the coach's final mortification. To the fundamentalist, the forward pass was a newfangled, if necessary, weapon, but the glory of the game came from toting that old pigskin, from bursting through the line, from ripping around end with big, fast blockers obliterating everything in their path. At heart Lombardi was still one of the "Seven Blocks of Granite," a man who preserved as much of the old way as he safely could, who knew that with the right horses he could set back the clock and overpower the flashy innovators who were springing up everywhere with their multiple offenses and their staggered defenses. Perhaps it was this inbred conservatism, this resistance to fancy football that made him the devotee of technology, of astroturf, exer-genies, universal gyms, domed-in stadiums, and sauna baths. It was as if he selected these external signs of modernity to conceal the conservatism of his approach to the game itself.

And, of course, the man who had been so serene, almost acquiescent on the plane ride back from San Francisco, was once again remorseless, unyielding, and ferocious when Tuesday arrived and the Cardinals were coming. On Thursday that week there was a driving rainstorm, and Lombardi splashed about happily in the squishy turf, driving the team through a two-hour practice, snarling at the runners who could not cut in the mud, at the linemen who could not break from the quagmire at the line of scrimmage, at the receivers who let the slippery ball slide off their fingertips. He was dressed in a Napoleonic cape and a plastic headdress to ward off the rain. "This is like shooting fish in a barrel," he rejoiced on a pass, as a defensive back skidded to the ground on the slick grass.

Before the Cardinal game, Lombardi activated Joe Rutgens, the veteran defensive tackle who had hurt his knee the first day of training camp. It was hard to tell about Rutgens. He still limped and had an ungainly sway as a result of his monstrous beerbelly and skinny birdlegs. His arms were thin, and he had no width across the shoulders to speak of. But then, he had never looked like much in the past, either, and had been one of the premier tackles in the league. In spite of his misshapen physique, Rutgens had a handsome, Roman-bust sort of head. And he was the archetypal "grizzled veteran"—matter-of-fact, hard to faze, inured to the breaks of the game.

"Never been on a winner in my life," he told me philosophically over a glass of beer. "University of Illinois where I played first string three years, we never had a winning season, never had a real bad losing one either. Four-five-and-one was the best we did. That was my junior year, and we finished a half game behind Wisconsin for the Big Ten title. Wisconsin got clobbered in the Rose Bowl anyway, 44–17, something like that, by Washington. Kinda glad it was them and not us, to tell you the truth.

"Funny to think of playing football all my life and never being with a winner," he paused, running his tongue across his upper lip and pondering the significance of that observation. "Sometimes I wonder if I don't jinx a team," he finally said.

"When Otto came, I thought he'd be able to win for once. We had some good ballplayers, number two in the league in defense the year before, and we had Sonny and those receivers. But the same old story, we ended up 7–7, the closest to a winning season of any team I've ever been on. When you've never won in your life and you're thirty-one, you can't even guess what it must be like.

"In '66 there were more injuries, some guys retired, and I had my back operated on after I got off to a good start. Then in '67 we figured it was our year and, damn, we had a good team, except we kept losing all the time in the last couple of minutes of a game. In '68 what could you say, we just didn't have nothing. Terrible. We just fell apart. Maybe that '67 season bothered us. It's got to have a deep effect on you, it's got to give you a sense of a letdown when teams are scoring on you at will in the last minute of play. The offense gets a little leery of the defense, and you can't blame them.

"Well, this year starts, and you got Vince Lombardi coaching; you figure you got a pretty good shot at a winning season, and it's been a long time coming. And I go out there the first day of camp and hit the sled, spin off, and my leg goes. The cartilage popped and tore, so hell, I thought there goes another damn year. I'm still not 100 percent, but I'm ready.

"I'll say I have to wonder how much longer it'll be for me. Seems like these defensive players are getting bigger all the time. Hell, you got Carroll and Hoffman at 6'7" on the ends now. I'm 6'2" and I used to be as big as anybody when I first came up. I need my experience to survive. I don't know, maybe I won't survive."

"What has it been like watching the games from the side lines, not even suited up?" I asked.

"That Cleveland game was bad. Real bad. I thought we had them, thought we'd won, and then it trickled away. You think to yourself, Jesus, maybe I could stop them, but you don't know. I've played long enough to know you can't tell. But I've played long enough to know you got to try like hell to stop them.

"I still want to play, I'll tell you that. I've talked to guys who've retired, and they say those first couple of years are the worst, getting used to being an old man in your early thirties. This game gets to your pride. Even for us guys who've never won. You're thirty-one or thirty-two years old and you're finished, washed up. Christ! You're young, yet you're old, and it gets to a man's pride. You want to play as long as you can, just to prove that you haven't slowed down, but there's no doubt about it, you have and you do."

As I look back on what Rutgens said, I can sense the edge of doubt in his voice, the foreshadowing of the end of the road, the insecurity over the future. But at the time it was not that clear. Rutgens seemed no more troubled than others. Younger men in better health were also insecure, their futures suspended in the balance. For even though the season was well under way, there was a growing feeling that the team was not yet set and that the forty-man roster, normally an inviolable institution, was merely a legal formality that Lombardi could alter at any moment. The trading deadline was still almost two weeks away, and the team had not jelled, did not have that sense of interconnected solidity that made men sure of their places in the whole. Lombardi was, after all, satisfied with the San Francisco tie because that was as much as could be expected from this forty-man roster. There was nothing to say that a few alterations might not change things, might not make him think of wins instead of ties. Wins were what he liked to think about, liked to commemorate on the paneled walls of his den out in Potomac, Maryland.

Chapter 16

The Cardinal game was homecoming, the chance for the 50,000 fans lucky enough to have season tickets to see in the flesh what Lombardi had thus far wrought. RFK Stadium was set on the edge of Washington's black ghetto, hard by the banks of the fetid Anacostia River. The stadium itself, plopped down in the middle of a black swamp of asphalt parking lots, was oddly out of place in this atmosphere of natural and man-made squalor. Modernistic, with an undulating concrete rim around the top, the stadium nonetheless fell short of any architectural distinction that would make it seem more majestic than its surroundings. It was the sort of structure and the sort of neighborhood that people chose to visit for only the most momentous occasions, as the Washington Senators had found out to their regret. But in Washington, the Redskins were such a momentous occasion.

It was a gentle fall day with blue skies. Inside the stadium, tender pea-green grass shoots were growing in the Senators' infield, an Indian-nickel Redskin chief was chalked in profile at midfield, and "Redskins" was printed in dusty red and yellow letters in the end zones. Out on the field the Redskin marching band in its buff-white Indian buckskin uniforms was striking up "Hail to the Redskins." The Redskinettes, in their Indian-maiden mini-skirts, were prancing and strutting about the field.

The Cardinals won the coin toss and elected to receive. The public-address system announced the Redskin starting defense: "At left end John Hoffman, at left tackle Frank Bosch, at right tackle Spain Musgrove, at right end Leo Carroll, at left linebacker Tom Roussel, at middle linebacker Sam Huff (cheers), at right linebacker Chris Hanburger (cheers), at left cornerback Pat Fisher, at right cornerback Mike Bass, at strong safety Brig Owens, and at free safety Rickie Harris. Head coach Vince Lombardi and the rest of the Washington Redskins."

Aside from Huff and Hanburger, it was a 1–1–1 round of applause that went up from the full house of 50,481 fans. The defense had not banked a great deal of good will with the Washington fans over the years. Down on the side lines Carl Kammerer faced his line-up, rattled their shoulder pads, cuffed them lightly in the ears, and took his place on the bench.

Curt Knight's kickoff boomed deep into the end zone and was downed by Roy Shivers. The Cardinals started from their 20 and it looked like another one of those ghastly Redskin defensive travesties. Shivers carried for 6, Willis Crenshaw for 10, then Shivers for 9, Shivers for no gain, Hart for 5, Shivers for 4, Crenshaw for no gain. Seven straight running plays for 34 yards. This was Lombardi-style football with a vengeance. Then, to show he was capable of mixing his calls, Cardinal quarterback Jim Hart dropped back and hit wide receiver Dave Williams on a 9-yard pass. Johnny Roland carried for 2, came back for 6 more. It was third and two on the Redskin 29-yard line, and the Cardinals sent in another tackle to block —a gesture of rich disdain and an announcement to the stunned Washington crowd that the Cardinals intended to grind out the first down with still another punch into the enfeebled Redskin line.

This was surely insolence of the highest order, a show of *hubris* that would anger the gods. Lombardi sent in Marlin McKeever with the defensive call, the message that enough was enough, that pride would have its fall.

Crenshaw banged into the line, and McKeever stopped him a yard shy of the first down. Jim Bakken came in and kicked the 34-yard field goal, putting the Cardinals ahead 3–0.

The Redskin offense took the field, as they had so many times in years gone by, traumatized by the knowledge they would have to score every time they got the ball in order to win; it was not the sort of revelation that bred confidence.

The offense failed to deliver a first down, and the Cardinals got the ball back. But the machinery of fate had been set in motion. The Redskins held the Cardinals for no yards in three plays, forced a punt, drove downfield, and tied the game on Curt Knight's 37-yard field goal. The Cardinals put the ball in play on their own 26-yard line, and on the first play from scrimmage, Pat Fisher intercepted a Hart pass intended for tight end Jackie Smith.

The Redskins moved 39 yards for a touchdown in four plays, capped by a beautiful 12-yard run by Larry Brown. Washington had a 10–3 lead as the first quarter ended.

For the Cardinals, the worst was still to come. In the second quarter they got the ball four times and made only two first downs. The Redskin front four shut down their running game, pressured Hart to roll out of the pocket, to throw off balance. Rookie John Hoffman was overpowering the Cardinal veteran tackle Ernie McMillan with regularity, blowing in like Deacon Jones. Chris Hanburger was all over the field, tackling, knocking down passes. It was a transformation: the defense was suddenly a unit, turning the ball back over to Jurgensen and the now-inspired offense. The Redskins drove from their own 14 to midfield, had to surrender the ball to the Cardinals, but got it right back again. This time Jurgensen drove 63 yards for a touchdown in eight plays, one of them a 28-yard run by Larry Brown, who was suddenly looking better than those highly touted Cardinal backs. That made it Washington 17, the Cardinals 3.

St. Louis needed a quick score now to keep the game in reach. Hart missed on his first two passes, and Mike Bass intercepted the third on the Cardinal 32-yard line. The St. Louis defense stiffened and held the Redskins to a 28-yard field goal.

It was Redskins 20, St. Louis 3, with 2:21 left to play in the half, a respectable lead for the Redskins to take to the clubhouse. On fourth and one, at the Redskin 43-yard line, Hart went for broke and threw for the first down to Willis Crenshaw. Sam Huff—"old board-hands," they called him for his wooden fingers—caught the ball on the Redskin 36-yard line and puffed 32 yards upfield before stepping out of bounds, panting with exhaustion. Jurgensen worked the ball down to the 4-yard line with fifty-two seconds left on the clock. But the Cardinal defense perked up. Larry Brown carried to the 1-yard line, was stopped for no gain, a pass to Taylor was incomplete, and with twelve seconds left, Knight came in to kick his third field goal of the half, putting the Redskins up 23–3 when the gun sounded.

The Cardinals scored late in the third quarter on an 80-yard drive to make it 23–10. Early in the fourth period, the Redskins added another field goal. The defense held and turned the ball back to Jurgensen, only to lose it on a Charley Harraway fumble at the Washington 28-yard line. St. Louis took it in from there to make the score 26–17.

This was the Redskins' traditional moment to falter, to allow another touchdown, and then to drop the game in the closing seconds on a field goal. Suddenly a nine-point lead did not look so comfortable; Lombardi began to pace the side lines, bending over to extract clumps of grass.

Out on the field, the Redskins had the ball first and ten on their own 24-yard line; Jurgensen kneeled on one knee in the huddle, preparing to confound the faint-hearted. He marched the team right down the field, scoring on a third and goal pass to Jerry Smith, sliding across the end zone grass on his knees.

The rest was academic. Even John Gilliam's runback of the ensuing kickoff to the Redskin 15-yard line seemed no cause for consternation. Old Joe Rutgens was now in the game, with a great cheer from the fans. Two plays later, Rutgens, as in so many days gone by, broke a block and came swaying into the backfield, forcing Hart to unload a desperation pass that was intercepted by Brig Owens. The game ended 33–17.

It was a game to gloat over. Knight, with Jurgensen holding and Len Hauss snapping, had hit on four field goals, tying Charlie Gogolak's all-time Redskin single-game field-goal record. Jurgensen was 19 out of 34 for 238 yards, and had produced on twelve of twenty third-down situations. Charley Harraway carried for 75 yards, Larry Brown for 82, twelve of them on a touchdown run, bowling over two defenders. Vince

Promuto, who had dislocated his shoulder in the first half, Ray Schoenke, and Willie Banks had led the runners around the corners with Packer finesse and power. Bob Long caught nine balls for 110 yards, showing that Charley Taylor could not be put under double coverage with impunity.

The Redskin secondary had held Hart to thirteen completions out of thirty attempts for a mere 138 yards and had intercepted five passes. And the secondary had looked good because the Redskin line had finally discovered a rush. They had only dumped Hart once, but they batted down balls, forced him to roll out, and hurried his throws.

The locker room was exuberant, aglow with men strutting to the showers, sitting tall in their wooden folding chairs, ready to tell the reporters what it was like to overpower an enemy. Larry Brown, in one corner of the dressing room, was being discovered by the press, as demure as a starlet sipping a soda at a drugstore on Sunset Boulevard. Pat Fisher wore a smile of vindication, and not only because he had intercepted two balls on his old teammates. "The Cardinals," he said, "have a great team; the only thing wrong with them is Coach Winner. He's why I left St. Louis. He used to tell the reporters out there I was what was wrong with the Cardinals. He'll have to find another fall guy today. It was good, very good, to beat him today."

Lombardi relaxed in his dressing room, with its somewhat blurred photo of Richard Nixon on the wall, installed by the room's baseball-season occupant, Ted Williams. Lombardi sat in the corner, stripped to his undershirt and stretched out in comfort. He had too little control over his face to exercise restraint there, but he measured out his words with moderation, with almost painful humility. Yes, the Redskins had played "pretty well," but there had been some errors that could have been costly and could have "turned the game around." Those two fumbles by Charley Harraway could have lost a ballgame on another day. With paternal modesty he called the front four "our young people up there," but noted they had played very well indeed.

"You think you got a championship contender here?" a reporter asked. This was the nub of it all.

"What do you think?" Lombardi said. "I don't make predictions like that, Coach."

"You looked mighty good out there," the reporter mused. Lombardi fought back a blush.

"The first thing I do after the game is find out what the Cowboys did," Joe Rutgens said in the locker room later. The Cowboys had beaten the Falcons 21–17 for a 4–0 season start.

In so far as Lombardi feared anything, it was the unknown. And on Monday, the unknown became Fran Tarkenton, the scrambling quarterback of the New York Giants. The Lombardi Packers had beaten the Vikings in ten out of twelve meetings when Tarkenton was quarterbacking Minnesota, but that had been from 1960 through 1967, the years when the Packers were the Packers, and the Vikings were a mere expansion team. Even so, some of the Green Bay wins had been tight, too close for comfort.

Tarkenton had always troubled Lombardi, had been the despair of his organized mentality, what with Tarkenton's freakish scurrying and his capacity to thrive in chaos. Lombardi's apprehensions over Tarkenton were summed up in the relish with which he told of former Viking coach Norm Van Brocklin's efforts to convert Scrambling Fran into a drop-back passer. "Van Brocklin," he said, "put a tether on Tarkenton in practice, and when he would drift out of the passing pocket, the Dutchman would pull on the other end of the rope." There was a wistful note in his voice, a regret, perhaps, that the Dutchman had not tugged at Tarkenton a little harder.

"One game does not a season make," Lombardi poeticized. "I would like to say we're all set to go, but it is going to be a long hard pull. Games with the Giants have always been hammer-and-tongs. It will be a ding-dong battle here Sunday." This string of clichés was a sure sign that Lombardi was preoccupied with other things and was too distracted to bother with what he was saying, for normally, he was refreshing in his capacity to avoid the gnomic football platitudes that made listening to so many coaches a bore. Cab-squad quarterback Danny Talbott, like Tarkenton the son of a Southern Baptist preacher, enacted the scrambler's role at practice. Lombardi's strategy was to contain Tarkenton inside by having his defensive ends block off the outside and then stealthily penetrate toward the center, like two stadium cops trying to trap a stray dog on the gridiron. It was, on the whole, a keystone-cop kind of practice week. Talbott ran around in large circles in the middle of the field, darting in and out of the coaching staff and reserves, looking as puzzled as a squirrel on a treadmill. In the meantime the defenders and receivers were racing back and forth, running here and there in a furious jumble of patterns and moves. The linemen, both offensive and defensive, were lumbering and puffing around the backfield, jumping in and out of Talbott's way while he ran the elliptical course of his treadmill. Finally, when he could run no longer, he would loft the ball downfield.

Lombardi was not alone in worrying about Tarkenton; he presented special problems to the whole defense. Rickie Harris, the free safety, said Tarkenton was the toughest quarterback in the league to play against—not the best, but the most exhausting, the most likely to force an error in the secondary. "You run and run and run," Harris said, "and when he changes directions, you've got to reverse field. You're doing spirals back and forth, and the thing of it is, his receivers are trained to run patterns within patterns, to go certain places when Tarkenton gives certain moves. You have to be tight on those receivers all the time. I mean, Tarkenton can turn on a dime and throw anytime. The trick is to contain him with your ends, like we're doing in practice. Then you make it sort of like a rundown in baseball, with the space getting smaller between him and the two closing ends. The really tough thing about him too is that he throws better on the run than he does from the pocket."

"I'm still learning the Lombardi offensive system after three months," Vince Promuto said. "But the guys I feel for are the defensive linemen. They gotta learn a whole new system just for this game. The defensive line has built up this habit of staying in rushing lanes. But in order to get to Tarkenton, you got to break that habit you've been building up all year. Tough, real tough."

He was peeling long mauve strips of tape off his ribs and the shoulder that he had dislocated in the first half of the Cardinal game. He was clean-shaven on one side of his chest, curly-haired on the other. "How's it going to be?" I asked, tentatively patting a shoulder.

"It's the other one that hurts," he said. "This side just looks bad. But my knee hurts even worse. It throbs all day long and most of the night. The only time it feels good is during the wind sprints at the end of practice. It gets all warmed up by then. I'll be ready to play on Sunday, don't worry about that. Not going to disappoint the Old Man."

He sat in the folding chair in front of his locker, both knees grotesquely swollen, the tape marks clinging to his strangely shaven torso. "Hey," he called down to tackle Walt Rock, "you are really something, you are, Mister," parodying Lombardi's favorite expression. Promuto would play the rest of the season on two bad knees, a shoulder that dislocated with ease, and another shoulder that would need an operation after the season. Why did he submit to a life of pain like this? In part, because he wanted to play for Lombardi. In part, because that was the nature of his profession. You played with pain, and there had to be an almost lethal quality of it before the team doctor would intervene.

The pain and the physical beating were not the exclusive trademarks of Lombardi teams. All the teams in professional football had more or less the same ethic. They encouraged men to play hurt, intimating that, if they didn't, there would be no room for them in the team's future, and then left the choice of whether to play hurt or not up to the individual. There were few players who chose not to under those terms —there was face, security, and personal pride all riding on the decision to go, to play hurt.

The deck was stacked. It was stacked not because football men were primitives who rejoiced in exhibiting injured specimens to the public, but because the public craved injury, the risk of injury, the transcending of injury, as part of the football spectacle. The public did not want the blunt blood and gore of the Roman circus, where death and mangled corpses were the climax of the show; that was too brutal a reminder of human fate. What the public wanted was a spectacle that was violent, but that showed man's ability to overcome pain and crippling injury. Something savage but noble, something violent but not alarming to the squeamish. Football fulfilled this need better than any other sport. It had a contact, but it also had its intellectual, strategic, and moral overlay. It was like warfare, before the television screens brought it up too close for comfort. It was warfare that created no guilt, that allowed the fans to cheer when the wounded were helped from the field and to cheer even louder when they came back in a few plays later after an injection from the doctor, a whiff of smelling salts, and a pat on the ass from the coach of the day.

Ray Schoenke told me, "I've never been in the military, I've never been to war, but talking to veterans, it's the same feeling. They talk about when they hit the beach. The anxiety. The fear. The pressure and the pain you feel. We go through the same thing before a game. I leave my wife on Sunday morning, and she's tense. You're going off to war, to Vietnam for two and a half hours."

Flea Roberts said, "Football is a barbaric sport. This is the last of the gladiator-type things. It's an emotional game, like being in the ring as a boxer, and your manager tells you if the guy you're fighting drops his left really sock it to him. But he doesn't tell you how hard to hit him, he just says, sock it to him. Now, if the guy happens to go out for good when you stick him one, you're awful sorry, but how do you know whether you've socked it to him hard enough to kill him? I mean, how do you know if you're going to sock it to him to keep him out for ten seconds or forever? Do you draw a line? Is there a certain rate of speed you hit a guy? Football's no different than boxing, no different than being in that big arena with those damn Romans, I'll tell you. In football you got to hit a guy to wrack him up. You just hit him as hard as you know how. You don't want to hurt him, but you can't afford to hit him and let him run right on past you. So where do you draw the line? You got to just slam in there and try and knock his jock off, that's it, that's the only line there is."

"Football," said Tom Roussel, "is good for the country. Every American has that feeling inside him that he'd like to hit somebody. He can't do it in this kind of society. But he comes out to the ballpark and he's almost in the game. It keeps him from going soft. It's the fans' way of fighting for the country. It brings out the viciousness of your average man. The fans get involved, they really do. They love that blood, man, I guarantee you they do. They just want to see a guy get bloody, not hurt, you know what I mean."

"Well, not exactly," I said.

"It's like this. They don't want to *see* anybody get really hurt, they just want to see somebody get his *ass* busted."

I laughed. It couldn't have been said more succinctly.

"Like in football, it's this way," he went on, a lighthearted lilt in his drawl, "Somebody makes a beautiful, hard, bruising tackle, you can hear the 'ooohhs' and 'aaahs' all through the stadium. But if the guy don't get up for quite a spell, they simmer down.

"Football is a symbol," he said. "If it wasn't there, where would the fans take out their frustrations? A man who works six days a week at a desk, where's he going to let his energy out in this society? He gets out to watch a football game, he yells, he screams, he sweats, he does everything. It makes him feel like he can lick the world and go back and sit on his can for another six days. I tell you, it's just as well they leave the meanness to us. It'd be a hell of a country if everybody was as punch-drunk as some of your ballplayers."

Roussel had the reputation of being a shade too easygoing out on the field, an iota too courtly with the opposition. Not Chris Hanburger. He had the reputation of being a hard-nosed, mean football player, notorious for his blitzing and his high "necktie" tackles, those head-wrenching blows that left the ballcarrier woozy.

When Lombardi was in a paternal mood at practice he would chide Hanburger affectionately, calling him "Christopher." "That a way to go, Christopher," he would chortle. No one ever bothered to tell Lombardi that Chris was short for Christian, not Christopher. Certainly Hanburger made no complaints. He was an army brat, used to the peculiar ways of men with stars on their shoulders, and there was a military meticulousness of detail about him. Even his locker had a squared-away look. Like a true army grunt, he was a man who groused and complained almost steadily in the locker room, hardly ever smiled, and stood in the doorway hectoring his teammates to finish their sandwiches so "we can get this meeting in gear." This was a trait that would have been irksome in most men, yet, in Hanburger, it was strangely likeable, even charming. "Chris bitches so much it's funny," Roussel said. "He bitches so much because he is really mad all the time and because he knows everybody enjoys the hell out of listening to him bitch. You ought to hear him get on Sam when he's late to the meetings. I admire the hell out of Chris. He's his own man."

That was true of Hanburger. In spite of his military precision and organization, he was a loner, an independent man. It was this strange blend of discipline and the loner's independence and recklessness that made him such an exciting football player.

We were sitting together at the stadium one afternoon after practice, the week before the Giants game. Hanburger wore a checkered sports shirt open at the neck, a pair of cuffed gray chinos, and desert boots. He was the only member of the team with a flat-top. That, together with his 1950's wardrobe, made him seem a decade out of step.

"Why the crewcut?" I asked. "The army upbringing?"

"No, I don't think so. I used to have a D.A. with curls up front when I was a kid, but I got with the wrong group of people and got into trouble, so I decided I'd get it cut close like this, and I've kept out of trouble ever since. I keep hoping the crewcut will come back; everything else does." He gave a quick, almost shy grin; a rather dashing, if self-contained looking man, with sharp, clean-cut features.

I asked him about violence in football, for his celebrity was in that special field.. He pursed his lips, gave the matter some consideration, and then began in an exact, rather surgical voice.

"I love to blitz. This is a game where there are pleasures as intense as anything you can experience in life. Blitzing for me has always been one of the game's real pleasures. A successfully executed blitz denies a first and ten, or the chances are at least good that it will. When they're operating on second or third and long yardage, it means they almost have to go to the air."

"How about coordinating your blitz and your regular play with the guys in the defensive line?" I asked.

"Important. Very important. I know from playing with Carl Kammerer over the years what he can do, and he knows what I can do. We have certain little calls we use, terminology that's different from what the coaches give you. I mean, we're not going against the defense, but there are certain things I can see that he can't, and vice versa. For example, if a back cheated up on our side, and if it's a running situation, there's a good chance that he's coming our way to block and that the ball is coming our way, too. If I tell Carl this, he can be conscious of it. That doesn't mean he changes his defense. He can just keep the possibility of what that cheat might mean in mind.

"John Hoffman is at Carl's end position now, and John is going to be a tremendous defensive end once he learns some technique. He just overpowered people in the Cardinal game. But he's still a rookie, still learning, and I'm a little leery of talking to John the way I would with Carl. John may just go overboard if I tell him something and think, 'Well, they're coming my way, and I'm going to leave the defense.' Carl wouldn't do that. If a runner back is coming out of the backfield on a pass pattern, say, I'll just say to Carl, 'Clothesline.' Carl will know what I want. Because if a back's clotheslined, it takes a lot out of him and it will help me on a pass coverage tremendously. He can come out of that backfield a hell of a lot quicker free than he can clotheslined. Now John knows how to clothesline too, but it's a delicate maneuver, somewhat illegal at times, and I wouldn't want to burden a rookie with that kind of trick to help me out the way I would a veteran like Carl."

"How about the clothesline? Is it legal?" I asked.

"Yeah, if you do it right. You got to be cagey about it. You've got to have the right angle, and the back has got to have the right weight. You don't try and clothesline a 240 fullback, he'll break your arm. But a small player when the opportunity presents itself? Damn right. I see nothing wrong with it. You get in a good lick around the head area, it rattles the man. You can beat a dazed man easier than an alert one. It's that simple."

"You've been criticized," I said, "for not tackling consistently, for being a gambler with that head-hunting necktie tackle."

"Well, the opportunity to hit somebody high around the head area presents itself, I'm going to do it. Not that I'm a brutal ballplayer, but I have put some people out of the game by tackling that way. This is a game of legal contact. The killer instinct has got to be legal, and the best instinct a ballplayer can have on defense is to work as close to the illegal limit as possible. Let's face it, you go against somebody very good and put him out of the game, well, the number two man is not as good as the number one man. That's why that number two man is on the second string. Getting hurt is part of this game, and you just have to hope it doesn't happen to you, but to the other guy."

"As long as it's legal?" I said.

"Right. There's no excuse for a penalty. Say there's an opportunity to hit someone on a special team, and it's a hanger between a clip and a legal block, well, you ought to pass that shot up. The chance of a penalty and a serious injury is too high. You don't want to be branded as a dirty football player. There are a lot of mean ones in this league, but no really dirty ones. People like Dick Butkus, Alex Karras, Tommy Nobis— they love to hit people."

"And people like Chris Hanburger too?"

"Well, I like to try to be that way," he grinned.

Chapter 17

The Giants had lately fallen on evil days and, like the Yankees, had faltered in the mid-1960's and had kept on stumbling right out of sight. Allie Sherman had been fired as head coach just before the season began and Alex Webster installed in his place, the sort of sudden *coup d'état* that normally left teams a little jittery, a little uncertain of whether the things they had been told in pre-season training were to be forgotten or remembered. To the surprise of everyone, the Giants were coming to Washington with a 3–1 record, including a win over the now obviously powerful Vikings. They were the Redskins' oldest NFL rival and, more than that, they were Vince Lombardi's old team. This was a game the Redskins could be expected to want.

The Redskins won the flip, a modest sort of triumph they were to excel in all year long. Washington put the ball in play on their 29 and advanced it 20 yards before they had to punt it away. The Giants brought it back 20 yards and punted. It was settling into one of those drab afternoons, devoid of any great *éclat* or any sense of ferocious rivalry, one of those 20-yards-and-a-punt kinds of games.

In the second period, the Redskins started to work the ball from their own 41. Larry Brown fumbled on the first play from scrimmage, the Giants recovered, and Tarkenton took them down to score in six plays, the touchdown coming on a Joe Morrison 11-yard run right up the gut without a Redskin hand touching him. With a little less than four minutes in the half, Jurgensen had worked the ball up to the Redskin 42-yard line. It was third and thirteen, and Jurgensen went for broke, faked to one side, and lofted a beautiful floating pass 40 yards downfield. Charley Taylor was all alone, digging in step with the ball, the nearest Giant defender 20 yards behind him. A sure 58-yard touchdown pass. Taylor was still in stride, watching the ball's descent, his hands cupped in front of his chest. The ball landed right on target, bounced once in his palms, and dropped to rest on the turf at the 17-yard line. Taylor's momentum carried him into the end zone. He stood alone, eyeing the ball upfield for a moment while 50,000 people eyed the Grand Prairie Flash, the one and only, in his moment of despair. The Giants went to the dressing room at the half with a 7–0 lead.

They came out like a team inspired, taking the kickoff and moving 72 yards in fourteen plays for a touchdown that put them ahead 14–0. Tarkenton passed three times for 24 yards and ran twice for 15 yards, mixing his plays well and getting plenty of time to pass, his roadwork behind the line of scrimmage a great deal less rigorous and more effective than Talbott's enactment earlier in the week. The Redskin rush seemed timid, befuddled, their energy sapping rapidly.

It was now midway through the third period; the Redskins, 7½ point favorites at gametime, were down by 14. Boos were beginning to sound from the stands. Washington came back on a five-minute drive with Charley Harraway carrying the ball in for the score from the 1-yard line, behind a pulverizing Charley Taylor block. The Redskins got the ball right back, and Larry Brown reeled off a 41-yard run down to the Giant 24-yard line. Three plays later Charley Harraway swept end for the score behind another crushing block by Charley Taylor that bowled over two Giant defenders. Now it was Redskins 14, Giants 14.

Three minutes later the Giants were in a fourth-and-two punt situation on their 46-yard line. Ernie Koy got off his only respectable kick of the afternoon, a 40-yarder. The Giants were offside on the kick, and perhaps for that reason hustled downfield with less than full alacrity. In any case, Rickie Harris, who had been almost decapitated on his last effort at fielding one of Koy's boots, now caught the ball at his 14-yard line.

He squirted through the first wave of Giant tacklers, got a block or two, and suddenly was in the open, racing across the field toward the Redskin side line. Flea Roberts, who had thrown the first block downfield that had freed Harris, was now on his feet, dashing toward the southwest corner of the goal where Giant linebacker Ralph Heck had the only angle capable of stopping Harris. Roberts banged into Heck's chest, Hanburger hit him from the side, Ted Vactor leveled him, and Harris skipped into the end zone with an 86-yard punt return.

Harris was mobbed by the fans in the end zone seats; he broke loose, started back toward the field but thought better of it, turned to the side lines, and heaved the ball as far into the stands as he could.

That made it Redskins 20, Giants 14—on three Washington touchdowns in seven minutes. Knight came in to add the extra point and missed it. It seemed incredible, but there it was: the white painted zero still hanging on the scoreboard right behind the 2. It should have taken the Giants a touchdown and an extra point to tie; now it would take that to win.

"Knight was shaking so bad in the huddle, it's a miracle he didn't kick Sonny in the head," a member of the field-goal team told me later. Now thoroughly shaken, Knight's kickoff went out of bounds. He kicked again from the Redskin 35, the ball came down on the New York 17, and was carried up to the 32. Tarkenton, with plenty of time, hit Homer Jones for 17 yards, and all at once a Giant drive was on—3 yards, 2 yards, 8 yards, 8 more yards on a double flea-flicker, 5 yards, 4 yards, 1 yard, 11 yards. Suddenly it was first and goal at the Redskin 9, and that missed extra point was looming larger, a grisly conjuration of that still-recent Sunday afternoon in Cleveland.

Joe Morrison went down to the 3 before Sam Huff stopped him. Things looked pretty grim indeed. Nothing the Redskins had shown defensively to date indicated they could hold this late in the game, this close to paydirt. Don Fuqua went up the middle, was defended perfectly by Sam Huff, and gained less than a yard. Now it was third and goal at the 3. Tarkenton tried to put it in the air to tight end Freeman White, but Brig Owens was on him all the way. That brought up the fourth down. It was too late in the game to do anything but go for the touchdown.

Tarkenton dropped back to pass, and once again his receivers were sewed up. He rolled out to the right, still looking for someone. There was a gaping hole where the line had once been. Tarkenton thought he could make it, turned sharply, and headed right up the middle. Pat Fisher saw him coming, dropped off his man in the end zone, and hit Tarkenton right below the waist, dropping him cold at the 2. It was a tackle as solid, crisp, and perfect as any I'd ever seen. Huff and Spain Musgrove came over to pile on. Tarkenton, realizing he wasn't going anywhere, gave the ball a flip onto the turf, hoping to simulate a fumble, which some nearby Giant might scoop up and take in for the score. The referee blew the play dead. (In any case, the loose ball was pounced on by a Redskin.)

There were about three and a half minutes to go. Jurgensen had some time to eat up, working from his own 2 at that. He needed the first down badly. On third and nine he hit Jerry Smith on the 18, another of those clutch consistency catches that Smith prided himself on. The Giant defense finally forced a punt on the next series, but had to use up two time-outs in the process. Tarkenton got the ball back with a minute and a quarter showing, but was unable to do anything with it.

So the Redskins went down to the dressing room 3–1–1 on the season, in the thick of things, it seemed.

In the locker room Ray Schoenke asked, "What's happening with Dallas?" The answer to that question was that at the Cotton Bowl at half-time, it stood Dallas 42, the Eagles 0.

Lombardi was in a less than jubilant mood in the coaches' dressing room. He suffered through a few technical questions, his answers testy. "On that shotgun formation Tarkenton tried . . . " a reporter began.

"That was no shotgun," Lombardi snarled, shaking his head at the colossal ignorance that would prompt the use of such a term. Later I was looking at the Giant game's movie with Harland Svare. "Watch Fran on this shotgun," he said.

"Well, I guess the league will fine Harris a hundred bucks

for throwing the ball in the stands," a writer began, trying to ease the session into more convivial directions.

"Did he throw the ball into the seats?" Lombardi demanded. "I didn't see that. If he did, I'm going to fine him too." He stared cheerlessly through the tile wall in the general direction of Rickie Harris's locker.

"We were a better all-around football team last week against the Cardinals," Lombardi intoned. "But if you got better every week, this would be an easy business." Curt Knight's kicking, a perennial bone of contention between Lombardi and the press, was raised. How about the two missed field goals, the point after touchdown?

"It's disturbing," Lombardi grunted, and I wondered if this question had been what was eating him all along. "As long as the missed point didn't cost us the game, it's all right. If we'd lost by one, I'd be even more disturbed. I don't know, maybe Hauss snaps the ball back there so fast it's affecting Knight's kicking. We did some disturbing things, but we won. And you have to win on the days you don't play so well, too."

In the dressing room Knight was disconsolate, deeply shaken. "I don't think I've ever missed an extra point in my life before. No, it wasn't Hauss's snaps. They were fine, and Sonny got the ball down just right. I had an off-day, a terrible day. I kicked poorly, and it happens to me just when I thought I had the mental thing licked after those kicks in the Cardinal game."

He retreated toward his locker, seeking a sanctity that the open stall did not provide. Knight was a friendly Texan with light freckles on his face. Often referred to by Lombardi as the "kid kicker," he was, at twenty-six, a year and a half older than his cab-squad rival Charlie Gogolak. Although the season was five games old, Knight was still on probation, and he knew it, which gave him a moody and defensive posture. At best, kicking made men manic-depressive, and Knight was now tasting the lower depths again. He was using up all his credit rapidly. One more bad game, a game where a missed kick meant defeat, and he would probably be gone, would certainly be reading a clamor for his ouster in the press.

Over in his corner of the locker room, Charley Taylor was dutifully manufacturing explanations for his dropped 58-yard touchdown pass. He was not called "jingle jaws" for nothing. He had misjudged the ball, the spheroid had followed an abnormal aerodynamic path, it had nosed earthward prematurely, it had lost its speed, and he had been following it over the wrong shoulder. Each visitor got a different, elaborately circuitous explanation. Finally Taylor's locker neighbor Jim Snowden said, "Let's face it, Charley, you dropped the damn ball."

But even in victory there were some questions being asked. "Looking back on this game," a defensive player told me, "the coaches didn't get us respecting the Giants enough. The mistake was their saying the New York line was lousy. You end up not respecting their guys enough, you don't get up for them, and they outplayed us as a result. Christ, we worried so much about Tarkenton, and he only gained 30 yards or something on the ground. Their other runners carried for 150 or so, and we were so worried about sealing Tarkenton off outside that they ran on us at will up the middle. We were real lucky today, to pull that one out. Without Rickie's runback we'd of been dead."

Rickie Harris, a man ebullient even in defeat, passed by wearing his biggest smile of the year. There was a certain spring in his step. "I'll pay half the fine, Rickie," I offered.

"Which one? The league's or Lombardi's?" he asked, his euphoria tested by the uncertainty of the sum Lombardi might levy.

"I'm only a writer. Half of the league's is $100." As it turned out, neither the league nor Lombardi fined Harris.

Lombardi viewed the game films Monday morning and met with the press in a mood as dour as he had shown in the dressing room on Sunday. "We had gaping holes in the line," he explained. "The Giants ran against us at will [179 yards], and the coaching has to be blamed for that. I put too much emphasis on containing Tarkenton's scrambling, and the line wasn't aggressive enough, they hung back too much. ... They've got to be more aggressive. In another way we did all right on Tarkenton; at least he didn't hurt us with the long pass. But on balance, you'd have to say our problem was over-coaching."

"How about the Steelers next week?"

"They are physically tough. You beat the Steelers usually, but they punish you. They are a tough team and they are overdue. They've got a fine player in this kid Greene. It will be a difficult game, as they all are."

The week of the Steelers game, Charlie Gogolak and I went out after practice for a beer at the Polonaise Café, a suitably Eastern European name for Gogolak, the Hungarian refugee, who had learned his soccer kicking in a cow pasture in upper New York state. He was a small man with a puckish, good-natured face who had borne the indignity of the cab squad with philosophical good grace. Given Knight's game against the Giants, he was understandably itchy for a chance to kick.

"I can make out a good case for Lombardi," Gogolak said, "as far as picking between Curtis and me. He hasn't been unreasonable about it. I think I could have done a great job for him. Some of those blocked field goals during the exhibition season weren't my fault. I'd kicked two field goals against the Lions in Tampa. I felt hot, and up comes the third kick, a 39- or 40-yarder. I knew I was going to make it. The snap comes back, and it's a slow center, really slow. Well, Brig sort of put the ball down awkwardly, and after my first step I realized he hadn't got it on the ground yet, the laces were turned the wrong way, and he was rotating the ball just as I hit it. On top of that, one of our linemen got knocked on his can, and when the Lion player blocked the ball he was about four feet away. Well, you figure that lineman is 6'3" or so; what the hell, you can't talk about not having a high enough trajectory in a situation like that.

"Also, our kicking unit wasn't practicing under pressure. It was a lot of those little things, like why did Nixon lose all those elections? Well, you don't really know. *You* know that he did, so you brand him a loser. I had a lot of kicks blocked, so he branded me a loser. He figured let's try Knight, and Knight did pretty well. But whether it's me or Knight, I think Lombardi is mishandling the kicking game. His attitude is, 'God-damn it, you're a specialist, you're supposed to know what you're doing, kick the Goddamn ball right and don't bother me.' That's a strong mistake, because kicking is 90 percent confidence, and you get extra confidence when you feel part of the team. You should be kicking under pressure at practice instead of standing around all week and kicking a few when everyone goes in to take a shower.

"This is especially bad for Knight, who really needs confidence, a guy who over the years has never played a full season of kicking football. He's not used to the pressure yet, and Lombardi doesn't see that, or if he does, he doesn't care. It's funny, because Lombardi's greatest point is that everything he does is geared to prepare you for the pressure of the game, and he has this great eye for detail—except where pressure and detail come to bear on the kicking game. Oddly enough, kicking was a Packer weakness too. Hornung kicked four for twenty-two one year before they finally benched him and got another kicker.

"Look at the way they've gone about coaching the kicking unit this year. They've got Svare watching it, in charge supposedly, but he doesn't know much about kicking. He'll start us booting from the 35-yard line and then, all of a sudden, he moves back to the 52-yard line. That's silly. How often are you going to try a 52-yarder in a game? It doesn't do much for your confidence to miss eight of ten from the 52 in practice. But you make eight of ten from the 35, where you're going to be kicking from anyway, and your confidence is high; also, you get your timing down. You know you can put it through. Why did Knight miss that extra point in the game? An extra point! Hell, that's from this table to the bar. You just can't miss at that range. Curtis missed because he was really choked, didn't have the confidence that the right kind of practice can bring.

"I tell you, we're in a screwed-up business. I have to wish that Curtis screws up in Pittsburgh so I can play. Talk about confused loyalties, when you hope your team loses so that the guy who is responsible can be eliminated to make room for me. And don't think Curtis wasn't happy when I had that field goal blocked in Tampa. Can you imagine that A. D. Whitfield has to think the only way he'll get to play is if one of our backs gets hurt, I mean really hurt, so he can't walk. You've got to be pretty naïve to get sentimental over a game like this.

"That's the thing about football; once they get you hooked on it, they convince you this is the only thing you can do with your life. You play football and you make enough to live pretty well the year round for six months' work.

"I remember up at training camp my first year, it was ninety degrees in the shade, everyone is bushed, really dragging ass, and one of the veterans turns to me and says, 'Well, it beats digging ditches.' I said to myself, 'Holy hell, they got these guys psyched out.' I mean, you analyze it. Here is this guy twenty-seven, twenty-eight years old with a college education, he's a celebrity, people have heard about him, and he's talking about digging ditches, actually thinks that's the only serious alternative for him. They get everybody thinking like that, I'll tell you.

"It's funny, when Lombardi axed Theofilides, I thought the team would probably do badly. But now I'm not so sure we won't even do better. Three-one-and-one *is* better in fact, better than last year. Theo's departure really shook the guys, made a hell of an impact on most of us. We figured, if he can ax Theo that quick, what about me? Everybody thought I was pretty secure too in camp. So did I, for that matter. And then by the end of August, I was beginning to wonder. With Lombardi you can't be secure."

"Did you spend this amount of time talking obsessively about Otto?" I asked.

"No, with Otto you would be content to say simply, it's a damn shame he has to be the head of us. And that would be it. What else was there to say? Still, Otto was a very nice guy, a very nice guy."

"And of course," I said, "that's what made the Redskins such a wonderful ready-made situation for Lombardi to inherit. You had your nice guy, and look what he did for you.

So let's try a bastard and see what he can do. It's sort of a parable for the nation at large.

"How about the future?" I then asked.

"I don't know. I'd like to play. I don't like putting on my uniform at eight in the morning and sitting in the locker room and having people dump on me because I'm a cab-squad kicker. It's no fun to go out there and kick it and have the coaches look the other way, and then after you kick one or two they say, 'Okay, Curt, now you kick it.' It's discouraging when they come out and film Curt kicking and not me. It gets under your skin. And I've got great pride for what I can do as a kicker."

"Suppose," I said, "Knight has another bad game?"

"Oh, God, then I'd really want to play, very badly. I'd be tempted to say, either play me or release me. I really would."

Now that Tarkenton was out of the way for the season, practice slipped back into its deadly rut, the same drills, the same constant coaching, the same Lombardiisms, the "What the hell is going on heres" and the "You are really something, you are, Misters." I was sitting in front of John Hoffman's locker, the pair of us conjecturing over the team's chances for the division title.

"The Cleveland loss wasn't good for us, but at least it didn't cost us anything," John said.

"What do you mean?" I said. "It cost us a game."

"No it didn't," he said. "Only the games inside our division count. So we're 1-0 there, and the Cowboys are 3-0."

"Where'd you hear that?" I said, bewildered. "All the games count."

"Is that right?" Hoffman said, turning to Tom Roussel for an answer.

"You bet they all count," Roussel said.

"I'll be darned," Hoffman said. "That Cleveland game cost us. We better get on the stick."

"I feel I've made a contribution to the team now," I said. "Now that you know the Steelers count, you can whop hell out of them."

"Damn right. Hey, thanks a lot."

Later, after practice, we sat around and he told me how he'd come to the Redskins. "I asked for the minimum—the reason being that, when the cuts come, if it came down to me with the minimum and somebody else drawing eighteen or twenty thou, then I figured they'd say, 'Let's hang on to Hoffman. Hell, he's cheaper.' That was stupid of me because I see now four or five thousand bucks doesn't mean that much up here. Well, even though I asked the minimum, which is $12,-500, they signed me for $14,500 and a $1000 bonus. I mean, I would have signed for a smile and an autographed picture of Lombardi. I'm not any more loyal to management for it, though. I'm not crazy about management. Management everywhere exploits the players. But I am crazy about Mr. Lombardi."

"But Lombardi is management around here," I said.

"Yeah, I guess you're right. In that case, I am loyal to management around here. I think Lombardi's tremendous. He really likes the members of this team. He says he does, and he's got no reason to lie about it. Suppose he told us he hated us? What could we do about it? So when somebody tells me he likes me, hell, I believe him. Maybe I'm gullible, but I don't see why Lombardi would get any great charge out of telling us he likes us when he doesn't. What would be the fun in that?"

"Were you prepared for the sort of man Lombardi is?"

"I tried not to read anything about the man. I figured, before I came to camp, there was no point in psyching myself out by reading *Instant Replay* and finding out how mean he is. That would start me out from a hole. Hell, I'm scared enough of him without reading anything that makes me more scared. I'll tell you one thing I've learned about him, though: he makes use of his blunders. He'll say something, then he'll have to take it back. He'll accuse somebody of something and he'll have to eat his words. And he's figured out a way of lifting up everybody's spirits by doing it. Maybe it's his way of being human. In another coach you might lose respect for him, if he fined you and didn't make it stick. Lombardi does the same thing and improves morale."

"Give me an example," I said.

"Like in training camp, Fred Sumrall got caught eating a doughnut. And Sumrall has this terrible weight problem—can gain weight even on days when he doesn't eat anything—so we're all blocking the sled, and suddenly out of the blue Lombardi is standing up there on that machine, and he starts screaming and waving his hands around. 'That'll be $20 for that damn doughnut, Sumrall,' and he's carrying on like Sumrall just committed the worst atrocity in the history of sports, eating this damn doughnut. And Sumrall looked like he was going to faint dead away. I mean, it had been like twenty-four hours since he'd eaten the thing, and nobody'd said a word to him. And finally Lombardi says, 'Sumrall, how many of those damn doughnuts did you eat?' And Sumrall says in a tiny voice, 'Just one.' And Lombardi says, 'Okay, Sumrall, that'll only be $5.' Sumrall looked like he could hug him. And the whole team is giving a big round of applause. 'Way to go, Sumrall, way to eat only one doughnut.' I mean, it's ridiculous. But somehow he makes profit out of the fact that he's volatile and emotional."

"How'd you do against the Giants?" I asked.

"Well, I was really singled out in the films. And that gets you down. But there's nothing to do about it. It's all true, right there in front of your eyes. Of course, you can see that other guys aren't doing their jobs either, but you can't say, 'Hey, Coach, look there, that other guy isn't doing diddly-squat either. It doesn't work out that way.

"Of course, looking at the Giant films, our whole defensive unit looks awful. The defensive line is completely disorganized. Nobody knows where anybody else is going. It looks like we're just running around. I spent too much time studying Tarkenton. Now I know I should have studied my own man more and Tarkenton less. I figured I could adjust to my man during the game, but I didn't. I thought I'd be able to dope him out after the first series of downs, but by the end of the game I still didn't have it in my head what that guy was doing to me.

"Jim Norton was just jubilant at my performance on Sunday. I mean, he was really elated on Tuesday, all fired up and ready to go. And when Lombardi didn't put me down to the second team, Norton looked pretty perturbed. You can't blame him. I was the same way when Leo got ahead of me for the Cleveland game. Leo was just horrendous out there sometimes, and I was going, 'Yeah man, Yeah man,' to myself. It was just great to see Leo screwing up. And don't think Carl wasn't happy to see Leo and me making fools out of ourselves against the Giants. He wants back in there, too. It's a whole lot of money out there, and you don't get any of it, if you don't play."

"Well, you ought to feel safe out there for a while anyway," I said. "Lombardi's stubborn. He'll stick with a player for a long time and he doesn't like to have his mind changed."

Hoffman arched an eyebrow in interest. "You think so? Yeah, maybe he does stick with a guy. Maybe that's true. Maybe you got something there."

"Furthermore," I said, "having two guys as tall as you and Leo gives him some sort of sensuous pleasure. He loves that height."

Hoffman gave a soft chuckle. "Sensuous pleasure, eh?" he said, rolling the phrase off his tongue.

On Thursday's practice, the Redskins suffered their first major injury of the campaign. The lines snapped together, those big yellow pads flashing in the air and giving off the noises that were by now so commonplace. Walter Rock took a while getting up and was finally helped off the field by trainer Joe Kuczo. It was hard to know how seriously Rock was hurt, and one of the reporters ambled down to the training room to try to find out. He soon returned. "Rock's too scared to talk, won't even say what's hurting him," he reported. Jim Snowden was moved back to the right side, and Ray Schoenke came in to play left tackle. Schoenke had started as third-string guard when training camp began, had worked his way up to the first team by the end of the exhibition season, and had then torn a cartilage in his chest and been put back on the second team again. He had filled in when Vince Promuto had been hurt in a few games and had done well—had won two blocking awards, in fact. He had worked hard to make that first team in Carlisle and Gaithersburg, and I knew how badly he wanted to get back on it. This was his chance, not quite the way he had wanted it to come, but still his chance. He sat in the baseball dugout after practice, his hair tangled and sweaty, blood streaming across his forehead from the opened scabs that most of the offensive linemen wore as evidence of the driving, head-blocking style of Lombardi football.

"This is it, Ray," I said. "Give 'em hell."

Normally the warmest and most communicative of men, Schoenke sat in the dugout, abstracted, staring over the football field. He would have one full day's practice to get ready for Pittsburgh, where he would get his chance in an alien position. Football was indeed a game where men had to prove themselves all over again, every week, in less than ideal circumstances. Schoenke, whose versatility was underrated, would prove no disappointment.

The loss of Rock, rated by Bill Austin as the best member of the interior line, had to hurt, not only because of his personal absence, but because the Redskin reserves were stretched desperately thin. Dave Crossan, the reserve center, was recovering from a hamstring suffered during the Cardinal game. Backup guard Steve Duich had a badly swollen knee that would not bend. And with Schoenke playing tackle, there was no backup man available at guard tackle and center.

To make matters worse, the Steeler line was rugged, tough enough for Lombardi to post a clipping from a Pittsburgh paper in the dressing room that showed a picture of Mean Joe Greene, their exceptionally agile 270-pound rookie defensive tackle. The words from the clipping, "It came as an agreeable surprise to Joe that fewer guards block him low in pro ball than in college," were underlined in red pencil. It was not often that Lombardi resorted to this transparent high-school psychology to rev up his charges. As Wooten had put it, "You can't screw around with clubs like Pittsburgh if you're going to win it." And Lombardi wanted to win it; he had a string of two straight on the line.

On Friday, Rock didn't practice, and the press corps asked Lombardi if he'd be available to play.

"Yeah, he's ready."

"You're sure?"

"You don't think he'd have the nerve to make me a liar, do you?" Lombardi gave a large sinister laugh at that one. "Listen, you want to bet Rock won't play? He'll be out there if he has to wear crutches."

"Hell, I'm not betting," a reporter said. "You'd make him play just to see me lose my money."

"Let me tell you, Coach," Lombardi said, "Rock'll go out there because he wants to, not because I want him to."

Inside the locker room Rock looked something less than the image of lion-hearted readiness, as he limped about on a badly twisted knee. "Well," he noted in a faint voice, "the paper said that the Coach said that I can play, so I guess I'm ready."

As it turned out, Rock did not play. Lombardi activated defensive end Clark Miller and Dennis Crane, a defensive tackle, who had been put on the move list two weeks earlier and had now been converted into an offensive tackle. Crane had not blocked for four years and had been given a crash course in offensive line-play by Bill Austin. Austin's tutelage, never a factor to be dismissed lightly, normally required longer than two weeks to take hold.

To make room for Crane and Miller, Lombardi put running back Gerry Allen and Steve Duich on the move list. As we boarded the bus for Pitt Stadium, Duich appeared almost jaunty at the prospect of a two-week excused absence from combat to let his knee heal. Certainly, he could hardly have looked forward to regaling the Pittsburgh crowd with that grotesque stiff-legged run he had managed at practice under Lombardi's urging.

Allen's face was drawn. He boarded the bus without glancing at his teammates, staring straight ahead, set apart from the team he had belonged to only twenty-four hours earlier.

He had started the season in New Orleans, and when Henry Dyer had fumbled, Lombardi had sent Larry Brown and Charley Harraway into the backfield. They had been there ever since. Now, going into the sixth game of the season, Brown was the second leading rusher in the NFL, Harraway the fifteenth. It would be difficult to nudge either of them aside, but as long as he was on the squad, Allen still had a chance to carry in a play from the bench, to break off a long run, to redeem himself in Coach's eyes.

That possibility did not exist on the move list, and now climbing aboard the bus, Allen's face, normally alive with vitality and good humor, was bleak with defeat—all the more bleak, perhaps, because he had to face his teammates. When a man was cut, he was allowed to slink out of the dressing room without the shame of good-byes. The move list, while not as final as a cut, meant a man had to face his teammates in the moment of his greatest vulnerability as a football player.

I remembered how chipper Allen had been earlier in the week. Frank Angelo, the clubhouse attendant, a corpulent older man with a dead cigar between his lips, had been making the rounds of the locker stalls, cleaning football shoes. Angelo was known as "Sees All" because he "saw all and said nothing" in some thirty-odd years in the Redskins' and Senators' clubhouses. Allen clapped Sees All on the shoulder and told me, "Sees All tells me I'm one of the great ones. He's seen a lot of them come and go over the years. Don't forget that. He's seen some of the great ones, and he ranks me right up there. Right, Sees All?" Sees All grunted and continued on his rounds of the locker stalls, polishing the mud off the football shoes.

Allen gave a semi-believing chuckle at the prospect of having Sees All as a supporter. "Yep, one of the great ones, and Sees All's seen them all."

"Well," I said, "next time I see Coach, I'll tell him I understand he's got one of the great ones on the roster and isn't playing him. And he'll say, 'Who?' and I'll say, 'Allen,' and he'll say, 'How do you know?' and I'll say, 'Because Sees All says so.' "

"Atta way to talk," Allen said, chuckling to himself. "Don't forget to mention that Sees All ought to know. Hell, he's seen all of the great ones. He puts me right up there, right up there with them."

Now Allen was on the move list, beyond the pale for at least two weeks, beyond the intervention of backers more influential than Sees All. Now he was a man bereft of hope, that most obdurate of athletic virtues.

Chapter 18

The sky over Pitt Stadium was overcast; it was a gray, bleak late October afternoon with a snap in the wind that made the stadium seem even more ancient and tacky than it was.

Various Steeler immortals and old-timers were introduced before the game, each drawing generous applause from the fans. The Redskins and their coaching staff took the field swaddled in their Arctic benchcoats—all except Bill Austin, conspicuous in his tawny yellow polo shirt with "Redskins" sewn in crimson script across the chest. Austin had been fired as the Steelers' head coach at the end of the 1968 season. It seemed characteristic of him that he would defy both the weather and the Pittsburg fans by so blatantly announcing his presence; naturally, he was booed.

The Redskins kicked off, and Terry Hanratty came in to move the Steelers. He drove them down to the Washington 37-yard line before an interference penalty and a 10-yard loss forced a punt. The ball was downed on the Redskin 2. Jurgensen's third play from scrimmage was intercepted at the Washington 44-yard line. Don Hoak carried to the Redskins' 33 off tackle, and Hanratty went back to throw deep for a score to wide receiver Marshall Cropper. Brig Owens intercepted at the 1 and ran it back along the Pittsburgh side lines to the 10-yard line, suffering a concussion in the process. The ball changed hands twice before Charley Harraway fumbled on the Washington 20 and the Steelers went in for a touchdown six plays later to take a 7–0 lead as the first quarter ended.

The second quarter was uneventful, with neither Hanratty nor Jurgensen very effective in the air. The warnings on the

Redskin clubhouse wall notwithstanding, Mean Joe Greene was having himself a field day. He broke through twice to dump Jurgensen, was a key factor in leaving Sonny five for sixteen at the half, and helped shut down the Redskin ground game, which was only good for 37 yards. Hanratty completed only two of nine passes for a piddling 19 yards, but the Steeler runners carried for 120 yards and a 4.8 average.

The Steelers had been uneven enough to account for their 1–4 record. The Redskin defense had done fairly well, considering the field position they had inherited from the offense. But Jurgensen and the offense sputtered along, disorganized, and dispirited.

As the third quarter dragged along, the Steeler seven-point lead looked good enough to hold up, with neither offense clicking and both defenses yielding a combined total of 2 yards in the first two series.

Then Jurgensen sharpened, not with the electrifying bravura of years gone by, but with a steady, sustained drive that moved 70 yards in nine plays. At the Steeler 10 his receivers flared to the outside, the middle of the field parted, and Jurgensen lugged the ball in for the touchdown with Mean Joe Greene gaping in disbelief. Steeler Coach Chuck Noll apparently had neglected to post a clipping in the Pittsburg dressing room that the '69 Jurgensen would scamper when the need arose. Knight converted, and the score was 7–7.

Pittsburgh returned Knight's kickoff to their 18, Hanratty dropped back to pass on the first play, and Marlin McKeever, in at strong side linebacker for Tommy Roussel, was knocked to his seat by the force of the ball, yet somehow hung on to it, got back up, ran a few yards, was hit and lateraled to Bob Wade, who carried for 8 more yards down to the Pittsburgh 8. Two plays later, Jurgensen found Charley Taylor all alone in the end zone and threw his two-hundredth career touchdown pass. Only Johnny Unitas and Y. A. Tittle had thrown more. Now it was Washington 14, the Steelers 7. Late in the third period, Sam Huff was knocked groggy and led from the field, his jaw slack, his eyes dead.

John Didion came in to replace Huff, and the defense held together until midway in the fourth period, when linebacker Andy Russell picked off Jurgensen's third-down pass and ran it back 22 yards to the Washington 45-yard line. From there, the Steelers punched down to the Redskin 23-yard line on two Earl Gros runs off tackle and a 15-yard Hanratty pass. Two 5-yard penalties and two fine pass-defending plays by Mike Bass left it fourth and sixteen at the Redskin 33. A field goal wasn't enough now. Hanratty faded back to throw and drifted out of the pocket to his right. Didion dropped off to cover Gros coming out of the backfield, but lost the race to the goal-line. Hanratty swept to his right and fired on a line to Gros in the end zone. Didion dove, but too late, and remained face down in the end zone grass, his hands clutching the turf, not daring to rise and look at the scoreboard. But there was a yellow hanky on the Washington side lines, where the referee said Hanratty had stepped over the line of scrimmage to throw the ball. It was no score, and the Redskins took over on downs.

Now the game was Washington's, if they could pound out a first down to run out the clock. Brown and Harraway fell 4 yards short, and Mike Bragg came in to kick. The Steelers put in a single safety, Roy Jefferson, their league leading pass receiver who had been blanked all afternoon by Mike Bass. Bragg punted deep, a 48-yarder, Jefferson fielded it and brought the ball back to the 18 with a little more than a minute on the clock. Hanratty, who had displayed the rookie's uncertain hand all day, suddenly came to life. He hit on three of his first four passes for 71 yards, all the way down to the Redskin 10-yard line. Sam Huff was resuscitated for the occasion, squeezed on his helmet, and went in to try to prevent another Cleveland-style debacle. There were forty-three seconds left to play. Hanratty underthrew Gros in the end zone, missed Jefferson, and had his third-down pass batted down by strong safety Bob Wade, a Steeler reject now in the game for Brig Owens. That made it fourth and ten, thirty-four seconds left. Hanratty dropped back again, saw Gros on the Pittsburgh side line, and fired the ball home. Bob Wade dropped Gros on the Washington 5-yard line, and Sam Huff piled on for good measure.

Somehow the Redskins had won. How or why was another matter. Lombardi looked limp down on the side lines, a man beaten by this ludicrously undeserved victory. "You people are going to give me a heart attack," he announced in the dressing room and threw the doors open to the press.

Jurgensen was in an expansive mood, buttoning up his co-balt-blue shirt.

"How come you came back so well in the second half?" a reporter asked.

"Because there was no third half," Sonny said, arching his eyebrows and grinning at the band of reporters, the affable quipster of yore.

"How about that Mean Joe Greene?" Jurgensen was asked. "What did Mean Joe say to you when he helped you to your feet after those times he nailed you?"

"I don't think he said anything," Jurgensen beamed. "I guess he was helping me up because he didn't want me to leave the game. The way I was doing, you can't blame him. This is the second poor game in a row for the offense. We haven't been executing well. But the important thing is getting the winning habit, coming out on top when you play badly."

The old Redhead sauntered off to line up Mike Bass for his TV show. It was hard to avoid the impression that Jurgensen was beginning to sound like Lombardi, spinning off Coach's clichés with the true fervor of a middle-aged convert. Still, it had been a long time since Sonny Jurgensen had played on a ballclub that was 4–1–1, and a few tributes to Coach were not out of place—not as long as you won.

Willie Banks, the second-year guard Lombardi had been touting for All-Pro earlier in the year, limped up to his locker stall from the shower room. "How about that Mean Joe Greene?" Banks was asked. "Did Mean Joe talk to you on the line?"

"Yeah, he bad-mouthed me. Like he come up to the line and look at Hauss and me and say, 'You guys gonna stop Mean

Joe, or is Mean Joe just gonna bust right through?'" Willie shook his head and stared ruefully at his ankle.

I saw Bob Wade across the room. "I knew they were going to throw to Gros that last play. I just knew it," he said happily. "It was the same pattern Hanratty tried the play before, and I called a slide with Rickie."

"That's right," Harris said in his squeaky, excitable voice. "I dropped off to cover their tight end. I was too far away to help. I could only just pray, 'cause I knew and Bob knew where that ball was going. Man, he nailed him flat."

"I met him head on," Wade beamed. "Just cracked him as good as I knew how, and down he went. I don't know where he came down, but it was somewhere this side of the goal-line, I knew that. I stayed in front of that end zone, I'll tell you that. Damn, it was good to play again."

Getting on the plane, I told Chris Hanburger, "Somebody up there must like you guys."

"Either that," he said, shaking his head, "or Somebody's the head coach."

"Well?" Lombardi demanded on Monday, staring at the newspapermen.

"What can we say," a reporter shrugged. "You won."

"Yeah," Lombardi admitted. "I don't know. We're a team that's playing in spurts. The Packers used to win most of their games on defense, which is what we're doing. This team is not the Packers, though. I'd have to say the opponents are able to move the ball at will on this team. At will, but not into the end zone. We bend, but we don't break."

"Is it possible to keep bumbling and keep winning all the way?" a reporter asked. Lombardi gave the man a frosty glare. "They're playing with everything they got and once in a while they put it all together for a long drive. You can't give more than the best you got. But obviously we can be outclassed. We can be overpowered. The offensive line is hurt. The defense is young, and the Steelers went to work on our rookie defensive ends. It was brutal. The Colts are going to have some pleasant game films to look at, I'll tell you."

Lombardi was unusually close-mouthed the week of the

Colts ballgame. In part, it was the pressure of the winning streak, the need to maintain it if ground was to be gained on Dallas, and the knowledge that his team probably should have lost two of the three games in its victory skein.

But there was a deeper reason, I thought. Lombardi had always gone out of his way to sing the praises of Don Shula. Conceivably he regarded Shula as a great coach, and certainly Shula's record at Baltimore merited approbation. But perhaps having beaten Shula so often in the past, Lombardi was anxious not to rub salt in the wounds. For while Shula's Colts had the best won-lost record of any team in football from 1963 through 1968, Baltimore had won only one NFL title in those years, and no Super Bowls. From 1963 to 1967, the Lombardi Packers had two Super Bowls and four NFL titles to their credit. Lombardi had won the big ones, and it stood to reason that Shula ached for revenge.

Coaching is, after all, a profession that consumes the ego, and there wasn't a coach in football who didn't resent Lombardi's decade-long monopoly of the limelight. George Wilson, head coach of the Miami Dolphins, had spoken for his colleagues during the 1969 training camp when he had asserted, "I'm tired of all this Lombardi business. Every one makes him out such a great coach. Given the same material, I'll beat him every time. I don't holler at fellows to embarrass them in front of their teammates. That's just a big show."

Lombardi had claimed amazement at this unprovoked outburst, yet he knew that there were coaches who shared Wilson's annoyance with his legend. Lombardi knew that his fellow coaches would take a special pleasure in beating him, in tarnishing that highly buffed Packer legend, in humiliating him if they could. The Lombardi Packers had been remorseless, had given no quarter, and that was not easily forgiven. If George Wilson was laying for Lombardi, what then of George Allen, Blanton Collier, Tom Landry, and Don Shula? They were the coaches of the best teams in the NFL during the late sixties. They had all been laid low by Lombardi, and now in 1969 their chance for revenge was at hand. Collier had already taken it; Allen, Landry, and Shula were waiting in line to settle some old scores.

I remembered talking once to Lombardi about the 1967 Los Angeles Rams. That was the year when their "fearsome foursome" dominated the sports headlines, when Allen was being billed as more Spartan, more dedicated than Vince Lombardi himself. In 1967 the Packers were shooting for their third straight NFL title. Their over-all won-lost record was not glittering, but good enough to wrap up the Central Division title early. The Colts and the Rams, both in the Coastal Division, had the best records in football, were neck and neck for their Division title and the right to play the Packers for the Western Conference crown.

In the next to the last game of the '67 season the Packers met the Rams in Los Angeles. The Packers didn't need the game, but the Rams had to have it in order to stay alive for a showdown with the Colts in the last game of the season. The Packers were ahead 24–20 in the closing minute of the game, and in the final seconds Green Bay dropped back to punt. It was now or never for the Rams. They broke the Packer line, a linebacker shot the middle and blocked Donny Anderson's punt. The Rams recovered on the Green Bay 5-yard line and scored two plays later to win 27–24. It was a game that seemed to possess an irresistible symbolism. It appeared that the Rams had momentum and destiny on their side, and that they would go on to beat the Colts the following week, go on all the way to the World Championship.

The Rams went to Baltimore for the season finale and tore the Colts apart 34–10, earning the chance to meet the Packers for the Western Conference title in Milwaukee's County Stadium the following week.

I was setting this scene for Lombardi, describing it with as much buildup as possible. It had appeared, I told him, that George Allen was headed for super-Lombardi status, that fate was on the side of the Rams. As I was delivering this background recital Lombardi suddenly stiffened and gave that tense deathmask grin of his, totally absorbed in his own recreation of the event. He began to mumble under his breath, "But we beat them, we beat them in Milwaukee."

"And then," I said, "you played the Rams for the Western Conference title."

"We beat them in Milwaukee," he said aloud, his voice remote, intense, in communion with the past.

And the Packers had won. It was 28–7, and Green Bay went on to beat the Cowboys the following week for their third NFL title, and then went on to their second straight Super Bowl win against the Oakland Raiders the next week.

So it was safe to say that George Allen had not forgotten that game in Milwaukee, that Tom Landry had not forgotten the game that next week in thirteen-below-zero temperatures on Green Bay's Lambeau Field, that Don Shula had not forgotten the overtime sudden-death play-off loss to the Packers for the Western Conference title in 1965 and had not forgotten that he had lost seven out of ten games with teams coached by Lombardi. It was safe to say that all the coaches of the NFL were, in Tom Landry's phrase, "tired of sucking hind teat to Vince Lombardi."

I had been to Baltimore for the Colts' fourth game of the season against the Eagles, three weeks earlier. Then the Colt fans choked the sidewalks waving fingers in the air to indicate how many tickets they were seeking to buy.

It was drizzling at Memorial Stadium for the Redskin game, and now the fans stood outside waving extra tickets in the air, anxious to dispose of their ducats, whether disheartened by the rain or the prospect of Jurgensen manhandling the once beloved, but now spurned, home team.

Certainly, neither foul weather nor the hint of defeat disheartened Baltimore's number-one fan, Spiro Agnew, who arrived at the ballpark some moments before I did. Agnew had just recently returned from his "effete corps of impudent snobs" speech to a Republican fund-raising dinner in Mississippi, a speech conveniently timed to allow him to take in the Colts game at New Orleans over the same weekend. When I got upstairs, Agnew was in the press snack bar, a large man with an inflamed red face, fastidiously outfitted and groomed, resembling a salesman in a classy midwestern men's clothing store. He was all alone in one corner of the room, smiling hugely, as if to encourage company, to invite a chat, a little friendly banter back and forth on the state of the world, the status of the Colt defense. I knew that, as the chief executive of Baltimore country and later as Governor of Maryland, Agnew had been one of the boys around Memorial Stadium, a clubbable, amiable man who enjoyed chewing the rag about zig-ins, zig-outs, blast blocks, and the like.

Now circumstances had elevated him to a somewhat loftier position in life, and from the smile on his face he seemed to have few regrets, seemed to have happily shouldered the burden of high public office, to have seen as many football games as ever. Perhaps the smile he allowed himself was a reflection of the great distance he had traveled so suddenly. The image of A. D. Whitfield returning to that flashing stoplight in Rosebud to dwell on the improvement in his lot came to mind.

And it seemed to me no accident that Agnew and his chief should be such avid frequenters of ballparks. The ballpark was where the silent majority could be found. The fans were by and large old-fashioned patriots who belted out the "Star Spangled Banner" with gusto, who rejoiced in military marching bands at half-time. It seemed absurd that such displays of patriotism should become political acts, but there it was. The country was split, and the ballpark was on the right side of the fissure. The cars in the parking lot had American flag decals plastered on their windows and bumpers. The nation had arrived at the state where even the flag was taken as an affirmation of support for the political philosophy of Spiro Agnew.

The ballpark was home base for Agnew. The people in the stands knew him as one of them, just an ordinary guy who was fed up right to here and was recharging his batteries at the ballpark before sallying forth to continue his crusade in their behalf.

Unquestionably, the political appeal of football came from the nostalgia the game evoked, the suggestion of an orderly, disciplined past that was disappearing rapidly, the sense that only in sports were young people conducting themselves in a truly American manner. Professional athletes were the last of the good, clean entertainers, the last illusory vestige of American innocence. Joe Namath notwithstanding, ballplayers generally eschewed mutton-chop sideburns, shaggy hair, pot, peace demonstrations, and open sexual rebellion. They lived by the old American rules, and Middle America appreciated that, enjoyed coming out to the ballpark, secure in the knowledge that Vince Lombardi had the flower of American youth well in hand. Parents and college administrators were caving in to the "punks" and "kooks," but not Vince Lombardi, not Spiro Agnew.

Lombardi was the transplanted flower of Middle America. His upbringing, his education, and his professional environment had taught him the virtues of discipline, order, patriotism. He was by nature a conservative, an austere man, yet a man who hated to give offense—a "softie," as he put it. He was surrounded by fellow coaches, owners, adulating businessmen, and salesmen who sought out and encouraged his endorsements for their favorite causes. They saw in his pithiness and intensity a form of advocacy that had mass appeal, and it didn't take much prodding to elicit a ringing defense of law 'n order from Lombardi; it didn't take much urging to trigger an outburst against the moral decay sweeping the country.

I remembered being at a sports luncheon at which the reporters, by and large a deeply conservative fraternity, were trying to get Lombardi to say that sports was the last bastion of discipline in America, that the law and order he imposed in the Redskin clubhouse and on the field was a valuable lesson for the country at large. Lombardi quite naturally obliged them and allowed that there was plenty of truth in what they said. He was a man who wanted approval, who liked to tell people what they wanted to hear, who believed in law and order when it came right down to it.

Later I told him, "You know, law and order is two things. It's what the words really mean, and it's also a codeword for repression. Do you want to be identified with both meanings?"

"I make a statement, and people can read into it what they want to. I don't give a damn. I'm for law and order, all right. But freedom is such a loose word, really. I'm not for too much permissiveness, but I'm not for any repression either. I like discipline. But that doesn't mean I'm trying to say people don't have the right to be free, to do whatever they want to. To picket, to protest, to raise hell with the way things are. Behavior is for each man to decide for himself. But you have to have football discipline to be successful in this game. This is a game of rules—a receiver has to be disciplined in his routes, a blocker has to be disciplined on who he drives where.

He shook his head. "You know," he said , a note of irritation creeping into his voice, "I listen to other coaches talk and, Christ, they don't get into all this. Why the hell do I always get drawn into all these damn things?"

"You know the reason why, don't you?"

"No."

"Because you've got this quality of intensity that leads people to believe that you've got something important to say, something that goes beyond football. Because of that, and because you've been so successful at football, people want to listen to you impart your football philosophy as a philosophy of life."

He grunted and gave an awkward little laugh at that. I did not discount the fact that if he was willing to accommodate the sporting press with a law-and-order stand, he was also willing to accommodate me by softening it somewhat. Yet, it seemed to me that accommodation was perhaps the key word here. For all the rigidity, the unyielding discipline of his background and his football system, he was prepared to bend, to entertain some doubts as to what life was about. There was in him an element of tolerance, of accommodation, of insecurity even. He had dedicated his life to disciplining these elements, mastering what he saw as weaknesses, yet in a sense they were his strengths. He led by example, and the most touching thing about him was the visible struggle to impose meanness on softness, faith on doubt, Spartan discipline on the volatile Italian nature. It was this contradiction that gave him an over-sized humanity, that led those who feared him to like him from time to time, those who paid him unquestioned fealty for his toughness to gape disapprovingly at his periodic acts of compassion.

"Look," he told me, twiddling with a pencil on his desk, "I got all the temptations and habits of anyone else. I'm not better or less than the next man. But the thing about me is that I always knew what my acts would mean. I was lucky. I fell into football, really. I had some early success with coaching in high school. If I hadn't, I don't know what I would have done or become. But I had that success and I knew then as a young man the path I had to follow. Now, the earlier in life you know your track, the better off you are. I was lucky and found a singleness of purpose early on."

"And you had to wait twenty-five years for the big chance to come, to be a head coach. That's a fair length of time," I said.

"That was a long time, not a fair length of time, but a long time," Lombardi muttered, stretching out the sentence. "I had a long apprentice period. But I had that goal in mind. I was never envious of anyone, but I had great ambition, still have. And because I knew what I wanted in the end, and had a long time to prepare for it, I wasn't going to miss my chance when it came. I think in the long run, the time I had to wait helped me more than anything else. It's easy to have faith in yourself and have discipline when you're a winner, when you're number one. What you got to have is faith and discipline when you're not a winner."

Chapter 19

At Baltimore's Memorial Stadium, Agnew was in the Colts owners' box, Middle America was filing into the stands, Lombardi was on the field in his transparent plastic-bad-weather gear, the two squads were on the side lines—the Colts said to be losing discipline, the Redskins said to be acquiring it. It had stopped drizzling, but a fine mist was still in the air.

The Redskins won the toss, and the game began on a note of orderly control football, as Washington moved downfield for five first downs. They drove all the way to the Colt 15-yard line before Billy Ray Smith overpowered the injured Willie Banks and dropped Jurgensen for a 12-yard loss. Curt Knight made good on a 34-yard field goal to put the Redskins ahead 3–0.

I was in the Redskins' enclosed box with Dave Slattery and some of the cab squad.

"My God," Slattery said, "look at that Dallas score." Down on the scoreboard in the first quarter at Cleveland, it stood the Browns 21, the Cowboys 0. Suddenly there was ground to be gained, a chance to come within reach of the Cowboys. They would be coming to Washington in two weeks for the first of their two games with the Redskins. And if there was one team Jurgensen knew he could beat, it was Dallas. It was a team that had fallen to Jurgensen's artistry in the past, a team that had always been leery of Washington and had been hexed by Lombardi. The team had the finest roster in football, but was curiously unsure of itself. Anything was possible. All the Redskins had to do was get by the Colts, and they would have momentum, perhaps even destiny, on their side.

The Colts came back with two field goals of their own, the

first a 49-yarder that hit the crossbar and bounced over, and the second an easy 12-yarder. Then Baltimore intercepted a Jurgensen pass at the Redskin 49-yard line and ran the ball in for a score in four straight carries. The kick was good, and it was Colts 13, Redskins 3.

The Baltimore defensive line, an object of universal scorn before the game, was putting tremendous pressure on Jurgensen. Still, the Redskins were hanging in there. They were, as Lombardi had said in Pittsburgh, bending, but not yet breaking.

With a little more than a minute left in the half, Rickie Harris intercepted a Unitas pass and was downed on the Colt 36-yard line. Jurgensen promptly hit Charley Taylor for 13 yards, then lost 15 when Billy Ray Smith burst over Banks again, forcing Jurgensen to eat the ball. Jurgensen got the loss and more back on a swing pass to Charley Harraway, and it was third and seven on the Colt 21-yard line, with time for a touchdown-pass attempt and a field goal if that failed. Jurgensen's throw to Bob Long was broken up in the end zone, and the Redskins were penalized for holding all the way back to the Baltimore 43. Knight's 50-yard placement was short and wide to the left as the half ended.

According to the scoreboard, it was Browns 28, Cowboys 3, at the half.

"Do you suppose Lombardi will use the Cleveland score for his half-time speech?" I asked cab-squader Jim Norton.

"He won't have to. Nobody on our bench is going to miss that score."

Whatever the theme of Lombardi's half-time forensics, the Redskins came back fighting. Pat Fisher recovered a Willie Richardson fumble on the first play from scrimmage, and Jurgensen hit Charley Taylor on a 19-yard touchdown pass six plays later. Knight's kick was good, and it was Colts 13, Redskins 10.

The Washington defense held, forced the Colts to punt, and the Redskins took over on their own 27, the pendulum now swinging to their side. Then came a series of *opéra bouffe* disasters. Forced to punt on fourth and seven the Redskins fielded a ten-man kicking unit. After some confused milling-around at the line of scrimmage, the bench was signaled for an eleventh player. It turned out that Willie Banks, who had been taken out of the game at the beginning of the third period for his inability to stop Billy Ray Smith, had assumed he was benched until further notice, special team assignments included. The Redskins were penalized 5 yards for delay of game while Banks got his helmet back on and hobbled onto the field. They were next penalized 5 more yards for drawing the Colts' off-side. Lombardi looked on incredulously from across the field, but the worst was still to come. The ball was snapped, Bragg stepped forward to kick, and suddenly tight end Tom Mitchell darted through the hole Banks was supposed to be occupying. The punt smacked resoundingly against Mitchell's upstretched palms and rolled back to the Redskin 5-yard line, where the Colts recovered. They scored three plays later, making it 20–10. Two and a half minutes later they made it 27–10 on another Jurgensen interception.

"Three touchdowns to win," Jim Norton said, shaking his head. "That's a hell of a fourth quarter. You don't pull out that kind of rally very often."

The Redskins showed signs of making it such a quarter, however, as they drove from their own 10-yard line all the way down to the Baltimore 5-yard line, where Charley Harraway fumbled after an 8-yard gain. It was his fifth fumble of the year, raising the irony that he owed his job initially to Henry Dyer's fumble in the Saints game.

Perhaps the game was already out of reach, but the fumble turned it into a sterile academic exercise, a dreary rout. The Colts converted another interception into a touchdown. Henry Dyer took a Jurgensen quickie 69 yards down the middle for a score, bowling over two Colt defenders on the way, and the Colts added another touchdown drive to end the game 41–17, a score only a little less lopsided than the 42–10 Brown-Cowboy outcome posted on the scoreboard.

Interestingly enough, the final statistics were relatively close, with the Redskins gaining 357 offensive yards to the Colts' 359. Jurgensen had hit on almost three-quarters of his passes. The Redskins had lost on their own blunders, the blocked punt, Harraway's fumble, the interceptions, and the 89 yards lost to penalties in key situations—in short, the mental errors that Lombardi football teams were supposed to eschew. The Colts game had started as an important one, but once the Cleveland-Dallas score was flashed on the scoreboard, it had become more than that. It had become *the* pressure game. I could not help wondering if the Redskins were frightened, not exhilarated at the prospects that lay before them, all at once face to face with real contention for the championship.

The blocked punt had been the play that turned the game around. And, of course, I thought back to what Charlie Gogolak had said about the contradiction of Lombardi—the master of detail overlooking the kicking game and ignoring it as much as possible. It was true. The amount of practice devoted to the special squads was negligible; the damage the special teams had already done and were still to do was considerable.

In the basement of Memorial Stadium, the Redskin dressing-room doors remained shut for an inordinate length of time. The press corps strained an ear in the cinder-block passageway, trying to catch a phrase or two of the thunder inside. When the doors finally opened, the Redskins looked benumbed. After their loss to the Browns, there had been an undercurrent of rage and anger in the clubhouse. Now there was a silence far more withering and final.

"What did he say?" I asked a player.

"He said, 'You lost this game, the Colts didn't win it. Just remember that.'"

Lombardi was at the far end of the dressing room, in a small open cubicle reserved for the coaches. I had never seen him so angry, bitter fury on his face, the eyes flecked with rage. Even the other coaches were giving him a wide berth.

"We beat ourselves," he seethed. "We can't even operate our special teams without breaking down. We have some good people, we just don't have enough of them."

Someone asked if he'd seen the Browns-Cowboys score.

"Yeah, we all saw it. No, I didn't have to draw anybody's

attention to it. It would have been something to win today, with Dallas losing. But we're no worse off than we were before. One win doesn't make a season, and neither does one loss. We're still alive. We're going to battle like hell, I'll tell you that," he roared, his eyes suddenly dancing with defiance. He glowered at the wall, beyond which the team was showering.

I asked Jim Snowden how it had gone against Bubba Smith. He had been playing back on the right side since the injury to Walt Rock's knee and had said in Pittsburgh that it had felt a little strange to be back there again. "Bubba made me look pretty bad in that first half. He gives you that cuff on the ear, your head rings. Bubba's real quick, quicker than he looked in the films. Then in the second half I set back a little deeper and I'd see Bubba's hand swish in front of my face and I knew I had him. In that first half when I was popping him, hell, he was just bouncing off me. But when I stepped back a little, he started to try to run over me, and that's what I wanted, Bubba to become aggressive."

Promuto came by and cadged a cigarette. "This is the fourteenth straight time I've lost to the Colts," he said. "I got to give them credit. They had the pride to beat us. That tells the story. We both got good quarterbacks, a couple of superstars apiece, and the rest of the guys are about the same size and speed. So the difference is frame of mind. This is a mental game. Baltimore has the confidence when it plays us that it can beat us. I don't think there's anybody on the Colts that doesn't believe they can't beat the Redskins. So they beat us." The cigarette clenched in his teeth, he walked into the shower stalls.

"How come they pulled you out in the second half and sent Clark Miller back in?" I asked Leo Carroll. He gave me a baffled look. "All I know is what they told me. They told me they put Miller in there because he had a hamstring pull, and they wanted to find out if he could play on it." He started to lift his palms in supplication for some heavenly enlightenment, but thought better of it, and dropped his hands back in his lap, staring into his locker and shaking his head.

Willie Banks sat on his stool, gingerly picking at the tape around his right ankle. The season was slowly assuming the proportions of a personal disaster for him. Lombardi had touted him for the Pro Bowl at the beginning of the year, and now his hurts were multiplying, his performance deteriorating week by week. He had been one of the principal reasons for the loss to the Colts, and he had probably been reminded of that fact already.

"I thought I was replaced for good when they pulled me," he said. "And there was someone already in my position on the punt team, so I just lined up any old way, and the punt gets blocked. I didn't even know what I was supposed to be doing there, and I guess I sure didn't do it, either. Billy Ray Smith just made a meal out of me. With this ankle I'm getting 5 to 10 percent worse every week. Somebody like Billy Ray can work you over when you're like that," he said, wincing and jerking the tape off his ankle.

"What did Lombardi say?" I asked a player.

"I can't remember," he said. "All I can remember is sitting here and thinking it sure would be nice to be over in the Colt dressing room. This had to be a sweet one for Shula."

It was indeed, and over in the Colt locker room Shula was reported to have been less than gracious in victory. "We not only bent the Washington defense, we broke it," he announced with some force. Told that, oddly enough, those were the same words Lombardi had used to describe the Redskins' win against the Steelers, Shula nodded. "If you want to hear Lombardi, you can go over to the Redskin dressing room," he said. And he did not fail to point out that this was his second straight victory over Lombardi.

For his part, Lombardi avoided adding any fuel to the controversy when he met with the press on Monday. "As far as Shula's comment, what can I say? There's never been any bad blood between us. I admire Shula. What the hell, if you just run around and nobody likes you or dislikes you, you might as well be in a coffin."

It was a graceful resolution of that matter. No doubt Shula's remarks would be stored up and a revenge devised at a later date. Lombardi didn't enjoy having his nose rubbed in it any more than the next man. And he still had Tom Landry and George Allen to contend with.

"Aren't the next two games against the Eagles and the Cowboys must games?" he was asked.

"Screw the next two. We got to win them all."

It was not a boast, just a terse statement of will. Lombardi had his back to the wall; he had inherited a team with a fragile faith in itself at best, a faith that had melted away in Baltimore. Now Lombardi had to fall back on his own resources: his disdain for the odds against him, his confidence in his personal ability to withstand, even to reverse, the flow of events. This was a new kind of pressure for him—not the pressure of remaining victorious, but of preventing disaster.

All coaches analyze their games for patterns and tendencies. From Lombardi's standpoint, the message in Baltimore was clear. The Redskins had collapsed. They had faced the enemy with a three-point lead, had seen the foreshadowing of a Cleveland rout on the scoreboard, and had thrown the game away. The Redskins were afraid to win, preferred to pay the price of mediocrity, the price of success.

Their blunders argued a lack of mental toughness. Lombardi would not say it about the 1969 Redskins, but he had said it often enough in the past about football teams in general. There was a moment when teams had to play with posterity in mind, with a sense of their own destiny as champions. The Green Bay teams did so, the Redskins didn't. Sonny Jurgensen had had his classical 28-for-38 day, as he had had so often in the past, but he had lost, as he also had so often in the past. He was a master technician, a superb athlete, but not a winner; he could not rally the team the way Hornung could. Sam Huff, for all his will, was over the hill, and was in any case an assistant coach and could not lead the defense. So there was no one on the field to give the team soul or character. Those great Packer teams had been held together by more than Lombardi. Bart Starr and Paul Hornung, Willie Davis and Willie Wood were vastly different men, but they had a sort of leadership about them. In a sense, they represented different strands of Lombardi's own nature, the bravura and the shyness, the religiosity and the wildness, so that in their totality they made a team that was very nearly like Lombardi, all of the strands pulled together by Coach's desire to win. The Packers did not fall apart when the pressure was on, when they were one and a half games off the pace and had a chance to pick up a full game. They had faith.

Perhaps by design, perhaps unconsciously, Lombardi did a characteristic thing. He began importing ex-Packers to the Redskins midway through the season. Perhaps he thought the men he acquired were better than the men he cut. Perhaps he needed some exterior reminders that his faith was valid, that loyalists won ballgames. Perhaps he meant to jar the team's sense of security, to let them know that losing and complacency could cost them their jobs.

Lombardi's first move was to cut A. D. Whitfield from the cab squad and bring in Chuck Mercein, a fullback who had just been cut by the Packers and who had had that great pressure day on the icy turf at Green Bay for the 1967 NFL championship against Dallas.

It was a cold day when Mercein arrived in Washington, his presence unannounced, naturally. The Redskins were practicing on the badly worn stadium turf, and the writers huddled together on the side lines, trying to keep warm, anesthetized to the routine on the practice field. Tim Temerario had come out to watch practice and was telling us that he had been scouting the AFL teams for 1970 trades and that they all looked pretty powerful.

"Timmy!" Lombardi barked from the field.

Temerario gravely excused himself and padded out to Coach. Lombardi chatted with him briefly and then turned to face the press. "You're on the field, you're on the field. Get the hell off the field," he roared. "I don't want you to get hurt and us sued," he added, with avuncular consideration for our welfare.

Presently Timmy came sauntering back to the side lines.

"What did he want to tell you?" I asked.

"Funny. He didn't have anything to tell me. I guess he

decided to clear you guys out and didn't want to have to shout at me too." He pursed his lips and nodded his head, weighing the peculiarity of this hypothesis.

As practice broke up, I noticed a new man, Number 30, slinking from the field in the middle of a crowd of players.

It was Mercein, and now it became somewhat more apparent why Lombardi was shooing back the press. The puzzling thing, as always, was why Lombardi thought he could keep Mercein's presence a secret. Like a Byzantine emperor, his plots and machinations often seemed to exist for their own sake.

After practice Lombardi made one of his infrequent calls to the players' dressing room. "Get the hell out of here, get the hell out of here," a reporter yelled, his face carefully split from ear to ear with a smile that advertised the jest. There were appreciative sniggers around the locker room, the team amused, but hardly emboldened to laugh out loud.

"The team seemed to enjoy your yelling at us," Lombardi was told.

"That's why I did it," he chuckled.

He was reminded that he had told his first Washington press conference back in February, "If you're wondering what the Redskins are going to get from the Packers in exchange for Mercein, I am it." Now he was told that it seemed the Redskins had Mercein back as well.

"In that case, the Redskins got me for nothing," Lombardi sang out. He gave a huge horselaugh and stamped about the dressing room for a few minutes, winking at the astonished players. Then he snapped, "All right, let's get going in here. We don't have all day," and headed off for the film room.

I wandered over to Jerry Smith's locker. "A. D. got cut," he said, his voice torn.

"Jesus, that's too bad. I thought somehow he'd get back up."

Smith shook his head. "This is a brutal way to make a living. I had three really close friends on this team. Theo, A. D., and Brig. Now there's only Brig left."

"What's he going to do? Has he got any nibbles?"

"What can he do? He's hoping. I'm going to call a few

people I know. Jesus, it's a tough game. The physical beating's the easiest part of it."

I went over to see Whitfield at his office in the Black Economic Union a few days later. We sat in the conference room, Whitfield in a white turtleneck sweater and cowboy boots, fiddling with his tan Stetson hat on the table.

He wore an embarrassed, self-conscious look of solemnity, an admission that he was now an ex-Redskin, a man who could only talk about the past.

"If they lose this week, it's going to be miserable, unbearable for the guys. It could become an ugly situation for them." It was a wrench to hear him talk about his teammates in the third person.

"The insecurity and the fear?" I asked.

"Yeah. The fear is terrible. I've never seen it like this. The guys seem to rise on Sunday, but because of fear or because they really want the game? How do you combat fear when you're out there trying to do your job? It has to affect your play. When you're so conscious of making a possible error? And you know that if you make one it can be curtains? Some pressure? Yes, you've got to have it, but not to the extent that you start worrying about your job more than playing football. And the guys are worried. I went. It could be anybody next. And you can't tell what Lombardi is thinking."

I asked Whitfield to think about and recreate what his year had been like since Lombardi's arrival.

He looked over my shoulder, regarding the bare wall, letting it all come back.

"When the announcement that he was coming was made in February, I said to myself, gee, this man is fair, honest, and one hell of a coach. Geez, I'm finally going to get the chance of my lifetime, the chance to play for this guy, a guy who's going to bring out the best in everybody. You see, it's always been my ambition to play fourteen full games and see if I could make that 1000-yard club—1000 rushing, 1000 receiving. That was what I always wanted.

"Well, I was sort of reluctant to go down and meet him, but one day I was in the Redskin office, and he just grabbed me and put his hand on my head and cheek and rubbed me and said that scout Bob White had told him all I needed was a little confidence. So I went down to Bob White's office to thank him for the recommendation, and Lombardi came in and looked at me; he seemed fascinated with my size, the way I was built, and he looked me over from head to toe and he said, 'Hell, you're built along the lines of Charley Taylor.' Whitfield laughed slowly, huskily at that. And I thought this is going to be my year. I was just filled with joy, and Coach Bob White said, 'A. D. is a nice kid, he just needs a little confidence; and Coach Lombardi rubbed my head again and said, 'I'm going to put confidence in you.' And oh, hell, my head was just popping. And I came back home and I called Jerry in California, and Brig, and told them how happy I was going to be, how I was going to get a chance to show people what I was able to do.

"So I got right down to work, doing exercises and running miles and miles, doing ups-and-downs all through February, March, April, May, and June. I figured if hard work was ever going to pay off, this was the year. I was real excited in camp. I started off at first-team fullback, and the first few days he was saying, 'Attaboy A. D., way to go,' and 'C'mon, run on home.' After two or three weeks I was beginning to get downgraded. My body was fatigued out. I'd lost my legs. My legs had never been as dead before, because I was really working, coming out of the backfield quick as I could every time, because I wanted to show this man how much I wanted to play for him. I don't know whether he thought I was loafing or what, so one day he asked me, 'Do you really think you're running?' And I told him my legs were dead, and he said, 'I know, I understand.' Then, after a while, he started telling all us backs he was disgusted with us and was going to bring in a whole slew of new backs if he had his way."

"Did you ever think that your statement about your legs being dead stayed with him?" I asked.

"Maybe so," A. D. said wonderingly. "It's true that little things like that stick to his mind. Come to think of it, I don't think I ever was with the first team after I told him that. He really weighs what you say, you got to watch out.

"So we came down to the end of the exhibition season and the last cut. I thought I had a chance, thought maybe he wasn't disappointed in me after all. I didn't play much in Philadelphia that last exhibition game, just one series, and I ran well.

"Then on Monday after the game, I was driving around and not worried, and when I got home my wife said, 'You got a call from Tim Temerario. I thought, 'Oh, hell, this can't be no good news. I'm cut.' Tim said that the coach would like me to stay on the cab squad. So I talked to some of the assistant coaches I was close to, and they said it would be to my advantage to stay here. I already knew the system, had a chance to get activated, and Lombardi was going to treat me fair financially. When you're cut, it's a time you look for encouragement, so I stayed.

"And then when Gerry Allen got put on the move list, I thought they'd activate me for sure. And instead, he gets Mercein. Who is Mercein? He's never done anything to beat me out. I could run rings around Mercein. Knowing that, it hurt. It really hurt to be cut.

"You should never get too faithful in another man; respect him, yes. But don't count on him. I had such confidence in Lombardi that when I got cut I couldn't believe it would be done to me. It made it very hard to accept the reality that he didn't want me, but I guess I have to accept it. I'm unhappy now, but I'm not really bitter."

"Why not?" I asked.

"It's Lombardi, I guess. You have to accept the way he is. He can be the way he is and get results. Nine hundred and ninety-eight out of a thousand would try it his way and get nothing. Lombardi is the master of his technique, the others are just beginners at it. They lack something, and when those others start carrying on the way Lombardi does, you just say, 'Ah, the hell with you, buddy.' But you don't rebel against Lombardi. His method is worth it because you win. Players under him have never experienced a losing season. He knows what he's doing. He's an emotional, impulsive man, but he's a nice old cat. In his way. Hell, I can't hate him. It would be stupid to try anyway."

Whitfield put on his Stetson, gave the brim a snap, and moseyed on out of the room, another western marshall walking into the sunset.

The ethic of football was winning. I had begun the season accepting that credo, shrugging at the hundreds of minor humiliations and injuries that went into the weekly drama. If Lombardi drove hard to win, so did the coaches who faced him. It was a game with a dog-eat-dog set of rules, and the players and coaches were ,rewarded for abiding by them. Sometimes, though, I wondered if all of them knew what they were getting into, if they had weighed the real nature of their profession, if they had really assessed the transition from college ball to the pros. It often seemed that, as with the rest of us, choice and free will played a negligible role in their careers. For athletes were made young and had their fate shaped early by a cumulative chain of events over which they had no real control.

As Len Hauss told me, "It all starts when you're a little kid. Somebody says, 'Hey, you're so big you ought to play football.' So you're a kid and you go out and play high-school ball. Then somebody offers you a college scholarship, and you can't turn that down, so you play ball all through college. Then in your senior year, you're drafted by the pros, and they're offering money, so you take it. It's like any kid would do if a recruiter came to college and offered him a bonus to sign with General Electric. It's all laid out for you, and you go play ball without thinking about the why and how of it. You're just there, and most of us keep on playing as long as we're able. Don't really know what else to do with our lives in some ways."

Gary Beban told me, "For a football player, the normal life is a little scary. We're basically working off our bodies. In the real world your body doesn't matter; you've got to work off your mind, your personality, yourself. A lot of us will be over thirty years old when that time comes, and that is pretty frightening. That is why pressure and security are such painful issues for all of us."

Did A. D. Whitfield know what he was getting into? Was he forewarned of the risks involved? Probably not. All he really knew was that he was expected to play as hard as he knew how, and everything would work out for the best. He had done that, and now everything had worked out for the worst. I could not regard Chuck Mercein as any more deserving than Whitfield— less so, in fact. I had been prepared for ruthlessness when I had first joined the Redskins, assuming it was part of the game. I was not so well prepared for it to be exercised on people I had come to know and like. The season was past the midway point, and there was a gulf of doubt springing up between the team and Lombardi. Increasingly, I found myself on the players' side, wondering where the conflict and the pressure would end. I had to hope he would bend to the team and accept the fact that they were all he had. Their breaking point seemed perilously close to being tested.

There were several other personnel changes before the Eagle game. Willie Banks was banished to the move list in disgrace. Clark Miller was deactivated, apparently having demonstrated in Baltimore that he could not play on a hamstring. Steve Duich was brought back up to take Banks's place on the roster, and rookie linebacker Harold McLinton was activated to fill in for Marlin McKeever, who had suffered a bad hemorrhage above the knee during the Colt game and was a doubtful starter for the Eagles. On the decimated offensive line Walt Rock was now declared fit for action. Ray Schoenke would move from left tackle to right guard, taking Banks's place on the first team.

"Timing and luck—that's what makes or breaks a football career," Schoenke told me. "Lombardi feels that Willy can be an All-Pro guard, and he's right. Willy has all the potential, he's tough and he's quick. But he hurts his ankle—that's bad luck. Then he has to play on it against Mean Joe Greene in Pittsburgh and Billy Ray Smith in Baltimore, and they stomp all over him— that's the worst possible timing for a string of bad luck. So now Willy's benched, and I'm in there. And once things go sour for you in this sport they're hard to set right. You're rejected, labeled as a loser. I ought to know, it's happened to me enough."

There was, as always, the timbre of compassion in Schoen-ke's voice, a sense that fairness required an account of the outside circumstances that had triggered Banks's fall from grace. In an age when athletes were instant celebrities being packaged as high-minded candidates for public office, Scho-enke was that comparatively rare figure whose decent in-stincts and intelligence were evident without the benefit of promotion. He was half Hawaiian and half German and had inherited the jet black hair, bronze skin, and outgoingness of the Islands along with a certain Teutonic size and seriousness. As he had noted, bad timing and poor luck were littered across his football career. He had played his college ball at Southern Methodist University, where he was a second-team All-American on a team that won only four games in three years. He was drafted by the Cowboys, was one of their first-string guards in 1964, and got cut in 1965 because Tom Lan-dry said he was injury-prone. After sitting out the 1965 season, Lombardi signed him to a no-cut Packer contract in 1966 and sent him to the Cleveland Browns on a "make-the-team" deal four weeks into the 1966 training season.

"The Cleveland coaches were telling me I'd made the team and so I set up house on Euclid Avenue, and then I sprained the arch of my foot a week later, and the Browns released me outright. I had to come back to the house and tell my wife we'd have to move again. After Dallas cut me she wanted me to quit football. Maybe it's false pride, but I knew I had to play somewhere. I never had doubts about my ability, and I had to prove that the people who were cutting me were all wrong about me. I had a no-cut contract with Green Bay, but I didn't want to go back there because I knew it meant spending the year on their cab squad; I knew that if I didn't play in '66 I never would.

"When you're cut you get some brutal treatment. Art Modell called me into the Brown front office and he said, 'Schoenke, I can't believe Lombardi gave you a contract for this much money. You should have been signed for $100.' Then he laughed in my face and said, 'You're just out to exploit the league.' I had a pretty good relationship with Blanton Collier, so I went to ask him what he thought I should do, and he said, 'Well, I'd recommend you quit football and get another kind of job.' I mean, I was crushed. It turned out Landry had called Collier and told him I was injury-prone. And I thought back to Landry telling me at the beginning of '65, 'Schoenke, you'll never make my team.' And then, of course, he never gave me a real chance, so I didn't.

"Well, my wife and I were really down. Nancy said she'd lost faith in other people, but not in me, that I should give it another shot somewhere if that's what I knew I had to do. So I called the Redskins, and they said come down here right away. Four weeks later I made the Washington first team. And I was on it until the start of this year.

"This year I came to camp with one of the best grades from the '68 line, and they put me down on the third team along with some rookie. I forget his name. He wasn't around long. The first couple of exhibition games came, and I'm just sitting on the bench, looking around, not knowing what to say or think. I think it stemmed back to the 5.25 forty I ran in the time trials when camp began. I knew I was faster than that, but once coaches get the idea you're slow, it's hard to jar that notion loose. Finally, I had Don Doll time me again, and I ran a 5.1, but still they had me down on the third team. And, by God, I was fighting to get up on the first team, tackle, guard, even center. I didn't care where, just when. One day after the second exhibition game we'd just had a foot-race for the tackles and I'd won it, so I sidled up to Bill Austin in the shower room and said, 'What did you think about that race for a slow man?' And he said, 'You're starting the next game at left guard.' So I was first-team left guard the last four exhibition games.

"Just before the season starts, I tore a ligament in my chest and everything I'd fought for goes down the pipe. The pain was just terrible. I've played with all sorts of hurts, but this ripped ligament was the worst thing I've ever endured, just excruciating. Lombardi was going to get rid of me.

But the bluntness of it all, the fear that he meant it about cutting me, the panic that he's going to jot down in his little mental book that Schoenke couldn't take it, wasn't mentally tough enough, was unreliable. His philosophy is: If you can't do it, I'll get rid of you and get somebody else. He believes that. He actually believes he can get somebody else, even after the season starts. So he's fearless, completely fearless. Where most coaches might say, "Hell, if I get rid of this guy, where am I going to get anybody better?' Lombardi says, you either make it or break it right now. I got to say that Lombardi is the fairest coach I've seen about playing the best man. Yet, I know I had to play with my injury or get cut. And I didn't know if I could physically do it.

"And there's no one wants to play more than I do. I have had some dirty deals in football, the grind of the season is tough to live with. I live out in suburbia and I see these fathers out with their family on the weekends, playing with the kids, and I have to feel a little envious about that. I like that kind of life, but then I think about Sunday and what a beautiful day it can be. It can be just so fantastic. To pull out on a block and spring a long run for a back! In the Cardinal game I came charging out and I whapped a defender with my shoulder and turned him right around, and the back scoots right by for a long gain. It's a tremendous feeling, and I think how many men get that satisfaction. Does a man get that kind of feeling down at the office? I doubt it.

"And yet the season gets under way and I'm not playing. I played some in the Browns game and got 100 percent on my blocking, and I went in for Promuto when he hurt his shoulder in the Cardinal game and I got a blocking award. But that's only two games out of five I've seen action in. I wanted that first-team job back I'd won in camp, but the call still didn't come." I remembered Schoenke sitting in the dugout after practice when Rock had been injured before the Steeler game. I asked what had been going through his mind when the call came, what he had been thinking about when he seemed so abstracted.

He pursed his lips, recalling the moment, and then grinned.

"I wasn't thinking at all," he said. "I was too damn mad to be thinking. Just the day before I'd gone to Bill Austin and asked why I wasn't playing. Austin implied I'd start at left guard against the Steelers, so all that week I'd been busting a gut getting up for the Pittsburgh tackle I'd be facing, and then Rock gets hurt, so I go to left tackle instead of left guard. I've got two days to learn the moves of McGee, the Steeler defensive end, and since everyone else on the line is hurting I've got be ready to play both guards and the other tackle as well."

"That's a fair amount of pressure to have laid on," I allowed.

"Yeah. But I was mad enough that I was determined to show Lombardi and Austin I could do the job. I knew if I screwed up Lombardi would chew me, like I'd been there ten years. You want to get your chance with all the breaks going for you, but I didn't, and I was determined it wouldn't make any difference. The Steelers used a lot of multiple defenses on us, and our line didn't have much of a day, but after the game Austin told me I'd had one of the better blocking percentages on the line. So I'd figured I'd build on that and have even a better day at left tackle the next week against the Colts. I studied the Baltimore defense of end Roy Hilton backwards and forwards, was really up for him. The game gets under way, and Snowden is having a lot of trouble with Bubba Smith, so Austin told me to be ready to take Snowden's place at right tackle. So I'm on the bench trying to think how I'll work Bubba, then Willy's ankle's going fast. So they want me back in at left guard because Billy Ray Smith's having a field day, beating Banks to the inside. I felt like a juggler, thinking about how I'm going to work on three different guys, and I know I've got to keep concentrating on the guy I'm playing against right here and now. I knew I couldn't get rattled, couldn't make a mistake, had to show Lombardi I could execute. I had a pretty good day at Baltimore as both a guard and a tackle.

"So now Willy's gone, and I'm back at guard again, where I first started out. Even so, the pressure's still not off. Lombardi is driving and pushing all the time. You have to do it his way. He says we are all creatures of habit, and he builds a team on the basis of constant repetition, something mindless we can turn to automatically in a game. His philosophy is we're all kids. Well, it hurts, but it's true. We want the easy way out, ballplayers are humans, and most humans are lazy. I've always been able to get motivated without any outside pressure. With Lombardi you have to accept the motivation coming from him. It takes a while to get used to that, to forget your own personal pride in being a self-starter, a man with your own code, your own reasons for wanting to excel.

"When I was at Green Bay in 1965 I was just dying at training camp. At the end of the day I didn't know how I'd gotten through it. The Packer veterans were all having a good time, playing cards, sitting around the dorm joking. They were used to what the Old Man wanted; they'd accepted Lombardi's ego and drive in place of their own. I was tired because I didn't. It's helped me, that brief exposure to him in Green Bay. Still, I'm not used to him yet. Very few of the guys are. We're all running around trying to keep him happy, trying to not get chewed out. It's ridiculous. I try to figure him out, to analyze him. He never lets up, never bends or gives. Just when you think he will, he just pours it on that much harder. It's hard. But any man who has the discipline that this man has— what can you say? I don't think I've ever met a man like him. It's tough enough to play this game, even tougher to play it for a man like Lombardi. You play for him because you know he can make you win, because you know that sooner or later he's going to have a championship here. And that makes it worth it."

The Saturday before the Eagles, I drove over to Georgetown for a bite to eat with Jurgensen after practice. This was not Sonny's year for chitchat with the press. He had always ducked the writers after a game when he could—his views on "instant analysis" parallelling those of Spiro Agnew. But in years past he had always cheerfully obliged information-seeking reporters during the week and was said to enjoy sprawling out in a chair at his locker stall, offering reflections on football, life, himself. He was by nature a gregarious man, with his big boyish smile and his happy facility for a wisecrack. When

Lombardi had first met Sonny in February he had told him, "I only want one thing from you—be yourself." There was perhaps an implied rebuke in that pithy piece of advice, a hint that what he had been in the past was not really himself. Even in the full flush of his football youth Jurgensen had never been one of the boys in the clubhouse, had never been a Joe Namath or Joe Kapp kind of quarterback, who played with the guys off the field as well as on. He was not that sort of man; few quarterbacks were. Having been told that there was something missing in his way of being "himself," Jurgensen had set out to show the world a more subdued image of himself. The exuberant and chatty Redhead was not for publication this year.

As we drove toward Georgetown, he said, "The one thing that has always stuck in my mind that Bart Starr told me, and this is long before Lombardi came here, was that it was a pleasure to go out and play the games as a Packer because you had all this stuff built up in you that you had to use, had to do. That's the way it's been for me so far this year. More preparation than I've ever had before. Everything has a reason, a meaning. It makes it much easier to play the game."

I asked why, after all these years, he had suddenly taken a more standoffish attitude toward the press.

"Well," he said, "a lot of the past in Philadelphia was distorted. A lot of the things I said about Philadelphia were in jest. A lot of the things I said about myself were jests. I didn't live the way I supposedly lived in Philadelphia or drink as much as I supposedly drank in Philadelphia. I couldn't and play football. Understandably, that was something to write about. It made good copy, but it was exaggerated; it got out of hand, and I took offense at it."

We stopped at a red light, and there was an old woman at the street corner, with a bandana tied around her hair, a man's slouch hat on her head. "Hey," Sonny said, his mood of solemnity suddenly disappearing, "who does that lady look like?"

I looked at her and shrugged.

"Oh, what's her name. It's right on the tip of my tongue. Moms Mabley on TV. That's who. Doesn't she? Just like Moms Mabley."

I laughed, and we continued toward Georgetown, Jurgensen chuckling and shaking his head, a man who knew his TV performers, it seemed, a man who enjoyed staying home in the evening and watching the tube with his family.

"About the publicity," I reminded him.

"Yeah, well, even here in Washington when they write about Sonny Jurgensen, they go back to Philadelphia and dig up those stories. It's like poor journalism to have to plagiarize stuff from the past all the time. I mean, people change. What you do or say eight or nine years ago isn't what you do or say now. Take that Joe McGuinness piece in the *Saturday Evening Post.* That thing made me look bad, like I was undermining Otto Graham. That closed team meeting. I had nothing to do with that. Williams brought the club in. It was obvious we were divided. That was no secret. It was like a camera coming on TV, and nobody knew what to say, aaah, eehh, aahhh, oohhh, welll, uhhh.

"My wife, Margo, says she can look at an article about me and know exactly what it's going to say. There'll always be the Cutty and water, the bartenders in Philadelphia wearing black arm bands, me drinking with my left hand instead of my right. That stuff."

Jurgensen twisted the wheel in a neat little U turn and parked in front of the Georgetown Inn, a staid establishment, with a middle-aged clientele.

Perhaps he was trying to tell me something about his life style. Heads turned around as we came in; the maître d' hôtel escorted us to a table, Jurgensen smiling, nodding at a table or two.

It was hard to know how many more great football years were left in the Old Redhead. He was thirty-five years old now and was an extraordinary athlete, his build, his apparent lack of muscle tone, notwithstanding. If men like Charley Conerly and Y. A. Tittle had played into their late thirties, perhaps Jurgensen could too, but even so, when the end came to an athlete at that age, it was sudden and sometimes total. Jurgensen was clearly playing from game to game. I asked him what he planned to do when his football days were done.

He gave a sad smile. "I'm not sure. I'll play as long as I enjoy it. It's still fun for me, even now, even at my age. It's been my life. I guess Lombardi'll tell me when I can't do it anymore."

"No ideas about the future, then, beyond football?"

"No. When it comes, it comes. Then it will be a challenge to find another career, another something to commit yourself to. Being a pro athlete is a unique situation. In some ways it's unfair. You come out of school and succeed in a hurry, and then it's over. And you're still young."

How often I had heard that refrain. Usually, it came from linemen, who were doomed to obscurity. It was a shade more poignant coming from Sonny Jurgensen—his looks, his profession, his very name an affirmation of youth.

"Going into athletics can be a tragedy. Someone like A. D. Whitfield. He's been on our team for years, it seems, and always done well and now he's out of a job. Sometimes I wonder what's on a man's mind starting out all over again, trying to find something new to do with his life. Maybe they're better off starting over again now than ten years from now. But it's a great profession, ball. The competitiveness of it, being part of a club of men who've made it all the way through. You can't regret that."

The waiter came by and announced in a foreign accent that he was "rewting for ze Eagles." Jurgensen laughed, and we both ordered hamburgers. An older man with silver hair and a florid face stopped at the table. "Do you think you'll beat those Eagles tomorrow, Sonny?" he asked gravely, rocking back and forth on his heels.

"No question about it. With all our fans pulling for us, we can't miss," Jurgensen said.

"You think that, eh?" the man replied, nodding and weighing this information. "Well, good luck," he said and returned to his table to report that Sonny was in fine fettle and foresaw a victory. "Does it bug you," I asked, "about never having a winning season — here in Washington? Do you have the sense that getting the championship would be the vindication of your being the best quarterback in the game?"

"The championship thing has never bothered me, really. It's one of the breaks of the game—a matter of being with the right team, the right personnel, the right attitudes."

"The right coach."

"Oh, yes. That certainly," he grinned.

"How about the Redskins, then?"

"Well, we've all got hope now. There never was that feeling under Graham, not even at the beginning. We were an explosive team in those days, but we were not a sound one. Now the people who've been pampered on this team in the past because of their exceptional ability, the people who just tried to get by—they've been forced to change. With Lombardi, cheating is out. You don't rest up for one play on the field and then put out on the next one. You don't run a pass pattern one time and not the next, block one time and not the next because you know the play is going away from you. With Lombardi, you do it every play, on every situation, or you won't be out there the following week. Look at the Colts game last week. We reverted to last year. We hadn't learned what he taught us.

"With him here, win or lose, you know you're going to be a respectable ballclub, know you can be proud at least that you played all out, because he demands that you have to play his way. Throwing to all the receivers as primary targets has been difficult for me. But I know I have to. He has got to stick to his system because he knows it so well. He can detect errors immediately. A coach has to be able to know what's wrong. What else does the word mean? And because he knows his system, no one can slip anything by him. He doesn't ask anything of his ballplayers that he won't do himself. That's maybe the key. He works harder than anyone, wants us to do well. You have to respect a man like that. He's total."

A woman came over to the table, obviously tipsy. She looked like she might stay a while. As she rambled on, Sonny smiled and nodded with resigned good grace. Her party was signaling desperately for her return, with embarrassed, apologetic looks on their faces. Jurgensen gave them a signal that it didn't matter and invited her to sit down. She talked for a while and then said that she was probably jabbering too much and was sorry if she was, but that she was going to have an operation on her tongue on Monday to have part of it removed for cancer, so she wanted to get all the talking done she could before Monday. It came out of the blue and had a ring of authenticity to it. The woman and Jurgensen chatted for a few minutes more, and she invited him over to her table to meet her family. He walked over, with that big boyish grin on his face and a look that proclaimed that this sudden encounter had made his day. He was a man who had a certain grace off the field, as well as on it.

Chapter 20

The Eagles came to Washington with a 3–4 record, a team that had to be beaten if the Cowboy game the following week would have any meaning.

The Redskins won the toss, and the offensive team trotted out to be introduced. There was a round of boos for Charley Harraway's name, a frank if harsh reminder that his fumble in the Colt game still rankled and that he was in a profession where bygones were never bygones. Harraway stood there for some seconds listening to the catcalls, then raised his hand and flashed a V sign, whether for victory or peace, one did not know.

The Eagles game was like the opening series in the Cardinals game all over again, except that this time Tom Woodeshick and Leroy Keyes were grinding out the yardage. It took them eight carries to run the ball for a score. In the Cardinals game, the Redskin offense had struck back rapidly, and their defense had then stiffened. Now the Washington defense stiffened somewhat, but the offense remained sluggish well into the second quarter, when Jurgensen mounted a 75-yard touchdown drive. The two key plays were a 27-yard run by Larry Brown and Charley Harraway's reception for 42 yards. There was a satisfying measure of irony to Harraway's catch, a certain retrospective dignity in his V sign. The drive tied the game at 7–7.

The action seesawed back and forth for the remainder of the half, both teams evenly matched in their becalmed languor.

The necessity of addressing a few glum remarks to the team kept Lombardi from taking in the half-time ceremonies. Its theme was Flag Day, and each fan had been given a miniature

"Old Glory" at the gate. Lombardi had imported this custom to Washington from Green Bay, where it was a spectacle of a few years' standing, dreamed up by three local housewives. No doubt its spirit was less pugnacious out in the American heartland than in the nation's capital three days before the beginning of the November Moratorium. The Redskins assured the press that the half-time show had been arranged long before the Moratorium. Nonetheless, the U. S. Army Band played martial tunes and a color guard from all the branches of the military service was on hand, as was Lt. Col. Lloyd L. Burke of the U. S. Army, a winner of the Medal of Honor during the Korean War, who led the flag-waving crowd in the Pledge of Allegiance. Needless to say, it was a ceremony divorced from its alleged theme, an occasion that called forth jingoism, not patriotism, and spleen, not homage.

Both teams took the field for the second half more energetic than they had been in the second quarter. The Redskins took a 14–7 lead on a touchdown throw to Harraway all alone in the endzone. The Eagles came back on a long scoring drive of their own. The Redskins got the ball back and spent the last four minutes of the third period and the first four of the second driving all the way down to the Eagle 3 before Jurgensen hit Charley Taylor for a touchdown. That made it Redskins 21, Eagles 14. Then, thirty seconds later, Sam Huff picked off a pass by Snead and chugged 18 yards to the goal-line, putting the Redskins ahead 28–14, with ten and a half minutes left to play. Although that seemed to salt the game away, the Eagles reeled off five first downs, 84 yards, and almost six minutes of playing time for a touchdown, making it Redskins 28, Eagles 21.

Still, there were only five minutes left, time to run out the clock if the Redskins could eke out a few first downs on the ground. Larry Brown was certainly running well enough to make this tactic appealing. That was apparently Jurgensen's thought, too. Brown carried off-tackle the first play from scrimmage, gained 3 yards, fumbled, and the Eagles recovered, with a little less than five minutes to play.

Carl Kammerer was now back in the game, having replaced

John Hoffman. On second and eight, Kammerer and Chris Hanburger dumped Eagle quarterback Norman Snead for an 11-yard loss, ultimately forcing a fourth-and-five situation at the Redskin 22-yard line. For some reason, the Eagles elected to go for a field goal. It was hard to imagine what good three points would do them with less than three minutes to play unless it was an announcement that they planned to get the ball back shortly anyway, that the Redskin offense wasn't going to get a first down, and might even fumble again. As it turned out, Sam Baker's 28-yarder was no good. The Redskins took over, a touchdown up, on their own 20 with 2:45 showing on the clock.

The Redskins succeeded in using up forty-five seconds on a holding penalty, three incomplete passes, and a 42-yard punt, which was taken by Eagle safety Bill Bradley on his own 33 and returned 5 yards to the Eagle 38.

The two-minute warning sounded. Snead moved inside Redskin territory with a quick 15-yard pass to Ben Hawkins. On third and ten, he hit rookie Leroy Keyes for 20 and moved down to the Redskin 27-yard line, where he called a time-out. It did not look good for the home team, but then the Redskin defense stiffened, the line put on a pass rush, and the secondary held firm. Snead missed two passes, even drew a 15-yard penalty for intentionally grounding the ball. That left it fourth and twenty-five at the Redskin 42-yard line. Snead's options were limited. You might say he was in a passing situation—not a little swing pass, not a quick zig-out to the side lines, but a go-for-broke bomb. He dropped back and looked around. There didn't seem to be anyone open. As pressure was beginning to be felt, he arched the ball high in the air for the northeast corner of the end zone, where Ben Hawkins and Mike Bass were standing. It was the old "Alley-oop," the ball hanging in the air for anyone.

Bass was behind Hawkins, they both went up in the air, and the ball dropped harmlessly to earth in the end zone. The referee had a yellow hanky in his hand: he flung it at the 1-yard line, signaling interference on Bass. Eagles' ball, first and goal at the Washington 1. Bass got up and remonstrated with the referee, jumping up and down in place. Lombardi stormed up and down the side line. Groans and boos sounded from the stands, hopelessness set in, and the Eagles scored to tie the game, 28–28.

Had Bass fouled Hawkins? By any logical scheme of things, the question was laughable. Every time a receiver and a defensive back went up into the air to fight for a ball, a foul occurred—offensive and defensive, and sometimes both. It was a judgment call. There were two contending rivals, placed in a random situation, both trained to stretch their talents as close to illegality as possible, so they jumped into the air and intertwined, or perhaps not. Who could really say? It was doubtful that Bass, for all his protestations of innocence, knew whether he had committed interference or not, and just as doubtful that Hawkins, for all his outrage, had the foggiest idea; it was even more doubtful that the referee could recall precisely why he had reached for his handkerchief in the first place. The nature of football, however, demanded that calls be made, and once made, there was no appeal.

The verdict was that the Redskins had been tied 28–28, a score that was an absolute refutation of Washington's title hopes.

The 28–28 tie made it obvious to everyone, to Lombardi, to the team, to me, that the team was dead. They were out of the race. The division title had passed to Dallas.

The Redskins had to turn to lesser pursuits: a winning season, a building program for 1970, a spoilers' role against another championship contender. It was a piddling sort of vision of the next six games, but what else was there? Like everyone else in RFK Stadium, I seethed and cursed the referee. But there was perhaps a difference. The fans suffered for the score; I suffered for the Redskins for I knew what this tie would lead Lombardi to demand from them, and I suffered for Lombardi too. He was a "nice old cat," as A. D. Whitfield had allowed. No one suffered a defeat more intensely, more personally than Lombardi.

Yet for all that, the game was not over. There were still fifty-five seconds left on the scoreboard. The Eagles kicked off to Jim Snowden, who fielded the ball uncomprehendingly on the 17. In the exhibition game against the Eagles he had gotten a kickoff, tried to run it back, and fumbled. A fumble was clearly in his mind, and he knew that a fumble at the Redskin 17-yard line could make the game even worse than it had already become. He took a couple of steps and then sat down with the ball. Rickie Harris came darting up, asked for a lateral, and got it. He headed toward the side lines to kill the clock and was stopped at the 19-yard line. Jurgensen fired a quick 19-yard pass to Charley Taylor and called a time-out. There were 0:38 seconds left, and the ball was at the 38-yard line. Jurgensen missed Dyer on a pass, then found Dave Kopay open up the middle, but Kopay bobbled the ball. Now it was third and ten. Jurgensen sent Charley Taylor deep. The ball dropped earthward at about the Eagle 35-yard line, and Eagle defenders Irv Cross and Joe Scarpetti closed on Taylor and scrunched him on the spot, like the jaws of an iron maiden. The referee reached for his yellow hanky, but thought better of it.

Lombardi was beside himself on the side lines, bellowing interference, his jaws snapping, his feet stamping. An interference penalty here could give the Redskins time for another couple of plays and a field goal to win. And interference was clearly merited, either against the Eagle defenders or Taylor. The only judgment was whether Taylor had sought to be sandwiched or whether the Eagles had zapped him to keep him from the ball. But the referee turned his back, the yellow hanky still in his hip pocket. The Redskins punted, and the Eagles took the tie, running out the last seven seconds.

Downstairs, the press was banned from the whole dressing-room complex for ten minutes. Some of the writers were to note that they could hear Lombardi cursing the referees through the steel door, the 50 yards of passageway, another steel door, another few feet of passageway, and a wooden door. And he did upbraid them. Later he told me, "I lost my cool in the Eagles game. First time it ever happened to me, first time I've ever gone after the referees. Oh, hell, I've always yelled at them from the side lines, but to go after them in their dressing room, I've never done that before. I'm sorry I ever did. If there's one thing I regret about this year, that's it."

It was not remorse, but defeat that was etched in his face in the dressing room. He looked haggard and old, a man shorn of hope. Those defeats in the exhibition season, the collapse in Cleveland, even the disaster in Baltimore were not games that had finality that precluded the hope of a comeback. Not so with this game; it merged the pessimist and the realist in his nature. He knew that it was all over, and that knowledge aged him. He waved a flip card in the air, glancing idly at the printed red rosters on either side.

"This has to be one of your disappointing games," a reporter said.

"Yes, it was," he murmured, and the anger, the frustration, the indignity of it all rose to the surface. "They played volleyball with Charley Taylor on that last pass. Sandwiched him. The official reached for his handkerchief and didn't throw it." His sudden rage subsided, and he turned bleak. "We got no damn defense. Today or any other day, for that matter."

"Was the pass rush better after Kammerer came in?"

"Yes, but you're being kind. Hell, after last week in Baltimore, they figured the Sisters of the Poor could run against us. What'd they gain on the ground?" He made a half-hearted gesture to retrieve the mimeographed game statistics on the table and then brushed that effort aside.

"Great half-time show," a reporter said.

"Yeah," Lombardi said, blowing the story of the Moratorium coincidence put out by the Redskin front office. "That's our answer to whatever they're doing on Wednesday or Thursday."

The dressing room was like a morgue. Clothes still hung in lockers, and most of the players were still in the showers. The few players in the clubhouse sat at their stools, not even talking to one another. The mood was so black that it beggared questions, and the press hung back in small knots around the room, talking to themselves, honoring the privacy of each man's defeat.

"Where's Bass?"

"Still showering, I guess. His clothes are still hanging up."

"Ah, he won't say anything, anyway."

"Screw him, what can he say?"

We hung on, not really wanting to talk to Bass, but using his absence as a pretext for waiting and for not bothering anyone else.

Charley Taylor came out of the showers, and a few people ambled over to get his views on the volleyball play Lombardi had denounced so ferociously.

"I had my eye on the ball. I saw it coming," Taylor allowed. "Then I saw them Eagles, and then I was on the ground."

"Could you have caught it, do you think, Charley?"

"Well, maybe I could have; then again, maybe I couldn't have. It was out there. Now, maybe I could have caught that thing, and maybe not." He got up and wandered back to take another shower.

"Well, we screwed your book up," a player said, flinging his wet towel across the dressing room. "Now you can tell what this damn place is really like."

That comment was, I thought, the quintessence of winning and losing, a telling commentary on the sporting code. You could only tell the truth about losers; winners were wrapped in protective layers of sham heroics. The truth, in short, was the vengeance dished out for losing.

Mike Bass was still in the shower, his teammates busily greasing the rails of his innocence. "Twice last year," Rickie Harris told me, "I let my hands rest back in tight situations to show the ref I wasn't interfering, and both times I got called for interference. Well, that's what Mike did. He held his hands back trying to show the ref he wasn't interfering. And the thing is, when you do that, they may think you're jerking your hands back because you have interfered. It makes you look guilty even though you're innocent."

It was as plausible as anything else, at least. Bass finally came out of the showers, took in the vulpine colony of newsmen, and announced he had no comment.

"Lombardi must have told him to clam up," a reporter muttered.

"This is the first time this year I've seen Lombardi really blunder psychologically," a player told me. "Before the game he told us, 'I'm going to lead this team to a Super Bowl. Maybe not this year, maybe not next year. It might have to be the year after. Some of you won't be on the team then.' You can't talk like that on this team, you can't get any football team thinking that far ahead. You've got a team that's looking beyond the Eagles to a Super Bowl in the distance somewhere. The problem with this team is that it's always believed in next year. Next year we'll win it all. Hell, it's the same story every year. I would have thought Lombardi knew that."

"What did he say after the game?"

"It was terrible. He was furious, on the verge of tears, and he said, 'Some of you won't be here on Tuesday.' All I know is I'll show up on Tuesday; no one's said anything to me yet."

"You know," another player said, "one of the guys was with the Packers told me this is the first time this year he's seen Lombardi like he used to be in Green Bay, the veins pulsing in his forehead, the screaming. It makes you wonder, Jesus, what's it going to be like around here?"

"What did you make of Lombardi's pre-game Super Bowl statement?" I asked another player.

"Myself, I thought, well, I'll be around for it in two or three years. But, hell, he picked the wrong time to talk about Super Bowls. You got to play them one at a time. And we're not out of it yet, not even now. We've got injuries, but we still had a shot for it before today's game. Still do. Hell, let's talk about the Super Bowl this year, if you got to talk about it."

"How was he after the game?"

"There were tears in his eyes, and his voice was real choked, and he did some screaming later on. He felt bad. Hell, I felt bad too. I gave it what I had. What does he want? And he told us that was the worst played football game he ever saw. He's just a poor loser. I hate to say that about him, but he's just a poor loser. It's as simple as that." He gave a soft chuckle, not without a certain affection for the man in question and a certain amused amazement that he had just uncovered the key to Lombardi's character, and that it should be so transparently simple.

"Well," a reporter said on Monday at the Redskin offices, "this is the day the Christian gets thrown to the lions."

"What? Who?" Lombardi said, emerging from a trance-like state.

"You," the reporter said, with something like impertinent delight.

"Jesus Christ," Lombardi grunted and shook his head.

"I was just kidding."

"C'mon, give me a rough time," Lombardi challenged. "I'm bloody but unbowed."

"Well, what went wrong?"

"When we should have controlled the ball near the end of the game, we didn't. Look at the statistics," he said, picking up the freshly mimeographed sheet. "Losing coaches always say look at the statistics, I guess. Looking at the stats you see that after eight games we've got an average gain per play of 5.3 yards, compared to 4.8 for the other teams. Now look at the number of offensive plays we've run. That's 465 compared to 523 for the other teams. There's a hell of a big difference between those two figures. We've got a good enough offensive team to win most games. But the defense lets the opposition keep the ball too damn long. This has got to be a team, and it's not yet. We've got a great performer at quarterback. Maybe the best the league has ever seen. He's all man. Stays in there and plays under adverse conditions. And I mean adverse, the way our blockers let the defense come in to get him. You grade our offensive line, they come up with pretty good marks. But they make their mistakes one at a time. It seems that one guy breaks down one time, another another. We'd be better off if they all broke down together."

"Speaking of breakdowns, how about the Packers?" someone wanted to know.

"Yes, their getting beat yesterday surprised me. The Packers usually beat you one way or another. They've got the players. Like Dallas this week, with their forty great athletes. We don't have forty great athletes here, I'll tell you. But don't get me wrong; I knew what I was getting into here. You'll never see me cry. I've played Dallas before. I've played them all before," he said, the gleam of past years and altered circumstances in his eyes.

Warmed by such memories, he embarked on an account of how he had installed a special hearing aid in Larry Brown's helmet. The Redskin rookie runner, it appeared, had been born with a defective right ear. Lombardi, the triumphant gadgeteer, had commissioned a special electronic helmet device to sharpen Brown's hearing in the huddle. The hearing aid had arrived on the Thursday before the Eagles game, and Lombardi described how he had tested it out on Brown. "We got at different ends of the locker room," Lombardi said, "and I began talking, first loud, then lightly. When I asked him if he could hear me, he said, 'Yes, Sir, but I could always hear you, even without any hearing aid.' " Lombardi had a merry laugh at this concession to his reputation.

"Listen," a reporter asked, "how come you're giving us all this information today? It's like you're happy to be talking to us for a change."

"Well," Lombardi said, "it beats looking at the Cowboys' game with the Saints."

After practice on Tuesday I went over to the brick rowhouse Charley Harraway and Henry Dyer had rented for the season on the edge of Washington's Negro Gold Coast. The place was unfurnished, shabby, and run down—hardly a pad for two pro running backs to share. Harraway's flight from Cleveland on Monday night had been held up in traffic, and he had not gotten to sleep until late Monday night. He was bushed, and he plopped down in the double bed in his bare bedroom; his hands were cupped under his head, and he stared up at the ceiling. I found an old upright chair, and Harraway started to talk, somnolent, with a drowsy smile on his face and his voice even more soft-spoken than normal.

"It's a mean way to live," he said, removing a hand from behind his head and waving it listlessly around the room. "I tried to bring my family up here from Cleveland, but roaches and more roaches. We tried three different apartments, and no sooner'n we'd go to bed at night, those roaches would come out of the woodwork. It's difficult, man, to get a place to rent for a family for two months. That's the game. I got a nice house I bought over in Cleveland, got a business over there. Only I'm not there any more, I'm here. Well, what are you going to do?"

"What about the fumbling?" I asked. "There are some who say you were a fumbler in Cleveland, and some who say you weren't."

He smiled ruefully. "A fumble is your fault; still, you don't have any control over it. That's the two things you got to remember about fumbles. I've been quite concerned about it. In fact, you see that ball over there?" There was a football standing on its tip in the corner of the room, and I nodded. "Well, I slept with that ball all last week, because I want to make my subconscious aware that that ball is part of me. I know Lombardi has given a few ballplayers a ball to carry at all times, although he hasn't asked that of me.

"Well," he said, "I have thought of that football day and night this last week. Before that, I tried to tell myself those fumbles I had were just freaks, things that could happen to anyone. But, hell, you get three of them, then four, then five, you begin to know it's more than that. And I began sleeping with that ball."

"Do you carry it to the neighborhood grocery, the drugstore?"

"No, not there."

"Why? Because people would take digs at you. Like, there goes Charley Harraway, thinks he's a big football star and has got to show he's with the Redskins."

"Yeah," he grinned. "That crossed my mind. But I'm going to sleep with it until it becomes part of me."

"How did you feel when the fans booed you last Sunday?"

"I anticipated the booing before the Eagles game, and I had the peace sign all set."

"It was a peace sign, was it? I didn't know whether it was a V for peace and conciliation or a V for victory and defiance, a 'Screw you guys, I'm going to win with or without you.' "

"No, for peace. Like when your wife is upset with you, you have to do something to win her back over. That's the way I meant it. I was very aware of the need to succeed during the Eagles game. Not for the fans' sake, you understand, but as part of the team. Up until a couple of weeks ago, I thought the team was coming together, but then I began to sense something wrong. It seems there is something, some alien force, which is trying to drive us apart. Not racial. Not dissension. Nothing like that. It's hard to explain. Hard to combat it when you don't even know what it is, but it's there, some alien force. I don't know what it's going to take. A big explosion to get us back to where we were, but there's definitely something bothering us right now. Something that's interfering with us."

He was looking up at the ceiling, his face in repose, the eyes crinkled in thought, a man on the couch trying to trace his way through the labyrinth of memory to get at the source of that "alien force." And it was there. Harraway was quite right about that. It seemed to me to be doubt, doubt that had always been there, but had been cast momentarily out of mind by the three-game winning streak and then surfaced with pervasive suddenness once the team lost. The doubt had to be there, personal doubt, team doubt. For the Redskins were a transitional ballclub made up of marginal veterans and pickups. They were only safe as long as they won, as long as they could stack fluke success on fluke success. Otherwise Lombardi would make changes, search for new people, increase the pressures and insecurity. At bottom he was demanding more than these forty players could deliver.

I returned to Harraway and Dyer's apartment the following day to talk to Walt Roberts, the "Flea," a former roommate who had moved to the suburbs when his family had come to Washington to join him. Flea was a small wiry man, about 5 feet 9 inches and 160 pounds, lively, mercurial, a man with a rich deep laugh and flashing white teeth.

Henry Dyer and Charley Harraway had gone out to a local Ford dealer to get a car for Dyer, and we went into his bedroom to talk. Flea sat on the bed, and I went and got the house's one straightback chair from Harraway's room.

"I hear you were blackballed around the league," I began.

"Blackballed by New Orleans? You can't tell. But I was their leading scorer. Yeah, I had a pretty good '67 season and when I asked for more money, they wouldn't give it to me. They never even asked me how much more I wanted. So I came to camp without signing my contract, and hell, let's face it, I'm no superstar going to sign for Namath money. All I was interested in was a couple of grand, and I figured my year deserved that.

"Well, they kept me on fifth string at camp and finally traded me to Detroit, and the word was out I was a black militant. I don't know what's a militant and what's not. I can tell you this, there are no Eldridge Cleavers in pro ball. I'm pro black people, yeah. I think black people have been catching a lot of hell, but I'm not the sort of guy who's going to go out and get me a gun and change things overnight. Well, I was a free agent and I tried the 49'ers and the Rams and the Browns, and they said they'd get in touch and they never did.

"Were they all full up, didn't think I was much of a ballplayer, heard I was a black militant? You can't know. And remember this, I'm a little guy. The little guy's days are numbered in football. The coaches don't dig little guys. They're leery of them. This is a big man's game. There are guys out there trying to hurt you, and you got to be big enough to hurt them back.

"Well, come this year, I wanted to play again, wanted to get my fifth year in for the pension. With Lombardi, my reputation of being a black militant didn't have anything to do with whether he wanted me or not. And I really appreciate that. Personally, I think he is a pretty fair guy, so I decided to come here."

I asked about the doubt that seemed to be afflicting the team.

"Being realistic, I can't say it helps a team to have a tremendous turnover of personnel. I played in New Orleans like that, and every day you looked up and saw a new guy in the locker next to you. And you'd size him up and figure, does he look like a lineman, a back, or a receiver. And you'd say, 'What's your name?' and in a real tiny voice, 'What position do you play?' Hell, a team doesn't have a soul when things are like that. Still, Lombardi's got to go get the kind of people he wants, his kind of people.

"It's like taking a hill in the army. You know you got to lose some men, maybe a third of your battalion. You know some men are going to get hurt. Lombardi knows he's going to make some mistakes and he's going to hurt some people, but in spite of that, he has experience in these things and he knows he's going to make fewer mistakes than most. He knows he's going to make the right decisions most of the time. Eventually he's going to have to have the guys he wants. He doesn't have time to sit up and baby-sit with guys. He's got that damn hill to worry about. So he figures he's going to have to trounce on some good guys, but that's the only way you can rebuild.

"Does he want me? How can you tell? Green Bay never had a history of small ballplayers. The Green Bay system is based on size. He likes them big. Those great big tight ends like Ron Kramer. Those great big flankers like Boyd Dowler. The day of the Flea, the Gnat, the Super-Gnat and the Mini-Max is drawing to a close. We're the last of a breed. And hell, yes, I worry about that. I know most coaches are going to figure I'm not tall enough for the quarterback to see. They're going to wonder, can I block?"

"You threw a beauty in the Giant game for Rickie's runback," I said. "There you go," he laughed.

Dyer and Harraway returned to the house, Dyer at the wheel of a new Maverick lent by a publicity-conscious Ford dealer. Dyer was a large man in an Afro, with blue-tinted glasses and a slow phlegmatic look. "The guy'll sell me a T-bird for $5000, $6200 list," he mused.

"He'd probably sell me one for $5100," I said.

"Yeah, I'm better off with the free one," he said, and plopped on the bed for a quick snooze.

"As I see it," Flea continued, "right now it's a case of Lombardi trying to find the right people, and contrary to what he says or the papers say, that search isn't over. He's faced with being the world champion, with building another dynasty. That's what's expected. That's why he's bringing all those ex-Packers in, I guess. Because they know the system, one. And two, he figures they can show us the way, how to win."

Dyer stirred on the bed, brought to life by the mention of those ex-Packers, Mercein—like Dyer, a fullback—being the latest among them.

Dyer said, "Every time you find a guy who's not playing, you'll find a guy who thinks he should be playing. You got to have emotions, got to think you're better. So me, I figure I'm a better runner than Chuck Mercein. Hell, yes, I do. Am I getting a fair shake on this team? Ain't noway I can think that and I'm not playing. Fair is what Lombardi says and thinks. That's fine. He's the coach. He get paid for deciding that. Now you look at Flea. Flea's a small man. Lombardi don't like small men. I don't care if Flea's open on every play, Lombardi wants a receiver that's 6' 3". That's what the man wants, so Flea don't get the consideration a man 6' 3" gets."

"But how about you?" I asked. " You're 230 pounds, built along the lines of a Lombardi running back, bigger even."

"The games I played in so far I ran well, I caught well, I blocked well. That's about all you want in a back. Come against the Saints, I fumbled once, and he took me out and I haven't had another real chance. That Charley Harraway over there. We're buddies. But Charley Harraway never did nothing to come in here and say this is my job. He never played in the exhibition season. I don't have any less ability than Charley Harraway. What's coaching? It's a personal thing. If a coach like your personality, or dig the way you run, or like the way you walk and talk, he likes you. Maybe the coach don't like the way I walk around the dressing room, maybe he don't like the way I carry myself, maybe he thinks I'm a hippie. He might even think I'm lazy by looking at me. Not by dealing with me! But I don't blame him as a coach. If I was a coach, there's certain things I'd look for in a player. I never been a coach, but I know from life that it's like women. Some men like big women, some men like small women. Some like

them with hips and some without. Each to his own, and if a
coach likes a certain thing in a football player, then that's
what he's going to play.

"Man," Dyer went on," it's tough being on that second
string. That's why I'm glad I'm not married. Like A. D. Whitfield gone, and Mercein here. What's the justification for ac-
tivating Mercein? Only one way. If Charley Harraway breaks
a leg or hurts his knee, and I go in there and royally mess up.
That's the only way Lombardi'll put Mercein in there. Because he ain't going to stick him in there over me and Charley
for nothing. Now, Mercein has still got to make you nervous.
Like, suppose we're behind 28–0, and Charley fumbles a couple of times, and I go in there and fumble once. They're going
to send me down to the third team, not Charley. That's what
second string means. You can't screw up once. Not one time.
I ain't complaining. That's the way it is. But it makes you
nervous. They can cut you from $1500 a month to nothing
overnight. I don't have no profession, no job. What can I do?
A $6500 education teacher, that's what I'm trained for. I
signed with the Rams for a $20,000 bonus. What can I do with
it? I was just a young kid, didn't know nothing. I don't have
no daddy I can say to, here put this twenty thou in your
business and make it grow. My daddy don't have no business
to put anything in, and none of my relatives either. There's no
way I can make that money work for me, no one gonna tell me
how, so I blow it. Now I'm a couple of years older and I've
learned that you make money on this high level in ball you
better live on this low level in life, so you can save some.
That's why I'm glad I got no family."

"He's right," Flea said. "I played three years in Cleveland
and got real smart and bought a house. I go to the Army for
six months' training and I was out in some foxhole at Fort
Knox and it was snowing, six below zero, and this guy come
creeping along in the snow and says, 'Hey, you Walt Roberts?
The Flea?' and I said, 'Yeah.' And he said, 'You just been
traded to the New Orleans Saints, can I take your picture?'
Man, I came back to Cleveland trying to salvage all the money
I put in a house I haven't even lived in yet. I did, but I'd never

buy a house now, I wouldn't dare. If I was Sonny Jurgensen, sure I'd buy myself a mansion on the Potomac, but not the average Joe Blow ballplayer. You got to save for the day some coach comes up and says, 'Hey, man, I'm sorry, but we don't need you any more. I tried to get you a job with the New York Giants, but they don't need you either. Good luck, fella.' I wish I wasn't married. I'd tell any kid to hold off getting married in this business. There's no security in it."

"Well," I said, "You've got the pension to look forward to."

"Hell," Dyer said, "men 6′ 3″ and 250 pounds don't live to be no sixty-five, anyway. You wait and see how many pensions they end up paying."

"What you're saying, then, is there's a contradiction here," I said. "Every coach in this league, not just Lombardi, but everyone, is trying to motivate a team to have faith and loyalty to one another, to be a happy, loving family. And what you've got are guys who're cynical about the business ethics of the sport, who're worried about their job, insecure and frightened. And to cap matters, you're asked to have trust and live in a sport that's brutal and impersonal."

"Football," the Flea said, "is like a preacher preaching against fornication, and you go over to his house and see him hard at it. Contradictions? Hell, yes, on Wednesday night. Now Sunday is something else again. You get out on the field and you don't care about your pension plan, or whether you're in a secure profession, you're out there to play ball. Whatever you do, you can't forget this is an emotional game; you get to love playing it. Lombardi is telling us we've got to have this love for one another and this morale, and I agree with him. It's crazy to talk about things like that. Yet in a way, it's not. You need it. You get it and you can't be beaten. What he's saying is you get the horses, you get that morale, and you've got it all. The security, the affection of the teammates for one another falls into place. Winning makes the difference. You bank $25,000 every Super Bowl, you aren't worried about any contradictions. You got plenty of love to go around when you're a winner. He knows that. Everyone knows that. But he wants it more than most."

"Yeah, he had it at Green Bay. You got to say that," Dyer agreed.

"You got to say he is a hell of man to play for if you're winning. And a hell of a man to play for if you're losing. It cuts both ways."

On Thursday I was paying a visit to John Hoffman's locker, shooting the breeze and enjoying John as I always did. He said, "That tie is real bad. Puts us two full games behind Dallas. We got to beat them to even stay close."

"Well, not that bad. A tie doesn't count. If we beat them, we'll be 5–2, and they'll be 7–2."

"Is that right?" he mused. "Ties don't count? I thought this sport was like hockey."

"No, they don't count. So the ties we got against San Francisco and the Eagles are a whole lot better than a loss to the 49'ers and a victory over the Eagles."

"Is that right?" he said, turning once again to Roussel for confirmation.

"Yeah," Roussel said.

I asked him what he had done wrong to have been taken out of the Eagle game and Carl Kammerer sent in.

"Kind of funny," he said. "They sent Carl in to replace Leo, but Carl got mixed up and told me to go out instead. Then, the combination of Carl and Leo seemed to be working, so I never got back in. Now Leo and Carl are starting against the Cowboys."

So much for the finely-honed logic on which football games were said to depend. "If you've ever been on a football bench, you'd know it was the most irrational place in the world," a veteran player told me. "The only one on our coaching staff who's sane during a game is Svare. Lombardi's so ape you can't talk to him."

But if Lombardi was not all reason and logic on the side lines during a game, by Tuesday practice he was able to re-fashion some stoical will, that second wind of reason that came to him like an endurance runner. Dim as the Redskins' prospects were, Lombardi started the title race all over again on Tuesday. On Monday he had said, "When things go bad,

Coach, they have a tendency to mount." Now, as the count-down for the Cowboys began, he worked not to reverse a tendency, but as if it did not exist. It was impossible to resist the energy, the growling, the strutting, the shrieking, the rock-like faith, and the missionary compulsion to spread it. If his charges were not altogether convinced of their destiny, that did not bother Lombardi.

"It seems like things are on the verge of coming apart," a player told me. "We're coming up to the real pressure games, Dallas, the Rams. All these new guys coming through the locker room. It seems like a lot of guys are afraid of their jobs and afraid of getting beat. The doubt is beginning to grow. Look around and you see sorrowful faces in the locker room. Hell, guys aren't even talking to other guys. We're afraid of what we'll admit to each other. We just don't know about ourselves any more."

"It gets so bad," another player said, "that I don't know who'll be around if we lose this week. I'm more worried about my individual performance than about winning. It's that bad, the security part of it eats at you so. Good God, if Lombardi would just bend to us, just a little. If he'd bend, I'm sure we'd respond and play for him."

"I don't know if we can get by Dallas or not. They're a hell of a team. But we got one thing going for us," a Redskin veteran said, "that we've never had before. We're so much bet er conditioned than we've ever been. That's got to tell at the tail end of the season. The last five or six games most teams are just pooped, playing all worn out, and can be easily hurt. You look at the Redskins in the past, always the same story. It comes to the last five games, we're dragging ass and we win or lose because Sonny has a hot hand that day or a cold one. Hell, in the huddle on Tuesday practices last year, you could hardly breathe, the fumes were so bad. You'd go in to see the Sunday games in the film room, the sounds and smells you'd hear from people with bad stomachs and hangovers! I'm no physical-fitness nut, but you can't play twenty foot-ball games in that kind of shape. The body just gives out. Lombardi's always talking about fourth-quarter shape; well, these last six games are our fourth quarter, we're in shape, and we may surprise some people."

On Wednesday Lombardi passed out the game plan. On its cover sheet were legends such as "Rush the passer" and "Intimidate this team to win." A paper target was taped to the cab-squad room wall, with the names of prominent Cowboys assigned different point values. The regulars who came in to use the universal gym lined up with a hard rubber ball to take their turn trying to hit Craig Morton in the bull's-eye. Each player had ten throws, and after eight throws linebacker Marlin McKeever was shooting for the team record. He missed the target completely with his last two balls. He made a gesture to strangle himself, to admit that he choked under pressure. Ted Vactor, a reserve defensive back, took ten throws and missed the target on all ten.

Later I was passing his locker in the main dressing room and said, "With an arm like yours, you ought to get into baseball."

"You think so?" he laughed.

Vactor was black, and a nearby white player said, "Only one colored boy in a hundred can make it as a pitcher. Science shows Negroes can't throw."

"Who says?" Vactor asked, his face hardening.

"It says so in a book one of the guys was showing me after practice the other day."

"Oh yeah?" Vactor replied in an offended voice.

"Yeah," the white player said, "it's by Lester Maddox. It's called *The Black Athlete in Sports*." He grinned. Had he been putting Vactor on all along, or had he devised this recovery at the last moment? It was hard to know. Certainly Vactor was not amused. It was one of the few occasions I overheard the faint byplay of racial tension in the locker room. Interestingly enough, there was another awkward scene the next day. Henry Dyer was prancing around the dressing room, trying to round up some extra tickets for the game, his clowning manner indicating that he regarded the prospect as an off-chance at best. He approached a white player on the scales. "Hey, man, how about selling me a couple of extra tickets?" The white player looked down and said in slow, clear voice, "I don't sell tickets to Negroes." Dyer looked up at the man and walked away.

It was axiomatic in football that the game just played was to be forgotten, driven from the mind, and replaced by the up-coming game. That state of mind was not so easy for Mike Bass. The Washington TV stations were rerunning the famed interference call throughout the week and the papers were printing sequential pictures of the penalty, none of them prov-ing anything. The CBS color man for the Redskins-Eagles game, Tom Brookshier, was quoted as finding the interference call a case of an offensive penalty on Ben Hawkins, rather than a defense penalty on Bass. It was a call that the public wanted to know more about, a call that Mike Bass compul-sively explored and had to keep coming back to.

I found him in front of his locker pouring over a *Washington Post* photo essay on the dispute. "You can tell from these photos," Bass said, looking up with satisfaction, "that I didn't commit a foul. If you look carefully, you can see that even if I did foul him, the ball should have been marked at the 3-yard line, because the photos show that no foul could have taken place at the 1, where the flag was dropped."

"What did the referee say?"

"That's a good point," he said, purring like a lawyer leading a witness down the primrose path. "Some of the other refs told me the call was all wet. And I talked personally to the official who made the call twice. The first time he told me I had my arm on Hawkin's shoulder. Then the next time he said that I pushed him. In essence, he admits he made the wrong call." He returned to the photos, seeking still more clinching evidence of an injustice.

Chris Hanburger was in the locker stall next to Bass. He had once told me, "I made a mistake two years ago I still can't get out of my mind. It was the last few seconds of the Cowboys game, and we had them beat. Dan Reeves came out of the backfield. He was my man and I forgot about him, and helped out on the tight end instead. Suddenly it dawned on me, where is Reeves? There he was behind me, all alone. I took off after him, but it was too late. He caught the ball for the winning touchdown, with eighteen seconds left to play. That's a play you can't forget." Now Hanburger looked down at Bass engrossed in his paper. "What did you do to screw up today, Mike?" he said. Bass jerked up his head, fright in his eyes. "What?" he said. Hanburger put on his bitching face. "What are those you're looking at, the Zapruder films? Maybe you can sell the play to *Life* magazine."

Bass laughed a little uneasily.

Hanburger gave the trace of a grin and shook his head, fondly suggesting the futility of Bass's quest for exoneration and its inevitability as well. He had been through it all himself and would be through it all again, soon.

Yet there was still the sense of that "alien force" gripping the team that Harraway had spoken of. The practices, for all Lombardi's drive and ferocious energy, were flat, error-prone, and lacking any fire.

The team was hoping Lombardi might bend. Instead, he turned the screws a notch tighter and cut Dave Crossan, whose hamstring, suffered in the Cardinal game, had never completely healed. Mercein's arrival had sent shock waves through the team, but Whitfield was after all a cab squader. Crossan was one of the forty-man team, a member of the roster. Dan Grimm, another ex-Packer, a former backup guard to Fuzzy Thurston and Jerry Kramer, was picked up to take Crossan's place.

One player told me, "Who are these guys he's getting from Green Bay? Mercein and Grimm, they never showed anybody anything. None of the ballplayers he's brought here from Green Bay ever had anything to do with the Packers winning. Now, maybe if he brought Forrest Gregg or Willie Davis out of retirement, I could see where you could say that these old guys are going to lead the way for us young Redskins. Gregg, Kramer, Hornung, guys like that can show you something. But Grimm and Mercein? How can a man lead you when he was nothing but a second-string follower himself?"

"I'm for bringing in a ballplayer who can help us," another player told me, "but to bring in someone who's been a Packer, just because of that? I'm very unhappy about this Grimm-

Crossan thing. I keep hearing what I suppose would be justifi-cations for the move. Grimm's supposed to be a better pass blocker, he would be a better guard or tackle. But hell, Dave played tackle for us against Dallas and did a great job on George Andrie. Anyway, how do you judge a guy like Grimm versus Crossan? If Hauss does his job, Dave's not going to play center, and if Schoenke and Promuto do their jobs, he's not going to play guard either. It's the same with Grimm. He might get a chance to play, but probably not. But talk about loyalty—you ought to stick with the guy you've got who's go-ing to do a good job for you, not some other guy from outside. At this late date it's impossible for Dave to get picked up someplace else. It's unheard of to cut guys this late. It makes everybody figure Dave must be a terrible dog for Lombardi to have dumped him for Dan Grimm."

The Cowboys game was to be on a weekend on which foot-ball and politics merged. In Washington, the Moratorium was in full swing all week long, and there were rumbling hints from the Defense Department that the National Guard would be mobilized over the weekend. That could conceivably mean that the Redskins could go up against the Cowboys without guardsmen Jerry Smith, Brig Owens, Bob Long, and Gary Be-ban—three of them starters, three out of the Redskins' six receivers.

In exchange for four borrowed players, the Pentagon was offering the Redskins another military display for the half-time festivities. Three busloads of marines in fatigues arrived at practice during the week to go through their paces after the team finished with the field. Lombardi greeted them raptur-ously, the first time I had ever seen him overjoyed at the arrival of strangers at practice.

But the decision to treat the fans to a Marine Corps Drum and Bugle Corps, the Silent Drill Platoon, three other ceremonial platoons, and a color guard had nothing to do with the Moratorium—a mere coincidence, really—according to Joel Margolis, the Redskin half-time director. The White House announced to the Redskins that President Nixon would take in the Cowboys game, the first President ever to see a regular-season NFL game. The Redskins-Cowboys game was to round out the President's football weekend, since it was also announced in advance that he would spend Saturday viewing the Purdue-Ohio State game on television. The meaning of this football weekend was not lost on the press or on the nation, for that matter. Football was the President's answer to the Moratorium, his definition of the bounds of useful protest. If you had some aggression to get out of your system, felt you had to raise your voice a little, the ballpark was the place.

I went to RFK Stadium on Saturday morning. It was Lombardi's ritual to have the players bring their kids along to Saturday practice, to loosen up the tension and make them feel one big happy family.

Lombardi, not an unkindly man, not necessarily a standoffish one, was nonetheless no natural charmer with children. His attention span was unusually short in this area, his grin overpowering. In any case, it could be assumed that the children of the Redskins had heard some reports from the office, some spine-tingling stories about Coach from their fathers. As a general rule, children above three snuck from view when Coach approached and looked distinctly uncomfortable if he tracked them down for a pinch on the cheek. On Saturday Pat Richter had brought his sons along, and Lombardi approached one of them, a boy about five.

"Well, here's a new one," Lombardi boomed. "Who do you belong to?"

This was normally a sign for a child to bolt for his father. Young Richter looked Lombardi in the eye and piped in a manly voice, "Hiya, Vince. How ya doing?"

It seemed almost enough to bring the team together, an echo of happier, more relaxed Saturday mornings out at Green Bay's Lambeau Field. Young Richter was the closest thing the Redskins had to Max McGee, the only person the Redskins had who could make Coach and the team laugh in unison.

Chapter 21

The National Guard was mobilized, but was dismissed in time for the four Redskins to get to the Stadium Sunday morning. Lombardi liked the team to show up at least two hours before game time, liked them to sit around the clubhouse and brood in solitude until the pressure of the week could be compressed into a personal will to win that matched his own.

The Cowboys and Redskins limbered up out on the field. Lombardi and Landry were wandering through their own ranks, at last meeting on neutral ground in midfield. They stood and chatted for a while, talking about their grandchildren, Lombardi said later.

The Cowboys won the toss, and rookie Calvin Hill brought the ball 70 yards to the Washington 30 on a kickoff return and two runs from scrimmage. The Redskins' defense held, and the Cowboys kicked a field goal to take a 3–0 lead. The Redskins struck back on a 77-yard drive, culminating in a 27-yard touchdown catch by Jerry Smith. The Redskins, who had not yet lost a game in which they had been scored on first, had a 7–3 lead with the first quarter half gone.

A 65-yard pass by Craig Morton to Lance Rentzel and Larry Cole's touchdown runback of a Jurgensen interception put the Cowboys back in front, 17–7, as the quarter ended.

Early in the second quarter, Bob Hayes returned a Mike Bragg punt 50 yards to the Redskin 3, and Calvin Hill took it in from there, making it 24–7, the apparent beginning of a Cowboy rout.

Suddenly, all of Lombardi's preparations, his solitary will, his reshuffling, the bullying, and his domineering energy seemed an impertinence, an absurdity. Further Redskin suffering and buffeting seemed pointless and cruel in such a context. It didn't seem the Redskins could be driven to play, driven to win.

The Redskins had the ball now and had worked it backwards to third and nineteen from their own 12-yard line. Jurgensen dropped straight back, as he had so often against the Cowboys in days gone by. Charley Taylor took off down the Redskin side lines, Mel Renfro and Phil Clark dogging his steps. The game was being beamed back to Grand Prairie, Texas, and Taylor liked to regale the home-town TV fans with a big play or so, a heroic reminder for all the girls he'd left behind. Jurgensen's pass was underthrown, Taylor looked over his shoulder, his eye on the sinking ball, and with abrupt catlike grace, he stopped in his tracks, doubled back, and hauled it in at the Cowboy 42. Renfro and Clark shot back to make the tackle. Taylor gave them a stutter-step and a loop and headed for the goal-line, with Renfro, a 9.6 sprinter in college, in hot pursuit. It wasn't even close. Renfro gave up around the 20, and the Grand Prairie flash put the Redskins a little closer, 24–14. As Lombardi had said, "No one really knows how fast Charley is." Reflecting on this question after the season was over he was to say, "Charley may be faster than Bob Hayes. There's no way of telling, but I would not be adverse to wagering on it."

The Cowboys took the kickoff all the way down to the Redskin 7-yard line before the defense held and forced a field goal, making it 27–14. Washington came right back. On third and seven at the Redskin 32, Jurgensen hit Jerry Smith for 10 yards, plus a 15-yard penalty that moved the ball to the Cowboy 43. A 17-yarder to Taylor advanced it to the 26. Jurgensen found no one open and lugged the ball over the left side for 9 yards, lowering his helmet for the first-down effort, like some turn-of-the-century fullback. He missed it by a yard. Bob Lilly and George Andrie stopped Harraway for a loss of one, and Jurgensen came back for 7 yards and the first down on a pass to Bob Long. It was first and ten at the Dallas 11, and Jerry Smith caught his second touchdown pass of the afternoon on the next play. The half ended with the score

Cowboys 27, Redskins 21. A touchdown and an extra point from the Redskin offense would make the Capitol Division a race once more.

Winning was a fragile creation that could be unexpectedly shattered at any time. That was obvious. What was surprising was that winning could be put together so quickly, so unexpectedly. After the Baltimore and Philadelphis fiascos, it had to be assumed that the Redskins were losers. Now they were within a touchdown of being back in it, within seven points of making it a race to the wire.

The seven points were not long in coming. Early in the third period, Rickie Harris fielded a Dallas punt on the Redskin 17-yard line and lugged it all the way, Chris Hanburger throwing what may or may not have been an essential block at the Cowboy 33 on Dallas linebacker Dave Edwards. A flag went down. Clipping, said the referee. No touchdown. No Redskin comeback. The ball was spotted at the Cowboy 48, and instead of going ahead by a point, Washington was still down by 6. A 15-yard penalty against the Redskins and five straight carries by Calvin Hill gave the Cowboys a 34–21 lead.

I had to think back to the clip, the call against Hanburger that had blunted the Washington chances for the game, possibly for the season, and even for the division title. There was, it seemed, almost a fugue-like repetition of themes in football.

I recalled Hanburger's defensive philosophy, the need for aggressiveness, for pushing against the very limits of illegality. I also thought of his enjoinder, "If there's an opportunity to hit someone on a special team, and it's a hanger between a clip and a legal block, you ought to pass that one up." From the press box, his block on Edwards appeared legal, and later the films showed that Hanburger had hit his target head on, that Edwards had twisted and had turned his back as he was hit. Hanburger was innocent, but the referee had dropped his hanky to the turf. That was it; there was nothing that could be done about it. Vince Promuto once told me that years before, he had tiptoed up on a flag dropped to penalize the Redskins and stuffed it in his pants. The official had walked around scratching his head, searching for his handkerchief, deeply puzzled. But even so, the penalty stood; stealing the flag was no answer.

Still, even though the Cowboys had a thirteen-point lead, the game was far from being over. The Redskins took the ball 75 yards in seven plays to score on Jerry Smith's third touchdown pass of the game. Now it was Cowboys 34 , Redskins 28, with a little more than a quarter to play.

The ball changed hands twice on consecutive interceptions by Mel Renfro and Rickie Harris. With ten minutes to play, the Redskins mounted a final drive from their own 21-yard line. On third and eight, Jurgensen carried for 12 yards and the first down, and then hit Taylor for 27 more, to the Dallas 35-yard line. Sonny Jurgensen was a hard man to defend that close to the end zone. The game was far enough along to give him four downs, instead of three, to keep the drive alive.

Twice hope had fled for the Redskins, but now it had revived once more. Larry Brown fumbled on the first play from scrimmage, and the ball was recovered by Dave Edwards, who was tackled by Charley Harraway. Hope died for the third time, except that there was a yellow handkerchief on the field. Offside on the Cowboys. Redskins' ball, first and five, on the 33-yard line. Jurgensen hit Bob Long for 2, and Larry Brown came back for 3 more, good for the first down on the Cowboy 27. The distance was about right—25 yards— deep enough to give the receiving corps room to maneuver, short enough to fit the limits of Jurgensen's extraordinary accuracy. He dropped back to throw for the touchdown. Bob Long was in the southwest corner of the end zone, a Cowboy cornerback on his heels. Jurgensen would have to thread the needle, but he'd done that before. He threw on a line for Long. It was low and hard, right into Dallas linebacker Chuck Howley's arms on the Cowboy 11. Howley carried it back 28 yards before Jurgensen knocked him out of bounds on the Redskin side lines. The Cowboys took it the rest of the way on the ground for the touchdown, to run out all but a minute of the clock, and won 41–28.

What could you say? That Jurgensen was 24 of 35 for 338 yards? That the Redskins had played on the same level with a vastly superior Cowboy team, had repeatedly fought back from sizeable deficits, and then had failed to win through questionable breaks and a handful of key errors? That was all true. And it was also true that they had lost and now stood 4–3–2 to Dallas's 8–1. The race for the division title was over. The Redskins would have to win six in a row, while the Cowboys dropped three of their last six.

Down in the dressing room, Lombardi was gracious, in command of himself. Perhaps he was relieved that the suspense was over. It was, after all, a more intense, more exhausting experience to believe in the Redskins than to believe in the Packers.

"It's not a tough one to lose," Lombardi said, "but it would have been a great one to win. I'm sorry we couldn't win it for the President. Dallas had too many guns for us. I've known Tom Landry for thirty years, and if I have to lose to anybody, I guess I'd just as soon it would be to him."

"How about that clipping penalty on Hanburger that called back Harris's touchdown run?"

"Did Rickie get into the end zone?" Lombardi mused. "He did, eh? That's too bad," he said, his eyes momentarily focusing on the past, the touchdown that could have been, the championship that might have been. There was an edge of that Lombardi defiance as he repeated, "Yeah, that's too bad. That could have put a different complexion on the game."

"Any one reason why you're not winning?" a reporter asked.

"You got to be kidding," Lombardi snapped, and then added more philosophically, "Our special teams have been hurting us."

Someone wondered if the TV camera wouldn't have caught some unusual facial grimaces of Coach during the game.

"That's all the TV does, is take pictures of me on the side lines," he complained.

"Are you giving TV hell?" a newsman asked, with a smile.

"No," Lombardi said, his face suddenly lighting up. "That's for people in different positions." He gave a startling guffaw, filled with pain and the release of nervous tension. He strode out of the room, leaving us with the memory of Spiro Agnew's recent assaults on the news media at Des Moines and Montgomery, instead of with the ashes of the Redskin loss. Lombardi was, after all, a man who never dealt with defeat.

I did not look forward to facing the clubhouse now that it was all over. I had to wonder if I had ever truly had faith in the Redskins as a team, the sort of easy faith that thought ahead to the Eastern Conference play-offs, the NFL championship, the trip to the Super Bowl. Probably not, almost certainly not. I had, at best, believed at times in Lombardi's destiny, his overriding will. It ended there. But if I had never really found faith in the team, I had found a sort of faith in their gameness, their courage, the character they had as men. Thus I found comfort in the absence of defeat in the locker room that afternoon. They had played a hell of a game and they knew it. If they had to bow out, the Dallas game was no disgraceful note on which to do it.

"Well, we took the game to them," Ray Schoenke said. "They can't take that away from us. When we had the ball down in their territory before Howley intercepted Sonny's pass, I thought 'championship' for the first time this year. I thought we'd go all the way. And then I remembered, you can't think that way. I forced myself to say, 'One play at a time.' It was great to see Carl starting again. That's been one of the toughest things this year, coming up to have him pound my shoulder pads and him standing there, the tears in his eyes, really wanting to play so bad. I thought he had a hell of a day. We all gave them a hell of a game."

I went across the room to Carl Kammerer's locker. His face was splotched with red, with exertion, and with the sheer happiness of being back in the line-up. Three cold grape soda pops stood in his locker, and he was chug-a-lugging a fourth.

"It was good to see you back in there starting," I said. "Somebody just told me how bad it was watching the tears in your eyes while you were popping him, setting his pads."

"The emotion doesn't run shallow in me," Kammerer allowed, setting down the soda pop. "I love this team and these guys. There are some men with grit here. I like that grit. Back when I was playing college ball on the coast, Alonzo Stagg used to be our coach emeritus. The grand old man of football, he must have been ninety-five years old. He started coaching back in the 1890's at the University of Chicago and had been coaching for almost seventy years. Well, we were out practicing, and the center came off the ball real quick, charged forward, and hit Stagg right in the spine. Hit this ninety-five year-old man right in the back and dropped him to the ground. Stagg just lay there. We thought the guy'd killed him. And Stagg sort of fought his way back up to his feet and he looks at us, sort of woozy, and says in this creaky old man's voice, 'Boys, if we hit that hard on Saturday, we're bound to win.' Now that's grit. That's why a man can love this damn game."

Vince Promuto's father and brother were in the locker room, their faces gaunt and knit with worry. Promuto had popped his shoulder loose again early in the game, blocking Bob Lilly. He had lain on the ground for a minute or so, been helped from the field, his status questionable. He had popped that excruciatingly painful shoulder back in place and returned to the fray, playing the rest of the game. Lilly never got to Jurgensen again. That too was a show of grit, and I complimented him on it.

"You got to have charisma," he roared, rejoicing in his own private word for Lombardi's special brand of leadership.

The sun was going down when I left the locker room. As my wife, son, and I were walking across the empty parking lot to our car, we saw a National Guardsman in starched, sharply creased fatigues. It was Jerry Smith. "I spent the whole damn weekend in an open jeep, cold as hell, breathing tear gas all night. Saturday night we got back to the barracks about 12:30. About 1:30 I'm ready to turn in, and the company commander comes up to my bunk and says, 'You got to guard the ammunition dump between 3:00 and 4:00. So I finally fall asleep, get up, watch the damn ammunition for an hour, get back to sleep again around 5:00, my throat and eyes still smarting. Then they sound reveille and all morning I didn't know whether they'd let me go or not. That was the worst part of all. I was really getting mad."

Mad enough, as it turned out, to catch seven balls for 98 yards, three of them touchdown passes. Another man with grit.

Lombardi, who could never be accused of lacking true grit, for that matter, met with the press on Monday and talked gruffly and technically, not yet conceding the demise of hope. Finally he said, "You play a little better when you play the best. And Dallas may be the best. I guess that's what this team has to learn: to play their best all of the time. It could have been . . . " he stopped and gave a wan smile. "Oh, hell, I hate to say that. That's silly. Forget it."

Yes, it could have been.

Chapter 22

The Falcons were coming to Washington 3–6, a team in some ways tougher than their record indicated. They had routed the Bears 48–31 the week before, with Van Brocklin calling the plays from the side line for his quarterback Randy Johnson. They had four class backs and were number three in the league in rushing. They had lost close games to the Colts, the Cowboys, and the Rams. But they were playing without their great middle linebaker, Tommy Nobis, who was recovering from a knee injury.

It was a lovely fall day, crisp and bright in RFK Stadium, and temperate enough for the hearty Bill Austin to take the field in his Redskins polo shirt. Henry Dyer carried the ball back to the Redskin 18. Larry Brown ripped off a quick first down, but a penalty for delay of game killed the Redskins' drive a few plays later. The Falcons took over on their own 34-yard line after a mediocre Bragg punt. The Washington defense held, Kammerer, McLinton, Crane, and Bass limiting three Falcon carries to 8 yards.

Billy Lothridge punted to Flea on the Redskin 26-yard line; the ball popped out of his hands, dropped to the gound, and was recovered by the Falcons. They scored in six plays to stake out a 7–0 lead.

The Redskins came right back, however, Jurgensen hitting Long for 15, Brown running for 15 more, Jurgensen back to Long for 7, then 14, and Jurgensen to Smith in the end zone for 16 yards and a tie ballgame. The drive was effortless, a mere two-minute trifle, carried off without the inconvenience of facing a third-down situation, with only one second down needed.

It was too easy, like a magician's trick.

Knight's kickoff was fielded on the 11-yard line and taken back to the midfield stripe before Rickie Harris knocked Charlie Bryant out of bounds. The special teams were having one of their patented days. A 7-yard punt return on a mere 37-yard punt; a fumbled punt; a 39-yard kickoff return. The Falcons would not require an explosive offense to get on the scoreboard with that sort of head start. And sure enough, the Falcons began grinding out the small yardage against the porous Redskin line. The ball moved from midfield to the Redskin 48, then the 44, the 39, the 36, the 30, the 28, the 27, the 19. It was third and one. Randy Johnson dropped back to pass under heavy pressure, missed his receiver, and went down in a pile-up. He didn't get up and was finally helped from the field with torn knee ligaments, out for the season. The Falcon quarterbacking was left to a second-year free agent named Bruce Lemmerman.

Implausibly, with the score tied and the game only a few seconds into the second quarter, fourth and one at the Redskin 19, the Dutchman went for the first down. You could only assume that he had wanted to beat Lombardi badly; no squeaker would do—a humilitation was what he had in mind. Cannonball Butler carried for the first down. Then Lemmerman's inexperience began to tell. Two successive penalties—backfield in motion and offside—moved the ball back to the Redskin 28. Lemmerman rolled to the right, found no one, and carried for 11 yards down to the 17. He missed Paul Flatley, threw a 6-yarder to Charlie Bryant, and on third and nine Van Brocklin decided to go for the field goal, after all. It was good, and the Falcons went ahead 10–7.

The Redskins were forced to punt from their own 30, and safety Mike Freeman got a 12-yard return before Jim Snowden and Jim Norton tackled him. It was now Lemmerman's turn to show how easily a touchdown could be scored. He hit Butler over the middle, and Cannonball legged it all the way to the Redskin 6-yard line before being overtaken by Chris Hanburger. Wages and Butler carried it in two plays, making it Falcons 17, Redskins 7.

The Redskins drew closer with a laborious drive, featuring runs by Larry Brown and passes by Jurgensen to Bob Long. Brown took it in for a score in four straight carries from the 14-yard line, to draw within three points, Falcons 17, Redskins 14.

The next *faux pas* from the special teams was scarcely to be credited. Knight uncorked a booming kickoff that was downed in the end zone. The Redskins, it turned out, were offsides, and Knight tried again from the 35. His kick was high enough and came down at the goal-line. The Redskin defenders seemed to evaporate on the long dash downfield, and Cannonball Butler ran the kickoff back 61 yards to the Redskin 39 before Rickie Harris stopped him. There were only two and a half minutes remaining in the half, and Lemmerman, throwing somewhat erratically, nevertheless managed a first and ten on the Redskin 8. His arm went cold, and the Falcons had to settle for a field goal. Jurgensen maneuvered the Redskins from their own 24-yard line to the Falcon 31 in a half minute, and with sixteen seconds left in the half, Knight kicked a 38-yarder, once again narrowing the Falcon margin to three points. With eleven seconds left, Lombardi was taking no further chances on his special teams and instructed Knight to boot a squibbler, which was picked up at the Falcon 35 and returned 13 yards anyway. Fortunately, the gun sounded before the Falcons could do further damage.

After performances by the United States Army Band and the Marine Corps Drum and Bugle Corps in the past weeks, I had to wonder what half-time displays from the Pentagon were still available. It turned out to be the Marching Junior Midshipmen from the Leonard Hall School in Leonardtown, Maryland. These tykes, who appeared to be about ten, took the field with their white spats, epaulettes, miniature midshipmen's uniforms, and toy guns for some close-order rifle drill. They traipsed about, their tiny jaws jutting out and their black-billed caps pulled down deep over their eyes. It was an extraordinary sight, frightening in its Orwellian picture of the future, chilling even to the lusty, patriotic fans.

"Where in the world did they get these kids from?" I asked

someone. "Ed Williams's kid goes to the school," I was told. The two teams came back on the field, and the tiny cadets smartly hut-hut-hutted off the field.

Early in the third period, Jurgensen dropped back to throw under heavy pressure and lobbed the ball over to Harraway, his safety valve, in the right flat. Harraway seemed almost astounded to have the ball. There was no shield of blockers in front of him. Somehow he skirted the defenders and took off downfield on a zig-zagging course, 64 yards for a touchdown. He must have run 125 yards, looking at times as he puffed along that he might sink to his knees with exhaustion. It was a thrilling carry, its suspense lying not so much in the menace of a Falcon tackle, but in Harraway's physical capacity to leg it to the goal line. Harraway returned to the bench to gulp lungfuls of air from the oxygen tank kept there for such contingencies.

Knight's kick was good, and the Redskins went ahead 24–20. Jurgensen was extraordinarily hot now, eating up the last five and half minutes of the third period with a long drive that finally petered out early in the fourth quarter. Lemmerman was unable to move the Falcons, and the Redskins got the ball back and added a 27-yard field goal on the drive, to go out in front, 27–20.

With 5:40 left to play, Jurgensen passed to Charley Taylor for 17 yards and a first down. Harraway carried for 5, and Jurgensen dropped back to hit Taylor on the fly. Falcon defensive back Rudy Redmond intercepted on his own 28-yard line.

Lemmerman then went to air and had his pass batted down by Dennis Crane, but Hanburger was called for roughing the passer, and it was a Falcon first down at the Washington 44. Given the ineffectiveness of his passing game, Lemmerman wisely kept the ball on the ground, and his backs reeled off 26 yards in three carries when the two-minute warning sounded. Butler carried for 2 down to the Redskin 28, and Lemmerman hit Gail Cogdill for a 14-yard gain down to the 14. The Falcons called time out, with 1:24 showing on the board.

It was a situation too often staged in the past to leave much

margin for hope. Two time-outs left, first and ten at the Redskin 14—enough time left, enough time-outs left, enough
momentum generated. Yet, that was reckoning without a
green Falcon quarterback and a fired-up Redskin defense.
Frank Bosch and Dennis Crane broke through to drop Lemmerman for a 5-yard loss. Lemmerman threw off target under
pressure from Kammerer, then Crane blocked a pass, and it
was fourth and fifteen. For Atlanta, it was now or never. Lemmerman missed Harmon Wages in the clear. The Redskins ran
out the last forty-three seconds and went down to the clubhouse 5–3, a 27–20 win somehow under their belts. The victory itself was improbable, and the statistics made it seem
even more improbable that the Redskins had only won by a
touchdown. Jurgensen had an 81-percent completion record,
26 for 32 and 300 yards. The defense had held the Falcons
scoreless in the second half, had given up a measly 83 yards
in offensive yardage. And even if the Falcon backs had carried for a game total of 133 yards, the Redskins had gained
148, with 102 of them from Larry Brown. The difference, the
closeness of the score, was to be found in the contrast between the two teams' punt and kickoff statistics; there the
Falcons had gained 189 yards to the Redskins' 85.

As Lombardi said down in the clubhouse, "Our special
teams are killing us. And, hell, we're not deep enough to
use regulars out there. I don't know. When we're not aggressive out there, we don't do anything. When we are aggressive, we get penalized. Got to find a combination, I
guess." He smiled, secretly pleased, I supposed, at any evidence of aggressiveness, the penalties be damned.

He was wriggling his toes inside his sweat socks; there
was a red 13 printed on the wool at the toe of the sock.
"Do you realize you have a 13 on your socks?" a reporter
asked.

"Yep," Lombardi said, his eyebrow lifting a fraction of an
inch. "I wear size 13 socks."

Bob Long and Charley Harraway had gotten the game
ball. Harraway was nowhere to be seen, his pads and helmet hanging in his locker stall.

"How about that guy?" a reporter remarked. "He does something good, and you can't find him."

It was hard not to think back to the fans booing Charley before the Eagle game. It seemed unaccountably bush-league that the man who had flashed that big-league V sign to the grandstands would flee the dressing room in his moment of glory. Then I remembered that Charley, Henry Dyer, and Flea drove down to the games together, and it became clearer why Harraway had left. Flea was doubtless in no mood to face the reporters, to discourse on those fumbles, so Harraway had foregone his chance to exult with the writers, to detail the steps he'd taken to get his own fumbling under control.

If Harraway had fled for Flea's sake, Long, the possessor of the other half of the game ball, had stayed on to face the reporters. Like Harraway before the Eagles game, Long had been roundly booed as he was introduced at the beginning of the game, but he had not mustered a V sign or any other visible show of defiance or conciliation. He had, however, caught his ten balls, and that should quiet the annoyance of the fans.

The boos had been sounded because two of Jurgensen's interceptions against Dallas were thrown with Long as a target. And if he could not be blamed for that, he was a more suitable subject for displeasure than Jurgensen.

So the only two players on the team who had been treated to the fans' raspberries shared the game ball. I liked the team's delicacy of sentiment there. The reporters circled Long's locker. He turned to face them, his face drawn tight with anger. "You guys like to talk to me when I have a good day, and don't say anything to me when I don't," Long said bitterly, his eyes almost wild with emotion. "I've never been booed before, and I don't care what the fans think of me. I play this game for one reason. I play it for Vince Lombardi."

The reporters pressed closer, sensing the imminence of hot copy, a player with no restraint left. Long recapped his automobile accident for the reporters, his broken bones, the fluid he carried on his hips, the arm that was shorter than the other. The writers jotted the information down and wrote it up the next day, but as with all anguish and pain of a remote nature, it only had real meaning for Long.

A few locker stalls down the way, Dennis Crane was sitting in his undershirt and jock, still savoring his performance, a second-year man who had found himself at last after ten games of shuffling back and forth. His pudgy choirboy's face was still flushed and his blond hair dark with sweat as he sawed at the tape around his ankles with a razor blade. In the final defensive stand that had won the game, he had been the hero, putting on a big rush, batting down two passes. From the press box it appeared that he had stopped Lemmerman's third-down pass with his stomach. He had been helped from the field, doubled over, his hands pressed into his guts.

"Did you block that pass with your stomach?" I asked.

"No," he smiled, "with my hands. I stuck them up high and the guard got me right in the pit of my stomach with his helmet, full force. Nothing I could do to protect myself. Man, I'm really pooped. I'm in shape, but I never played a game like that before. I think this is the first time I've gone all the way this year. Boy, Coach Lombardi's the greatest. If he wants me to play defense, I'll play defense; offense, I'll play offense."

"He said last week he might want you to go both ways."

"I don't know about that. He's great, but playing both ways?" he smiled.

"How's the belly look?"

"Jesus, I've been afraid to look." He lifted his T shirt, and there was a great red welt on the baby-fat hanging over his jock. He looked at it and grimaced.

"What did you think of the game?" a player asked me.

"It looked as if we were going to blow another one," I said.

"You don't know the half of it," he said. "It should have been a tie. I was right out there on the Harraway touchdown pass, and Charley Taylor clipped, bigger'n life. It should have been 20–20."

"Ah well," I said, "they say Chris didn't clip against Dallas last week." "Yeah," he said, "only it doesn't quite even out. If they hadn't called that clip on Chris last week, we'd have beat the Cowboys. And if we'd have beat the Cowboys, we'd have killed these guys today. They could have called two or three clips on Charley, and we'd still have beat them. Hell, they could have had the Dutchman out there in his prime, and we'd have taken them. If we had beat the Cowboys, that is," he added, an admonishing forefinger in the air.

The Dutchman, for his part, was not overly taken with the Redskin effort. Asked in the Falcon dressing room what he thought of the new Redskins, Van Brocklin said, "Same old Lombardi crap, only this time little square-outs instead of Packer sweeps."

Paul Hornung, a man who'd run a few of those Green Bay sweeps in his day, and Max McGee, who'd had occasion to catch a square-out or two in the past, were Lombardi's house guests that weekend. They had been standing around in the clubhouse right after the game, appearing immensely old and strangely out of place in their street clothes.

It was not difficult to imagine Hornung, McGee, and the Lombardis streaking back to Potomac, Maryland, to gather around Lombardi's color TV set to take in the Cowboys-Rams game televised from the West Coast. Dallas, playing without Calvin Hill, Jethro Pugh, and Ralph Neeley lost 24–23. I had to imagine that Hornung and McGee had arched their eyebrows at that score. And perhaps Lombardi told them that he wished they were still on hand, that it was still not too late to make one last drive for the championship.

Certainly, such thoughts crossed my mind as I considered the Rams-Cowboys outcome. It put a different complexion on things; the season had come back to life again. It was easy to say that I should have known better, that I was close enough to the core of the team to have already witnessed its final shudder of defeat against the Cowboys and against the Eagles before that. But this was not the way it worked. The more you knew, the more you hoped, and the easier the imagination revived. In a sense, it was better to be a cold-blooded season ticket holder and judge these forty men merely on their football skills. Only in that way could you avoid the inconsistencies bred by proximity and affection. All of the Redskins seemed big enough, tough enough, fast enough. They all wanted to win, and it always amazed me when they didn't. I had the fatal tendency to ignore their opposition, to forget that the enemy was perhaps even bigger, faster, and tougher and liked to win just as much. The sort of faith that Lombardi drove to inspire also overlooked the opposition. He sought to induce the feeling that the opposition was irrelevant, so long as the Redskins believed in themselves, but there was an inconsistency there, for faith was not infallible. It didn't work every time, not even in Green Bay.

And, of course, the whole sense of the revival of the guest was not illogical, not without its facile sophistry. The "if" factor could hardly be denied. "If" the Redskins got past the Rams next Sunday. And "if" the 49'ers took the Cowboys on Thanksgiving Day. The Rams had won ten in a row, they had to lose one sooner or later, didn't they? The Cowboys had all those injuries, had only two days to prepare for the 49'ers, a rugged team that was long overdue for some wins. And "if" all of this happened, the Redskins would be 6–3–2 and the Cowboys would be 8–3. The Redskins faced the Eagles in their twelfth game of the season, the Saints in their thirteenth—neither real menaces. So it could all come down to that fourteenth game, the season finale, against the Cowboys in the Cotton Bowl on December 21.

On Monday, the press trudged to the Redskins' headquarters to hear a word or two on the Falcons and to hear more, if they could, about the Rams, who were coming to town next Sunday.

"I guess you caught the Rams-Cowboys game on TV," a reporter said, expecting an elaborate Lombardi subterfuge.

Lombardi, whose fondest boast was that he thrust football from his mind after the Sunday game was over, smiled sheepishly. For once, he was going to admit that football had been on his mind after a Sunday game was over. "Yes," he allowed, "I saw part of the Rams game. Just a spectator, you might say."

Were there any problems he could foresee from that brief and casual peep he'd gotten on the TV screen?

"The chief thing to beat is their defensive line. I guess

Gabriel has improved tremendously since I last saw him. I only saw a little of the game, but he seems as strong as a defensive tackle. Even with people draped all over him, he can complete a pass. Hell, I can remember him putting a stiff arm on a guy coming in on a safety blitz. That takes some strength when they're coming at you with that kind of force.

"For us there were some pluses against Atlanta. We've been shuffling the defenses around and we've finally come up with something that looks decent. McLinton was very strong against the run. McKeever was impressive. Sam is ready to play, and Sam gives us a lot of smartness out there, but I guess he won't play next year. Harraway blocked very well for Brown. Harraway can be as good as he wants to. The offensive line gave Sonny good protection, the best he's had this year. The defensive line was heartening. Dennis gave us the best playing we've got out of him this year. He started to move his damn feet at last. Maybe playing offense some helped. And Kammerer had his best game, Kammerer was fine."

It seemed an occasion to have a beer with Kammerer. When we had last talked, after the Browns game, he had been downcast, and I had promised that I would get together with him again when he was feeling better. It had taken a long time.

Football, as Lombardi had said, is a game of clichés, and perhaps America loved football because it made the clichés come true. Certainly, I learned to be moved by clichés during my season with the Redskins. Appropriately, Kammerer began with a cliché that was strangely moving.

"My high-school coach—Giomi—used to knock the air with his fist and say, 'Can you hear it, can you hear it?' He wouldn't make any noise, just knock the air and say, 'Can you hear it?' And then he'd say, 'That's opportunity knocking, and you can't hear it, but if you do hear it, you'd better be ready.'

"That's the way it was for me, waiting on the bench. I kept myself ready. It hurt, but I tried to maintain the readiness."

"What was it like to be benched in Frisco?" I asked.

"That was the worst of personal situations. Humiliating. No other word for it. There were some ninety-four of my friends, family, neighbors, people I went to school with up there in the

stands. They'd come out to see me play, and then to be
yanked! To be sat down on the bench after one quarter and
not to get back in! I don't know what it was like for those
people. I didn't ask. They wouldn't have told me. For me, it
was just pacing up and down the side lines and watching the
play in the right defensive end slot. And watching it, I just
knew with objective academic looking that very soon I would
be called back. But I wasn't. I never got back in.

"Then came the Cardinals, and I sat out that game entirely.
Then the Giants, and I didn't get in at all. Then came Pittsburgh, and I have a very long history against the Steelers'
tackle John Brown. In fact, my first game as defensive end was
against Brown. I've always had good days against Brown.
Christ, Bill Austin had to know that. Mike McCormack knew
it, and I knew for all the world that I'd play in Pittsburgh.

It wasn't a question of getting in. It was a question of going
the whole damn game against Brown, of beating him dead.
Even though the evidence at practice that week was going
against me, I knew, just knew, I'd get the call in Pittsburgh.
And I didn't get called. I didn't know where to turn. Then
Clark Miller comes in; that puts me another notch down the
ladder. Now, there were four active defensive ends, and no
NFL team keeps that many active defensive ends.

"Then came the Colts, and Miller started there. I would see
a trap play made and I'd feel I could have done better. I'd see
a sweep coming from where I was standing on the side lines,
and I'd know in my heart that I would have been there to stop
it, either forcing the play deeper so someone else could make
the tackle or stripping down the blockers and making the
tackle myself. You know you'd be there. Just know it. Yet
somebody's not allowing you to be there. My chin strap must
have been buckled the whole game. I knew they'd have to call
on me, the way the Colts were turning the corners on us. Just
knew it.

"And there was one point in the game Lombardi came over
to Svare and McCormack and asked about somebody, and I
was back, sitting on the bench, and I couldn't hear the conversation. I just knew they were talking about the defensive right

end and when I heard Lombardi raise his voice and say, 'Get him the hell out of there,' I sprinted up behind the coaches ready to go, and they turned around and called for Bob Wade. They weren't even talking about the defensive end. They were talking about the safety. Somebody had hit Brig in the head, and he was woozy, not recognizing things quickly enough. I was on the field, I was past them, when I heard them say 'Wade.' And I stopped and came back."

"Did they say anything?"

"No. No, they didn't say anything. But Lombardi does things for a reason. He is *the* Coach in football, and I knew that he had me out because he didn't think I was able to do the job.

"The truth was, I guess, that I wasn't playing their defenses the way they wanted me to. It's a new defense they've brought here, and there are basic changes expected of you. What I was trying to do was compromise, to perform their defenses and still be me. You would think at thirty-two I would know better, but I didn't.

"I am no Deacon Jones. The great skills are not there. But I've always been an effort player; I have desire and I'm a sixty-minute football player. A Lombardi-style player, I thought. But I wasn't sticking to the defenses.

"So finally I went to Svare and asked him where I stood as a football player on this club. You see, I knew the job wasn't getting done. Svare knew it. Everybody knew it. Our line was not producing.

"The name of the game is the defensive line. The job is to secure the run so you know, and they know, and the whole world knows that they're going to have to pass on third and long yardage. But what was happening to us was we were giving them the run, and they were lining up against us second and five, second and four, when they can do any damn thing they want.

"Svare said he thought I was good for the club; he said he recognized my desire, but still, he had other ballplayers to think about, that he couldn't have a change for change's sake. That I'd had my chance and I hadn't done what was required.

He couldn't just put me in the ballgame until someone proved that he couldn't do the job required of him. Well, that was fair. I couldn't deny it was fair. And I waited, just like Giomi always said.

"And finally that chance came, late in the Eagles game. And it came in our home city, and there were 50,000 and some odd people out there, and when I went out on the field some of those people expressed their feelings. Yes, they cheered. Well, it filled my gas tank, that's what it did. And I tell you, I may have even overplayed those defenses somewhat. I just knew I had to show them that I would do what they wanted me to do out there."

A small dapper man with a faintly conniving look passed by our booth and eyed Kammerer curiously for a minute.

"Hey," he said, "are you George Izo?" Izo was a Redskin backup quarterback long departed.

"No," Kammerer said.

"You know who George is, doncha? He's a Redskin."

"Yeah, I know George."

"You know where George is, doncha? George is down in the Bahamas."

"Yeah," Kammerer said, "involved in some high-rise project."

"Right," the man said. "Well, I know George very well."

"You do, huh?" Kammerer said. "I was involved in that deal down there too."

"What is your name?" the man asked, cocking his head.

"Carl Kammerer."

"Oh, for crying out loud. Hey, I've met you. I mean George looks just like you. I mean there's a similarity, let's put it that way. You still with the Redskins, Carl, aren't you? Are you or aren't you?"

"You're close," Kammerer said.

"Aren't you still playing?"

"Yes."

"Christ, I've been out of town. Just got back. Been a little out of touch. What's *your* name?" he asked me, somewhat warily, I thought.

I rose slightly from the chair and held out a hand. "My name," I said, "is George Izo."

That cheered Kammerer, and I felt he merited it. The lineman's lot was not that happy a one. I'd learned that at least.

Thanksgiving was the Cowboys-49'ers game, and after trailing for the whole game, Dallas finally pulled out a 24–24 tie in the closing minutes of play on a leaping Lance Rentzel touchdown catch. The tie meant the Cowboys would have to lose either to the Steelers or to the Colts, while the Redskins beat the Rams, Eagles, and Saints, in order to make the season finale in the Cotton Bowl meaningful.

"We were invited out for Thanksgiving dinner," Ray Schoenke told me on Friday, "and there were the 49'ers ahead in the third period, and the people wanted to turn the set off and eat dinner, and Nancy and I were yelling, 'Go 49'ers,' and the people got mad, so we had to go home and watch the rest of the game. The Cowboys pulled off a tie, I haven't had Thanksgiving dinner yet, and I've got to shut out Merlin Olsen on Sunday. It's been some week."

So now the Rams were coming to town, 10–0, the only undefeated team in the pros.

"What movie do you want to see Saturday night?" Walt Rock asked Vince Promuto.

"I don't know."

"How about John Wayne in *The Undefeated*?"

"Nah," Promuto said, "we're going to see the undefeated on Sunday."

None of his listeners bothered to add, "They won't be on Monday."

Chapter 23

It was a cold, bitter day at RFK Stadium, not Rams weather. The Redskins won the toss and, with the help of three penalties, moved down to the Los Angeles 12-yard line before a third-down pass failed and Knight kicked a 19-yarder to give Washington a 3–0 lead. The Redskin defense was tough, the special teams were tackling, and the Redskin lead held for the first quarter. The Rams mounted a long drive of their own down to the Redskin 13 in the second period, where Gabriel missed a third-down pass. Bruce Gosset kicked a 20-yarder, and the score was tied.

Now the Rams' "fearsome foursome" began to show their heralded stuff. Rick Cash, Roger Brown, and Deacon Jones dumped Jurgensen for an 8-yard loss. Sonny got it back again on a pass to Jerry Smith. Merlin Olsen and Roger Brown nailed Sonny for 8 again, and on fourth and seventeen, Bragg came in to kick. He got off a 46-yarder, and Dave Kopay, together with Bob Wade, one of the few legitimate headhunters on the suicide squad, threw the Ram safety for a 4-yard loss. Tackles by Bosch, Norton, and Owens forced a Rams kick. Then the Rams defense held in turn, and Bragg had to kick. It was not, as advertised, a struggle between Jurgensen and Gabriel, but a standoff between the Rams' great line and the Redskin defense, suddenly mildly fearsome in its own right.

Didion's snap was wide to Bragg's right, he reached out for the ball, brought it back in, took his two steps, and got the kick off, right into the hands of Willie Ellison. The ball squibbed around the Redskin backfield, Ellison recovered, was hit, fumbled, and Dave Kopay fell on the ball. It was ruled that Ellison had never had possession, so the ball reverted to the Rams, first and ten on the Washington 22. Gabriel took it in from there three plays later on a 1-yard pass to Bob Klein.

Now it was Rams 10, Redskins 3. With a little more than two minutes left in the half, Jurgensen got the Redskins a first and ten on the Los Angeles 12. Finally, with one second left, Knight's field goal was good, and the Redskins went to the dressing room down by four points.

Both defenses held firm for most of the third quarter, the Redskins giving up two first downs, and the Rams one. Then, with five minutes remaining in the quarter, the Rams began to move on the ground, punching from their own 37 down to the Redskin 3 as the quarter ended. Gabriel hit tight end Billy Truax to go ahead 17–6 four seconds into the fourth period.

The Redskins came back with a 67-yard touchdown drive of their own, and with nine and a half minutes left to play, they trailed by four again, 17–13. Knight's kickoff was carried out to the Ram 23. Marlin McKeever stopped Ram rookie Larry Smith at the line of scrimmage. It was second and ten, and Tommy Mason carried for no gain, but the Redskins were offsides, making it second and five. Mason carried again for the first down.

The defense held on the next series, stopping a Gabriel rollout option a yard short of the first down. Pat Studstill got off a 50-yard punt that was downed at the Redskin 6. Harraway reeled off 9 quick yards, but the play was called back on a holding penalty. Jurgensen, working from his own 4, found Bob Long for 14 yards and the first down. There was a little more than five minutes left, hopefully enough time to mount one last drive and to eat a good slice of the clock in the process. Two plays later, a Jurgensen pass for Charley Taylor was intercepted by Jim Nettles. The Rams went to work on the Washington 29, and the Redskin line snapped at last. Having played almost a whole game at a standard not far below the powerful Rams, the Redskins came apart at last. Los Angeles drove for a touchdown in three carries from scrimmage.

So it was 24–13. Now the Redskins got off a long drive, but it came one series too late, a welcome but elegiac sight. It took

Washington six plays to cover 78 yards. Larry Brown led off with a 24-yard run, and then Jurgensen fired five straight completions to put the ball on the Ram 11-yard line. Jurgensen hit Taylor for a touchdown, but Taylor was ruled to have been in motion, and the play was called back. Four more passes failed, and the game ended, the last drive a scale model of the Redskins' afternoon: close, but not close enough.

The Cowboys' tie in San Francisco on Thanksgiving Day had a certain backdoor flavor that could not be crowed over. The Redskin loss to the Rams had an air of gallant doggedness that could not be belittled. It seemed a graceful moment to come to terms with second place, that spot in the athletic hierarchy that Lombardi had once called "meaningless."

In the locker room I overheard a player trying to line up a ride home on December 22. He spoke not with a furtive "Pssst," but openly, without apology. Who could blame him? It was over. Even Lombardi in his cryptic way was beyond pretense.

"What were your impressions?" he was asked.

"I am not without impressions."

"Well?"

"Well, they overpowered us defensively. I'm not pleased with not winning, but I'm pleased with the progress we've made. This was our best defensive effort. They've got a hell of a defensive ball club, tremendous pressure on Jurgensen. How many times did they get him?"

"Six," someone noted.

"On top of that, Sonny told me he had a lot of people open, but two or three times they had so much heat on him he couldn't see to find them. It would have been nice to have that last score. I'm kind of proud of those special teams."

At that point he leaned over and delivered a tremendously hearty slap on the knee to a reporter who'd been writing critically of the Redskin special units. The force, the startling suddenness of the blow almost knocked the man off the desk top where he was perched. Lombardi chuckled to himself, for what reason it was hard to know. Certainly, the reporter didn't know. He wore a starchy, affable sort of look, not quite certain if he were being complimented or attacked. As far as Lombardi's dealings with the press went, it was always wise to give full weight to both possibilities.

"Of course, you've beaten the Rams before," someone mused.

"Yes," Lombardi replied, "I've beaten the Rams before—but under different circumstances." It was clear from the wistful sound of his voice what those circumstances had been. For Lombardi to conjure up the memories of the Packer days of glory in the company of a roomful of writers who had come to deal with the here-and-now was unmistakable evidence that he conceded the present and the short-term future—perhaps, in an irrepressible burst of frankness, even the long-term future. He said, "My Green Bay team in 1959 was a great deal younger than this team. Kramer, Thurston, Gregg, Hornung, and we traded for some good young ones: Willie Davis and Jordan, and then we got a player from Washington, too. I forget his name."

"Chuck Mercein," the reporter with the throbbing knee sang out in jest. Lombardi laughed. "And we had Max McGee, who wasn't young, but he played six or seven years for us anyway. I would have liked to have come up with a winner here. I'd still like to come up with a winning season."

Later, after the season was over, Lombardi told me, "After the Rams game, we were one game above .500, three games left, close to having a winning season. And I think that, really, was the first time I didn't have much selflessness. I had never had a losing season, never coached a team that lost over a regular schedule. And suddenly, keeping that record intact became very important to me. I don't really think it was important at the beginning of the season. It wasn't even important in the middle when we were winning. Not even in the middle, when we started losing. But at the end, yes. Those last three games, yes. They were important to me. Personally. And I've never felt quite that way about games, that it was a personal matter. That those games counted to keeping Vince Lombardi's string intact. I don't say I'm proud of feeling that way. But that's the way I felt."

I had sensed something of that confession on the practice field during the last three weeks. The team had too. Some wanted to pull it off for Lombardi. Some wanted to pull it off because only then would their lives, their off-season, their thoughts of 1970 in Carlisle be endurable. Most of them, perhaps all, wanted to pull it off because in the end losing was a damn sight less pleasant than winning.

Yet, wanting a winning season, as Lombardi did, meant that the pressure had started all over again, at a time when men were lining up those rides home for December 22. Still it was a different sort of pressure, the focus of which was outside the players and resided in the unquenchable ego of Vince Lombardi. When you still had a chance to make a run for the championship, you could motivate men with Super Bowl loot, NFL championship rings, lofty sentiments on the glory of being number one. But pressure to finish number two, to finish at best 8–4–2? What did that mean?

"This is different pressure," a player told me "Before it was pressure on the team, pressure to play for all the marbles as a team. This is pressure on people. There aren't any marbles left. Dallas has picked them up. What he's saying now is the team didn't make it. So now you're going to make it these last three games, or I'll know the people who didn't. The fear is here now in a different way. The element of fear is not being cut this year, but not being back next year. That's why the fear is so personal, you see."

There were not many Redskins who could be certain of a job on the basis of past credentials. One of the few was Len Hauss, a six-year veteran out of the University of Georgia who was considered one of the league's three or four fine centers. So far Hauss, a courteous man with a quiet manner and a Deep-South voice, had not had an outstanding season. Partly it was because his knees were bothering him and because he had a pinched nerve in his neck that was atrophying one of his arms. Partly it was because the Lombardi system called for the line to set back deeper for blocks, making it more difficult for him to get around his linemen when he pulled outside.

"Learning the Lombardi system has been tough for me," he

told me. "It's been tough for everyone. It incorporates some very basic changes in blocking attitudes. And you look at our line. Vinnie is in his tenth year. Schoenke and me in our sixth. Rock in his seventh. "Snowden" in his fifth. It's not easy to change the habits of all those years. We've had some uncertainty about what we're doing. It comes down to doubt. And if you line up to start a play with even a little bit of doubt in your mind, you're in trouble. Not doubt about who to block, but how to execute it. Who to block you can find out easy enough. But how is where the habits come in.

"Plenty of times I'll come up to the ball and think, did Sonny say rollout or bootleg? If he said rollout, you block one way and bootleg, it's the other. And if I can't remember, I just turn to Vinnie next to me and I'll say, 'Vinnie, am I coming or going?' I mean, sometimes you can almost get to the point of lining up and saying out loud, 'Okay, I got him,' and point at someone across the way. So the guy knows you got him. The defensive tackle is lined up right over Vinnie, so he knows that either Vinnie'll block him or I'll block him. Possibly Snowden. The defensive tackle knows that. If I say to Vinnie, 'Are you pulling?' and he says 'Yeah,' then the guy knows it's not Vinnie, so it's probably me.

"I mean, deception is fine, but a guy isn't necessarily going to beat me or stop the play because he knows I'm going to be coming at him. And, of course, we'll line up and pass the wrong information sometimes to keep the defense honest. Like in the Cowboy game, for example, we came up with a third and short yardage, and the last time we were in that situation we ran a straight running play up the middle. So Sonny called a pass this time, and I got over the ball and whisper, 'Wedge, wedge.' And Vinnie says, 'Wedge here,' and I point my helmet and say, 'You got him.' So Lilly is thinking, 'They're coming right up the middle at me again, eh?' I can't remember what Lilly did that play, but he didn't dump Sonny, because he only got Sonny one time all day, the time Vinnie dislocated his shoulder."

"How about the pressure for these last few games?" I asked.

"We've got to have a winning season. That, at least, we've

got to have. To play for him is tough. To play for him and lose could be unbearable. It could be more than a man could take. Personally, I'm kind of sensitive, too sensitive maybe, and this year has been hard, hard emotionally for me. A friend of mine —well, last week Lombardi was screaming at him, and I felt tight for the guy, for the agony he was going through, and while Lombardi was screaming this guy poked the player next to him and said in a calm voice, 'Hey, hand me that ash tray, would you?' And there is Lombardi yelling at him, and it's like this guy has a shell around him, an invisible shield that's keeping all this stuff off him. I couldn't believe it. If it's me he's yelling at, I've got both hands on the seat and my butt is scrunched up so tight I want to explode. No, to be frank, I'm not sure I've got the innards to face Carlisle again if we have a losing season."

"I haven't seen anyone very happy right here and now, never mind Carlisle," I said.

"Being happy? That's a product of winning. When you're losing you can't kid around much. Say a guy goes out for a pass and gets hit in the back of the helmet with it. This would be funny if you're 8–0, but not if you're 0–8. It's nothing to laugh at then. In fact, it's probably why you're 0–8 in the first place. So if you're not winning you suppress jokes and highjinks. You keep it to yourself. There's got to be a butt for a joke, and when you're not winning everyone is too vulnerable to be a butt. You can't make light with a guy when you know he may be cut or benched."

"Do you have any doubts about yourself? About the nature of the game?"

"Doubts? They're always there, but you don't think about them until someone brings them up. I play the game because I enjoy it. Money, yes, and the recognition too. Why does anybody play? Number one, to prove to myself that I can do it. Number two, to prove to the guy next door that I can do it. Number three, because I enjoy it. Number four, for the money. Yet, I've learned some things from the game I'm grateful for. It's funny, here I am engaged in the most violent profession there is, but I've learned from football to be a more peaceful, tolerant sort of person, I think. I come from Jesup, Georgia. And I hear some people back home talk about hippies, and they want to beat them up. I would have too at one time. Now, I don't want to beat anybody up.

"When I came to the Redskins out of the University of Georgia, I wouldn't sit at a table with colored guys in camp. I had never sat with a colored person before. This didn't bother anybody but me, and I was pretty quick to learn that avoiding the colored players was only going to make life tough on me. Hell, they didn't care if I avoided them. So the next thing, you're sitting with them and suddenly you're finding out all kinds of things you never got a chance to find out in Jesup. The people I run into back home can't understand my feelings any more on racial things. Those people have never known, or even been around a Bob Mitchell, Jim Snowden, Rickie Harris. These are fine people, just regular guys, and if it hadn't been for pro ball, I'd have never known that. You don't learn it in Jesup."

Saturday morning, December 6, Richard Nixon flew off to Fayetteville, Arkansas, to award a plaque to the winner of the Texas-Arkansas game, a team to be declared number one in the nation by executive fiat. The same morning, the Redskins shoved off to Philadelphia by Metroliner to play the Eagles. If they won, Washington would clinch second place in the Capitol Division. Lombardi had once called the NFL's "Runner-Up Bowl" a "hinky-dinky game for hinky-dinky teams." How infinitely more insignificant a game that could merely wrap up a second-place finish in a four-team division, how inglorious to be accompanying Lombardi—the advocate, the architect of total victory—to a game of such piddling, if not demeaning, stakes. How improbable that a football game played in Fayetteville, Arkansas, would attract presidential preference on a weekend when a Lombardi team was competing even closer to home.

After the team disported itself on the astroturf for an hour or so, once again selecting their own shoes for the next day's game, we bused out to the hotel, where Coach could while away the afternoon watching the Arkansas-Texas game.

I sat down next to Lombardi in the front of the bus and asked how he figured the team had reacted to pressure until now.

"There's pressure and there's real pressure. The first kind is routine, the kind you face all the time in football, the play-by-play pressure. On that score we've picked up tremendously. At the beginning of the year, every time they faced a little pressure they snapped. Now they've learned to react a little better to ordinary pressure. But they're still no great shakes at reacting to the real tough kind of pressure, the kind that comes inside the two 20-yard lines, the kind that comes late in the game when you're a little behind or a little ahead, when you need to keep that ball and drive, when you need to get it back and hold it. Last week, against the Rams, for example, we made the crucial mistake. An interception late in the game when we need to drive for a touchdown to win. That's bad enough in a pressure situation, but then we let them score on the very next series, let them run the ball in for a touchdown that puts the game away. I have to say they had two pressure situations in succession, and they didn't react to them. Then, later in the game, Charley Taylor catches a touchdown pass, and it's called back on a penalty. The closer you get to the goal-line, the more crucial the situation, the more perfect you should be as far as errors are concerned. That's pressure."

"How about the element of fear? Is it a bad thing for a ballplayer?"

"I'd have to say there is quite a bit of fear of making mistakes in this club. In the end it's bad, if you keep on making them. Not so bad if the fear keeps you from making them. Hell, I can't just sit around and see an error being made and not say anything about it. I like to think I've had some experience in this business, and you don't win when you're making a lot of errors. Nobody wants to be told they're making errors, not the way I tell them," he added, with the shade of a grim smile. "But they got to be told and told until they get to the point where they don't make them any more."

"How about the fear of losing your job? From the player's standpoint, I mean."

"I suppose there are certain players afraid of their future. The Packers over the course of time came to see that my wrath was not as dangerous as it sounded."

"Do you think the Redskins have got that message yet?" I asked innocently, armed with almost a consensus to the contrary.

"Well, I hope they're beginning to realize that my anger is easily forgotten."

"By you?"

"I hope by them too. And I got to say this. What I criticize people for is mental errors, not physical ones. At Green Bay the mental errors disappeared quicker. And, in fairness, I got to say that the game wasn't as complex ten years ago as it is today. The defenses are more complex now. Ten years ago, you were able to innovate more than you can now. The coaching has gotten a lot stronger around the league. Coaches are more dedicated now than they were ten years ago, certainly much more than they were twenty years ago. It's a profession today. In the old days it was a part-time job for people who wanted to work outside."

"Tell me," I said, "is one of the reasons you like football that it's one of the last jobs around where, if you're lucky enough, you can run the whole show? Have absolute control over a corporation?"

"You mean a one-man operation sort of thing. Yeah, I like that. That's one of the things that makes it interesting. It's a five-million-dollar business, and there are very few positions that big where one man has so much say-so. Can put his own stamp on things. I like that."

"Have you made any serious mistakes you'd change if you could?" I asked.

"If I had it to do all over again, I might have done some things differently than I did. I've made some errors in placement of personnel that I'd correct. But I guess you're talking about bigger mistakes than that. It's always hard to look back and see your major mistakes. Especially when the season isn't over yet. But I guess if there's anything I'm a little leery about, it's that I'm inclined to give them too much, too quick. I may go at it too strong. But that's my way."

"How about all the Green Bay people you've brought in?"

"I picked up the Green Bay people," he said with some asperity, "because we had nobody good in those positions. This club was not rich in talent when I came. I'd say we've got less of it than any team in the league. I'm not just saying that. Take a look at them. They're fine people as people, but in a football sense they're cast-offs. Everybody. I thought getting the Green Bay people would have a multiplier effect. They know my system already."

"How about cutting Dave Crossan in the middle of the season? That shook a lot of people," I said, as offhandedly as possible. It was a question that contained much of my own ambivalence, my admiration for Lombardi's fearlessness, energy, and solitary will poised against the ruthless, often unpardonable price it all exacted from a team I felt fond of. The Redskins might indeed be cast-offs, bargain-basement rejects, but they were good men. Yet, at the same time, I knew that none of the seeming ruthlessness of winning came easy to Lombardi. If there was a thin man trying to get out of every fat man, there was a shy, insecure, accommodating sort of man trying to be submerged in Lombardi. Perhaps only in football could he suppress these characteristics, could he cut Crossan and not cringe at the violation of part of his own nature. And given Lombardi's nature: his ambition, his discipline, his fear of failure, his terrifying will, perhaps he could only operate successfully in a profession where the code was harshness, where winning was the end that justified, even exalted, the means. With him the mastery of his own character had to be total, the rules he obeyed had to be absolute; otherwise the man he was trying to submerge would get loose. And he feared that, feared it as only a man who had devoted the better part of his life to overcoming his doubts and weaknesses could.

Confronted with Crossan, whose departure was indefensible in human terms, Lombardi fell back on the football ethic that made it all simpler to cope with. He said, "Any time I can get an improvement, I'm going to do it." He held his thumb and forefinger to the light, a crack of space between them. "Even this much," he said, peering through the tiny chink of light.

We loaded back up on the team buses the following morning for the drive to Franklin Field. A kempt young man with a trimmed Assyrian spade beard passed by the window. "Look at that guy," Sam Huff said, implying that the only explanation possible for such a growth was a serious "mental error."

"Sam," I said, "they'll be playing ball in beards in five years' time."

"Not for Lombardi, they won't," Sam said.

"I don't know," Harland Svare said. "Maybe it'll be crew-cuts football coaches won't want in five years, Sam. The younger generation is always going to the dogs. Forget the beards. The important thing is can they play football?" I gained the impression that Svare at least would be willing to suit up the House of David in 1970 if they looked as if they could go to the Super Bowl. All things considered, I imagined Lombardi and even Sam Huff would share a certain exasperated toleration for Jovian beards if they came on real, honest-to-goodness linemen.

As the bus wended its way through Philadelphia, Sonny Jurgensen, in the seat behind me, kept up a steady soliloquy on the sights at the side of the road, recalling the monuments and parks of the city he had once inhabited. He had begun his career in Philadelphia some twelve years earlier, a fourth-round draft choice, who had quarterbacked a running Duke team, where the opportunity to hum that football had not been great and his talents not yet obvious.

He had once told me, "I only threw the ball fifty-three times my senior year. We played strictly a tight T formation —both ends tight and three backs—and you can't pass very well from that formation, because it kind of cuts down the zones that everybody has to play. So we weren't a throwing team. But I had a God-given ability to throw that football. When I got in the pros I knew it, and they knew it.

"I played four games in '57, my rookie season, and we won three of them. I think I threw three touchdown passes against the Redskins in one of them. I think they intercepted a few balls on me, too. Quite a few.

"Then in '58, they brought Van Brocklin in. Playing behind Van Brocklin was an experience. It wasn't any secret to me that I wasn't ready when I saw Van Brocklin pass. Van Brocklin was an artist, and he could teach—a great teacher. I owe him a lot. Then came the Eagle world championship in '60, and Van Brocklin working with me more and more, teaching me, because there was a possibility he was going to take over as coach and general manager. But he went to the Vikings instead, and it was my turn to throw in '61."

It was indeed. Jurgensen threw 235 completions out of 416 attempts for thirty-two touchdowns, all Eagle records. His 3723 yards in the air broke the NFL record. In the four years he was with the Eagles, he never had a better season, in part because of injuries. But even so, he was that rare vision, an electrifying athlete who could dominate a game on a given day. Three times with the Eagles he passed for more than 400 yards in a game. Yet, he was—if you believed the stories—a trifle on the zesty side for Philadelphia. The fact that the Eagles had losing seasons in 1962, 1963, and 1964 did not help matters.

The Philadelphia fans were legendary for their boorishness, the sheer vituperation they could lavish on a home-town jock who had fallen in disfavor. Moreover, the men they always chose to attack were the stars—like Richie Allen and Sonny Jurgensen.

So when Joe Kuharich took over the Eagles before the 1965 season, he dealt Jurgensen to the Redskins for Norman Snead, a quarterback whose life style was said to be on the bland side.

Jurgensen had not been notably happy those last few years in Philadelphia; he was a man who understandably resented being the fall-guy for churls and snobs. As the bus crept along through slums and spacious parks, he identified the sights in the tone of a man revisiting some distasteful, but still vivid, boyhood haunt. And in the best sense, Jurgensen had a sort of boyish, happy-go-lucky attitude. It was this, at bottom, that gave him the imperturbable confidence to drop back and hum that football into a crowd. It just never occurred to him to doubt that he could do it. At thirty-five he still had the supreme artistry of youth. He was a grown man who excelled at a boy's sport, and all the grown men in the nation, from the President on down, envied him for it.

We passed through a decrepit blue-color neighborhood, the massive wooden tenement houses gray with encrusted grime. "Hey, look over there," Jurgensen sang out in a voice loud enough for the whole bus. On the corner was a dingy neighborhood tavern, a few corroded beer signs tacked to its facade. The lettering on the window plate said "SPIRO'S PLACE."

"So this is where it all began," Jurgensen cried with delight. The bus ploughed ahead into a Negro ghetto. There were a few men idling the morning away on a street corner; one of them wore a jacket and a pair of white silk football pants.

"Hey, they've got a game, too," Sonny said.

The man in the football pants peered at our bus with a singular absence of curiosity.

"That's where you'll be next year at this time, Sam," Sonny said. "Just standing on the corner in a pair of old football pants trying to get a game of pick-up."

Huff looked dolefully out the window.

"Better pick your corner," Sonny said, "or I'll get there ahead of you."

Chapter 24

The sky was overcast, and as gametime drew nearer, the gray clouds pressed closer to the emerald stubble of astroturf on Franklin Field, giving the fiber grass an almost supernatural glow. Some fans dangled a stuffed effigy of Jurgensen from the upper-deck seats. There were "Vince Who?" signs in evidence and a lusty round of boos for Coach when he took the field. So far, a fairly mild crowd, by Philadelphia standards.

The wind had a cold snap to it, just a degree or so above freezing, and by gametime the drizzle had turned to heavy rain. The Eagles kicked off to Rickie Harris at his own 5, and he returned the ball 54 yards to the Eagles' 41. The Redskin first-down bid and a Knight field goal failed, and the Eagles took over on their own 20. On third and fourteen, Norman Snead hit Ben Hawkins for 51 yards down to the Washington 13. Tom Woodeshick knifed up the middle to the Redskin 2, and rookie Leroy Keyes carried it in from there. Sam Baker put the point after right through the uprights, the ball soaring up toward the dummy hanging from the stands with the Number 9 on his jersey.

The Redskins started working from their 37. Larry Brown broke a beautiful 37-yard run around left end to the Eagle 26. A few plays later, Jurgensen passed 12 yards to Taylor in the end zone, and the Redskins tied the game 7–7.

The rain was still coming down, and by the end of the first period the footing on the field appeared a little slick. Early in the second period, the rain had turned to sleet, and a pale white crust began to form on the astroturf. The Redskin defensive backs, playing the zone, were having trouble maneuvering on the frozen surface, and Snead moved the Eagles down for a touchdown early in the second quarter to go ahead 14–7. Late in the quarter, Jurgensen was nailed in the Redskin end zone, and the Eagles went up 16–7.

The Washington defense held, and with a little less than four minutes left in the half, the Redskins took over on their own 20. Jurgensen threw to Taylor for 17 yards, then Larry Brown turned right end for 53 yards down to the Eagle 10. Charley Harraway carried the ball to the Eagle 5, and the two-minute warning sounded. Jurgensen missed Taylor in the end zone and then threw to Jerry Smith—also incomplete.

But there was some question in Jurgensen's mind whether Philadelphia safety Nate Ramsey had interfered. Jurgensen marched over to have a word with the official.

"Look here," he was told, "it doesn't look good you running up here and grabbing me. This game is being televised."

"I'm not doing it because I like you," Sonny explained. "They were hugging the hell out of Smith. That's not going to look good on the TV playback, either."

The official proved an unrelenting fellow, and Knight had to come in and kick a field goal, narrowing the Eagle margin to six.

After Knight put the ball through the uprights, in the general direction of the dangling effigy, Jurgensen went over for another pow-wow with the official. This was the moment the Philadelphia fans had been waiting for, a chance to let the Old Redhead know what they thought of him. The catcalls sounded, and Jurgensen responded with a gesture of his own, —a raising of the arm, a clenched fist, a tentative gesture of Redhead Power. That brought down the house, the jeers resounding, the choicest oaths unloosened. With sixteen seconds still left to go in the half, Jurgensen dropped back to pass, slipped on the now hopelessly icy astroturf, and when the tacklers unpiled he did not get up. Finally he rose to one knee, stood up, and limped from the field.

Frank Ryan appeared mesmerized on the side lines. The call had finally come, midway through the twelfth game of the season, and he stood frozen in disbelief. A thirty-three-year-old former All-Pro quarterback with a Ph.D. in mathematics, a man with poise and maturity, he suddenly began looking to all sides for his helmet. To all appearances he might have been George Plimpton, suited up for the hell of it, just lolling on the bench jotting down notes for a book. Suddenly he was called on to go in, second and ten at the Eagle 40, twelve seconds showing in the half, the Redskins down six points.

The year had not been an enjoyable or a satisfying one for Ryan. He had come to Washington with the understanding that Jurgensen was the number-one quarterback, that his job would be to spell Sonny when he got tuckered out, to come in late in the game and lead the Redskins when the contest was out of reach either way. There was a sense of utility, of satisfaction in such a role. But it had not worked out that way. Jurgensen had hung in there all season, tuckered or not. Now Ryan was in for his first play of the year, and I longed to see him rear back and zip one to Charley Taylor on one of those beautifully run, breathtakingly timed post patterns. Instead, the Eagles put on a hard rush, Ryan dodged a tackler, and hit Charley Harraway for a 4-yard gain. Ryan called time out, and Knight and a limping Jurgensen came on for the field goal, good from 43 yards out. The Redskins trailed 16–13 as the half-time gun went off.

Down in the dressing room at half-time, the Redskins changed shoes, most of them fishing around in duffel bags for their regular cleats. Snead had thrown for 153 yards in the half, and under some prodding from the secondary, Svare agreed to drop the zone defense and let his backs revert to man-to-man coverage.

Both defenses turned stingy in the third period, allowing no first downs, turning the ball back to the offense four times in a little more than six minutes. With eight minutes showing in the quarter, the Eagles had a second and seven on their own 13. Defensive tackle Jim Norton broke through and dropped Snead on his own 8, then on third and fifteen Snead dropped back into the end zone to throw. Carl Kammerer blew in and racked Snead back in the end zone turf, jarring loose the football. John Hoffman fell on it for the touchdown, and with Knight's kick good, the Redskins went ahead 20–16.

The Eagles added a field goal to draw within a point. A puny kickoff and a face-masking penalty gave Jurgensen the ball at the Redskin 42, and he drove in for the touchdown in ten plays, the last one an extraordinary catch by Jerry Smith in the corner of the end zone.

The Eagles added another field goal midway through the fourth period to draw within five points, at 27–22. But Jurgensen came back to put the game out of reach with a 70-yard touchdown drive, hitting Charley Taylor repeatedly on the Eagles' side lines. The pride of Grand Prairie, Texas, was maneuvering on the ice like Nanook of the North.

The Redskins now led by 12 points, 34–22, with only two minutes left in the game. Four straight Snead completions and a Redskin penalty brought the ball from the Eagle 11 to the Redskin 17, first and ten. Snead missed Ben Hawkins, was dumped for a 7-yard loss by Kammerer, and missed two more passes. The Redskins took over with less than a minute to go. Charley Harraway fumbled the first play from scrimmage. The Eagles recovered, and Snead threw for a touchdown with twenty-five seconds still left to play. Washington held on to the kickoff, and with the score 34–29, Jurgensen ran out the clock with a keeper.

The win guaranteed the Redskins second place in the Capitol Division; third place in the Eastern Conference, good for almost $1000 a player in also-ran money; and at 6–4–2, assured no worse than a .500 season. From Pittsburgh came word that the Cowboys had wrapped it up, 10–7, over the Steelers.

The sleet had turned back to rain, and I went out onto the field to inspect the astroturf. Frozen granules of snow stuck to each tuft of false grass. I touched one shoe-toe to the surface, like a swimmer testing the water, then stepped onto the field. It was indescribably squishy and slippery. I longed to hear Coach's thoughts on astroturf and walked across the field and the track that bordered it toward the dressing room.

A gamut of fans had formed around the entrance to the two locker rooms, and I wedged myself among them. The fans seemed a respectable cross section of Philadelphia society.

The man standing next to me was in his early thirties, soberly dressed in a tweed topcoat, a junior executive, perhaps.

The Eagles started down the file the police cleared between the fans. The air was suddenly filled with oaths from the fans. "You bums, you dirtballs," the man next to me was yelling, his voice hoarse with rage. I stared at him, his face now red, the veins along his neck swollen. "Woodeshick, you stumble-bum," he bellowed. Tom Woodeshick, who had run for 102 yards, slipped by to the dressing room, glancing anxiously from side to side. The effigy of Jurgensen still swung from the upper deck.

The Franklin Field dressing room was unusually cramped, and the press hemmed in Lombardi.

"How about that astroturf?" someone said.

"Nothing wrong with it. It was fine once we got the right shoes on," Lombardi frowned.

"What'd you think of your team?"

"Spotty. We've got this penchant for making errors; thought we might make one more too many at the end there. But we made it."

"How about that Brown?" someone sang out in tribute to Larry Brown's 136 yards on the ground.

"Brown has a real knack for picking his holes. He's a comer."

"What about that old Number 9?" a Philadelphia writer asked.

"He's a comer too," Lombardi laughed.

"And how about you? What have you done for the Red-skins?"

"Not a God-damned thing," Lombardi roared with delight. In the bus to the train station, Jurgensen asked, "Did you see that Number 9 effigy hanging from the upper deck? My ex-wife was probably up there jiggling the string." Jurgensen grinned from ear to ear, showing no regret to be leaving the City of Brotherly Love. The train trip back to Washington was a bacchanalia of sorts, as cheering as the fusty, dilapidated rolling stock of the Penn Central would allow. The beer flowed on beyond two cans, and there were even a few private flasks in evidence, the contents generously shared around.

"That astroturf was something," a player said.

"Lombardi said there wasn't anything wrong with it," I said. The player stared at me. "Did he really say that?"

"Yep," I said.

He blinked rapidly, shook his head, and wandered off to convey this latest evidence of Lombardi's eccentricity to his teammates. Presently, another player tapped me on the shoulder. "Did he really say the astroturf was all right?" he asked in a marveling tone.

"Yep," I said.

"I'll be damned," the player said. "Anyone asked me, I'd say today set the stuff back twenty years."

I was talking to Pat Fisher, the Redskin cornerback, who was having one of the best years of his nine-year pro career. Fisher, at 5'9", was exceptionally small even for a defensive back, but a bulldog of a player, as tenacious and pugnacious as the lines of his face, with his broken nose and determined jaw.

"I don't know what the word is for the feeling you're supposed to have about your coach. Respect is not quite it. But whatever it is, Lombardi has it. He may have been tough and driving, but it looks like we're going to have a winning season, and he's been himself, he's been the sort of man he says he is. He makes no bones about being all business.

"And there is a paradox there too. I'll have to admit it. If you can be traded to help the team, then bam, you're gone. Yet, you're supposed to have loyalty toward the team and the coach, and you ask, where is the loyalty that's supposed to be flowing back to me?"

"Yes, it is a paradox," I said.

"Right. And it's bothered a lot of people. And how can you expect people to remain stable emotionally under such an arrangement? You can be gone tomorrow, yet you're supposed to have this strong feeling about the Washington Redskins. Well, it's a problem. He's talking about very lofty, noble things, but how do you instill them when the underlying concern is insecurity?

"Yet, I contend that Green Bay didn't win its championships because of that part of Lombardi that shouted, drove, and criticized. The Packers won because of the personality you don't read about, the part you see when he's joking. He can be damn funny. It's peculiar, because his jokes are usually terrible, but he puts so much of himself in them, he's so determined that they're going to be funny, that they are. Maybe that's his real personality. The screaming is all put on, his way of moving people and getting something out of them. You have to get to the point where his yelling doesn't effect you, drive you into ground. But until you know him, the yelling and all is the only way he has to motivate you. Once he gets his team built, you may see the good things in Lombardi, and that'll motivate us, too. But at least he knows we've got to be motivated, got to be led. He knows that, and I've seen coaches who don't."

"How about leadership and motivation coming from the team itself?" I asked.

"Well, it hasn't been there. It wasn't there last year. You see, a team's personality has to come from its leaders. Leadership evolves, you don't assign it. It has to come from the real football players. And we have one player who is so good the leadership must be his. Sonny leads by his performance on the field. He doesn't opt to play the leader's role in the clubhouse. That is Sonny's nature. Say, for example, in the locker room the fellows were riding somebody. There isn't any man on the club except Sonny who could just yell, 'Knock it off,' and it would be done. Sonny could do it in a flash. He commands respect because he's such a great football player. If Lombardi can get us winning, I mean starting off fast, then Sonny could take it from there, giving us leadership from his performance. Winning resolves a lot of problems.

"I think he can win next year with what he has here now. He's molded the team already, taught us three years' worth of football in one.

"Yet you wonder if things will ever be the same for Lombardi, even if we win a championship. You can never really get the past back again. Love, loyalty, the Spartan qualities he talks about are easier to build in Green Bay than here. Green Bay is a Spartan town to begin with. Washington isn't. Apparently, the Packers had a sense of intimacy as a team. Was it because of their environment that brought them together all of the time? Or did the intimacy come first, so that they sought one another out?

"Either way, I don't know if you'll ever find that in Washington. The players are scattered out all over town, we don't socialize together as a group, most of the people don't live here during the off-season. If we have a championship team, it won't be because of player intimacy. We'll just be a championship team. Nothing bigger than that. Sometimes I wonder whether a championship alone will satisfy Lombardi, whether he doesn't need the other things that Green Bay was associated with."

Fisher had an interesting point there. Lombardi could never fully escape his past, those doughty Green Bay years, nor, for that matter, would he ever fully recapture it. Time advanced and circumstances changed too rapidly for it to be otherwise. With the season nearing completion, I sought out a few Packer veterans to see if they could tell whether Lombardi had changed in Washington, if he still seemed to know what he was after, and if he had gotten it.

Chuck Mercein was still languishing on the Redskin cab squad, his hopes for activation focused on 1970. As he put it, "I know if I can do the job he'll be impressed, because he has been impressed before. I'm not saying ecstatic, but impressed." He had a Slavic look with high cheekbones, a gaunt face with a prominent nose and deep-set eyes. He was one of the handful of professional football players from the Ivy League, and, like the majority of those, a Yalie. The Ivy League background no doubt set him aside from his fellows, just as his Packer past made him an outsider on the Redskins.

"You see, in a way Lombardi was Green Bay," Mercein said. "Who else was there? Everyone was obsessed with Lombardi but in the end they got used to him. Here they're not used to him yet. The Redskins ask me all the time, 'Was he this way in Green Bay? Has he always been like this?'

"Like this Saints game. We need it to guarantee a winning season. He's really chewing this week, really on them. And they ask me if I've ever heard him like he is this week. They can't believe that he'd put this much on them this late in the season. Well, from his point of view, this is *the* pressure game. You got to win it. It's like a championship game. And no matter what, he wants people who are used to pressure, because eventually he knows they *will* be playing in a championship game. It takes time to determine whether a guy can play under championship pressure, but if Lombardi has one thing, it's an eye for that quality. Pressure is linked to not making mistakes, particularly in crucial moments. I guess you've heard him say this."

I had to admit I had, that even the words sounded distressingly familiar. Mercein laughed.

"Well, this team doesn't really know Lombardi yet. It just tickles the hell out of me to see somebody smile from ear to ear the way Lombardi does, just like it scares the hell out of me to see somebody get as mad as he does. And I've seen him on the edge of tears through anger, where he can hardly talk, and, well, when you're used to him, you react to him. You react strongly to his emotions. The game can be a pleasure and a misery, but you're involved, you're reacting.

"You see, Lombardi thinks football is all about emotion. Some coaches have gone so much to technique and science that they've taken the personality and fire out of their players. Not Lombardi. And sooner or later he's going to get to these fired-up people here. It's just written that we're going to have a championship here. He refuses to accept defeat, even when he is defeated. I think he really believes that if the game goes on for another five minutes he can win. It makes a difference to play under a guy like that, I'll tell you."

"Has Lombardi changed and can he recapture what he had in Green Bay here?" I asked.

"That's what everyone asks me. Hell, he made a real mental error, a real mistake in judgment in leaving coaching in the first place. I think about two or three weeks into training camp last year he realized it. He was sort of lurking about, peeking around corners, seeing what was happening, and very reserved about it, wouldn't show himself too much. And once the season started, he looked tragic, no other word for it. Just tragic. And when he came to Washington, I understand he told the team at Carlisle, 'The reason I came back is because of you guys.' The players. I think he believes that.

"I came here and I realized, Christ, the man is happy once again. I mean the difference from the way he looked last year, just moping around the front office. I mean, I'd never seen him so happy. I've heard him talking to himself, whispering, 'We're going to have a hell of a team here one of these days.' And the funny part of it is, he's happy and everyone here thinks he's mad. They're just not used to him yet. They think he's going to breeze into practice all smiles on Tuesday after we've won on Sunday. He never lets himself get complacent with a victory. We won three championships in a row in Green Bay. I don't think anybody thought we could do it, but he sure as hell thought so, and he drove us like a demon, and we did."

Mercein had played for just one of those championship teams. In a sense, the mediocrity of his career before Green Bay seemed a symbol of Lombardi's capacity to turn dross to gold, to sense some quality in a man, get that man, and induce a big game from him when the chips were down. He was the essence of the Packer drama.

Bob Long had been with the Packers for all of their three consecutive championships. He had banked the big money, but despite his years with the club he was an obscure figure. He had ridden the bench, a backup receiver who had come in to spell Carroll Dale or Boyd Dowler from time to time. Long was the essence of Packer steadiness, the unsung reserve who came in during a pinch, a man who had the championship money and the rings, but not the fame. He, if anyone, was in a position to judge whether Lombardi had changed in Washington.

I tracked Long down on the Saturday morning before the Saints game at the D. C. Armory, where he was putting in a part of his weekend as a National Guard office orderly.

"I've felt, I guess," he said, "that it was hard for me to belong here because I came from Green Bay. And I'd guess it's fair to say that most of the ex-Packers have not been totally accepted. And I've felt badly about that. Maybe it's been worse for me, because I'm the one who's played for him at Green Bay and who has started here.

"But, I mean, everyone knows that I admire Lombardi, and I get the feeling that some people think of me as a favorite of his. Guys have said little things like 'Why don't you go ask Coach Lombardi for us, Bob?' or 'Why don't you go talk to the Old Man and find out for us?' Or even, 'Do you go to his house for dinner sometimes?' "

"How about Vince Lombardi in Green Bay and Vince Lombardi in Washington?" I asked. "Any differences?"

"He's still the same man. He hasn't changed that much for the team over the course of the year. But the team has changed more for him. They'll relax a little more and come over to him as time goes by. The guys have picked up little things he says, like 'You are really something, you are, Mister.' That's to the good. You need things like that.

"Vince Promuto is the best there is at it. You know, we were talking earlier in the season about there being no Max McGee on this team. I said it would help to have one, but we didn't yet. Well, Vince Promuto may be the Max McGee of this club. He's keeping us loose."

Two days earlier, after Thursday's practice, I remembered Promuto and Walt Rock conspiring in the tunnel outside the locker room, whispering together like excited boys, rolling their eyes and flashing giant grins at some anticipated jape. They finally walked into the clubhouse arm in arm and entered the training room.

Presently, halfback Dave Kopay came slithering out of the training room, great swaths of tape stuck to his sweat togs, binding his arms and legs together. His arms were tied behind his back and held in place by strips of tape that circled his neck. Rock and Promuto sauntered out of the training room, grinning. "You are really something, you are, Kopay," Promuto said, striking a Lombardian pose of jaw-jutting irritation over the supine Kopay. The cry resounded in the locker room, picked up here and there. "You are really something, you are, Mister."

Mike McCormack came into the dressing room and regarded Kopay on the floor red-faced, immobile, and smiling. "Who did this, the defense?" McCormack asked with manifest pride in his front four. "No," someone said, "the offense." McCormack frowned in disappointment and walked on to the coach's dressing room down the hall.

It was the first show of high jinks, of spirited mischief that I had seen in the clubhouse all season long. I thought that was to the good and would help to jolt the team out of private doubts and personal anxieties. But like all schoolboy tricks, it went on too long and was carried too far. Kopay was now panting on the floor, struggling to release himself, obviously reaching the uncomfortable point where a prank was passing into indignity. No one made a move to cut the tape. I thought of Pat Fisher saying that only Sonny could intervene decisively at a moment like this. But Sonny was in the shower. Jim Snowden surreptitiously dropped a tape-cutter in Kopay's fist, so he could saw himself free.

It was an incident meant to break the tension that had almost ended in an inner tension of its own, yet that was natural too. It was a week of tensions. Christmas was less than two weeks away, the team was thinking about going home, and the season was over—except that the schedule called for two more games. They would have to be played, but it was useless to pretend that they had the urgency, the physical exhilaration of the early autumn, when so much was unknown and a championship was still possible.

There was a natural ebb and flow to a football season, and for the Redskin team the tide was going out.

Lombardi was relentless and brutal during the week of the Saints game. Strutting, prancing, disgusted. "You're the same old Redskins," he cried. "Just standing around. What kind of angle of pursuit is that, Dennis? Move your feet in there, McLinton. What's wrong with you damn people?"

Yes, Lombardi wanted this game. The Saints had to be

beaten. After a dismal season's start, they were coming into Washington as winners of three out of their last four ballgames. The Redskins would be facing those big Saint runners with a defense that was still the worst in the league against the run. For their part, the Redskins had Jurgensen still leading the league passers with a 62.7 passing percentage for 2720 yards. Charley Taylor, with his ten catches in Philadelphia, was back in the pass-receiving race in second place with sixty catches. Smith was in sixth place with forty-nine, and Long in eighth with forty-six. That was a predictable, even a habitual Redskin trait. With Jurgensen quarterbacking your team, you expected to lead the league in passing. A more surprising statistic was Larry Brown's 795 yards rushing, good for fifth place in the league. Brown had already broken Charley Taylor's Redskin rookie rushing record of 755 yards, and with two games still to play had a slim chance of going over a thousand yards with two big days.

Brown, a mere eighth-round draft choice, was one of the team's few serendipities. Oddly enough, he had been noticed originally because of his blocking ability, rather than as a runner. His virtue was that he had been drafted low enough to be what was known as a hungry ballplayer, someone who knew from the outset he would have to pull out all the stops to make the team. Brown was a solemn young man, invariably outfitted in a pea-green suit, a little astounded with the year he was having, the sudden showering of fame and attention.

"How did the Redskins get wind of you?" I asked him.

"Beats me," Brown said. "I used to get letters in college, sometimes from Dallas, the Rams, and the Colts, but that's all. Dallas stayed in real close touch. I was really looking forward to playing for Dallas. Why, once they even tracked me down to my uncle's house in Columbus, Ohio. I don't know how they found it, 'cause I live in Pittsburgh, was just visiting in Columbus. I remember the first few days of the college draft last year, I was waiting for the call to come from the Cowboys, and then the phone rings and a voice says, 'Congratulations, man, you just been drafted by the Washington Redskins, and we're looking forward to meeting you and having you in our training camp.'

"I thought, the Redskins? Where the hell did they come in from? So the man hung up, and I started to do some reading and find out about what kind of running backs the Redskins had. Then a few weeks later, a guy at school come up to me and says, 'Man, your head coach is now Vince Lombardi.' I thought, Jesus Christ! Nothing has ever come easy for me. Sure enough, I catch all the hell. I'd read all the articles about Coach Lombardi and I was really scared. I really didn't want to be tested by that man. I figured he sounded too severe for me. I figured Lombardi was a real mean mother."

"Well, was he?"

"Well, he's all work, but he's not as bad as you read about. And being a rookie I was lucky in a way, because I wasn't noticed so much at first; like, I was down on the fifth team and I was able to know a little something by the time I worked my way up to his attention. But by the time I got up to the second team, suddenly, man, every mistake I made seemed like it was noticeable. I was confronted with the Man. This is along about the third or fourth week of camp. He was on my back all the time, and I began to have this resentment of him. 'Larry,' he used to shout, 'you're running in the wrong damn hole, you'd better learn your assignments.' And you know him. He can really yell. And I'd think to myself, 'If he'd just give me time, time, more time. I'm just a damn rookie. And I'd have my head hung down and then suddenly after a while I began to notice he'd be saying, 'Larry, you're a good boy.' Or, 'Keep up the good work, there.'"

"You were still chiefly a blocker then?" I asked.

"Well, I was a halfback, but I was blocking pretty good, too. I guess it was the blocking that caught his eye, 'cause one day I walked into the lunch room, and the rookies were supposed to stand up at their table and introduce themselves and say where they went to college and what their position was and sing their school song. So I stood up and said, 'I'm Larry Brown from Kansas State and I'm a halfback and now I'm going to sing you my school song.' And as I caught my breath to start in singing, comes this voice, 'You ain't no halfback anymore, Brown; you're a fullback now.' And it was Coach

Lombardi and it kind of surprised me, and I didn't sing my song too good. Fullback? Hell, that kind of worried me. I don't go that big. A 195-pound fullback? I'd rather be a halfback, because they carry the ball more. The fullback gets those hard-nosed inside plays and is the key blocker.

"The thing that helped me was that the system was being changed, and the veterans had to change their habits. Me, I didn't have any habits. I just had to learn. I had pretty good quickness with the ball. At first I was a little too eager to run, to hit the holes. And it was mass confusion for me running over blockers and not being able to control my speed. But after a while I was able to get so I could delay a little to read my holes and to make that quick decision and then accelerate."

"How about that thousand-yard club?"

"Wouldn't that be something," he breathed. "A 105 this week and 100 next week, or the other way around. I don't care which. But that would really be something."

After practice the Friday before the Saints game, I was having a beer and a bowl of clam chowder with some of the Redskin linemen. There was a certain pall in the atmosphere. Finally, one of the veterans told me, "Joe got cut this morning." I realized as soon as he spoke that it had been in the cards for several weeks. Rutgens's knee was hurting. He had been openly campaigning for an operation before the end of the season, so that he wouldn't have to return to Washington in January for it. He knew he wasn't helping the team, but had somehow thought that he would either go on injured waivers or be allowed to remain on the bench for the last few games. He had miscalculated the degree to which Lombardi wanted the New Orleans game.

So Rutgens was cut, and Willie Banks was brought up from the move list to take his place on the roster.

The Saints game was the home closer. It would be Bobby Mitchell Day, and I had to think of the irony of Rutgens not even being on the bench, just quietly fading from view the same weekend that Bobby Mitchell was being honored. Rutgens had come to Washington the year before Mitchell. You would have to say that Mitchell was much the greater athlete, had done more extraordinary things. Yet Rutgens had doubtless been at least as popular with the fans, probably more so. With Rutgens, you only remembered his good plays, his flying shirt-tail. He played a less noticeable position. With Mitchell, the fans remembered the great plays, but they also remembered the dropped balls that had always darkened his career.

There were few "Days" dedicated to retiring linemen, it was true. The backs and sometimes the linebackers were the ones who got the gold watches on the platform at midfield with the home-town faithful looking on. But, even so, Rutgens's departure was wrenching. He had not even been allowed to retire, but had been waived through the league, and no one had wanted him. It was a harsh epitaph, even for a lineman.

The players spooned up their soup and decided to go pay a call on Rutgens. Vince Promuto and I were left alone and he said, "You can feel sorry for Joe, but can't feel upset about it. This has happened a thousand times, getting cut.

"You feel bad about it, bad about Joe. It's like somebody in the fraternity house is gone. I know Joe Rutgens. I know his wife, I know his kid. I know how he thinks, and he knows how I think. Yet it's part of the game. I won't complain when it comes to me. It happened to Joe today and it's going to happen to every one of us. It'll happen to me sooner than it happens to Larry Brown."

"Okay," I said, "So Joe can't get the job done. He's got to be cut. You can see that. But how do you square cutting him with this talk of love for one another and loyalty?"

Promuto thought for a while, then he said, "You remember that sermon Martin Luther King gave, it had the phrase "I've been to the Mountain Top" in it? Well, King made the distinction in that sermon between loving and liking. He says God says you have to love everybody, but you don't have to like them. You have to respect people, that's love. You get respect among football players all for each other, that's love. That's what Lombardi's after. That don't mean you can't dislike parts of what he does. As you play and play with the same people that respect grows. That's the love he's talking about. And the more you play with them, the better chance you got to even like them. I figure if you play with Lombardi long enough love don't sound so fruity. It's not like you're talking about forty fags. You're talking about forty ballplayers who have learned that respect for each other. The kind of love Dr. King was talking about."

"Not badly put," I agreed.

"You see," he grinned, "you're going to end up a disciple of the Old Man yourself if you don't watch out."

I laughed. "I'll watch my step," I said. "He's really been something this week, hasn't he?" I added, falling into the cadences of Promuto's favorite Lombardi imitation.

Promuto gave a short whistle. "It's like we're all rookies the first week of camp all over again. He feels now that we can't get any higher in our standings. We can't overtake Dallas, we can't lose out to Philly. So now he feels he has to put the pressure on to keep us up, to give us a reason to play. Those films on Tuesday of the Eagles game. He was really ferocious. The team was stunned. It was like he was in training camp again. He'd just yell and then try and find a reason for it afterwards. I can see it. I've always said this: the American type of society is basically lazy. When you get hurt, you want to sit down and rest. When you get hurt a second time, you want to lay down. And when it happens a third time, you want to call an ambulance. Well, we been hurt physically, mentally, every kind of way. It's getting to the end of the season and we want to be lazy. The thing he sees is that to play football the way it should be played is a contradiction to all that. That's why he has charisma," Promuto said, relishing the sound of that last word as it rolled off his tongue, giving the dark secret smile of one Mafioso contemplating another.

Chapter 25

"Grass is like people; it got to have room to breathe," Joe Mooney, the head grounds-keeper at RFK Stadium, said. "You hit people in the shoulder all day, they're going to be bruised. Same with grass," he said, casting his eyes balefully over the stadium turf. There was not much of it left. The Senators' infield near the western goalposts was now frozen mud. Cleat marks were pocked in the ground everywhere, and clumps of turf as large as golf divots lay on the playing surface.

It was a bruised field, all right, and the weather for the Saints game was cold and wet, with a layer of snow covering the city from the night before. Even Lombardi took to the side lines in a pair of rubbers, hardly a Spartan picture. The Saints won the toss, and Lombardi formed the teams around him in a giant circle. I peered down at him with my binoculars, and he seemed to say, "Okay, let's go get them."

The Saints were expected to run. Andy Livingston and Tony Baker were having big years, both of them over 500 yards on the ground. Behind them, Tony Lorick, Ernie Wheelwright, and Tom Barrington were also powerful inside runners, the kind that had moved the ball on the Redskins all year long. Joe Don Looney, having failed to "Shape up" once more, had been cut.

Late in the first period, the Redskins jumped to an early lead on a 12-yard touchdown sweep by Charley Harraway. The offense having drawn first blood, the Redskin defense came alive and didn't allow another first down for the rest of the first quarter and most of the second. Rickie Harris intercepted a New Orleans pass midway through the second period and ran it back 47 yards to the Saints' 27. Jurgensen passed to Jerry

Smith at the 15 for a first down, but New Orleans held, and the Redskins had to take the field goal for a 10–0 lead.

The Washington defense turned the ball back over to Jurgensen with two and a half minutes showing in the half. Jurgensen threw a 30-yarder to Charley Harraway for the touchdown four plays later, making it 17–7 Washington.

First-string quarterback Billy Kilmer went out of the game with a stomach ailment, and rookie Ed Hargett was now quarterbacking the Saints. In less than thirty seconds, Hargett moved the club from its own 20 to the Redskin 37. He missed two straight throws, and with nine seconds showing, he threw a swing pass to Tony Baker, who carried the ball down to the Redskin 5-yard line before Brig Owens brought him down. The gun went off while Baker was still carrying the ball, so the Redskins went to the locker room with a 17–0 edge. Except for the Cardinal game, it was the only comfortable half-time margin they had had all year.

The Redskins began the third period with a six-minute drive that finally fell 4 yards short of a first down at the midfield stripe. Bragg came in to kick, got some pressure on the outside from charging Elijah Nevett, and unaccountably decided to run for it. He tucked the ball under his arm and swept around right end at a good pelting pace, appearing to have a long gainer in mind. He was nailed 1 yard shy of the first down, and the Saints got the ball back with good field position. Andy Livingston and Baker ground out the yardage with an occasional passing assist from Hargett. Four minutes later, it was third and goal at the 1. Don Shy carried it in for the score, putting the Saints down by 10.

The Redskins got the ball back and, with the help of a roughing-the-kicker penalty, worked it back to midfield again. This time it was fourth and three, but Bragg got his punt off. Marlin McKeever downed the ball on the Saints' 3-yard line.

The Redskin defense had had a good first half, had shown signs of containing the Saints' runners and of putting some heat on Hargett. The Redskin offense's third-quarter performance had been disquieting. Jurgensen's passes were off target. Larry Brown was being thrown for losses, didn't seem to have the faintest notion of where his holes might be, seemed to be almost leisurely about striking off for daylight. Something seemed askew.

The ball was now down at the New Orleans 3. To have the Redskin defense back on the field seemed an attractive alternative, a chance for Lombardi to juice up the faltering offense. There were three minutes still to go in the third period. The defense held the Saints to a third and six at the New Orleans 7, which meant a pass. That deep in their own territory, it meant the Saints would be operating at a distinct disadvantage, and might be somewhat rattled. It was a situation pregnant with thoughts of safeties and interceptions.

Instead, Hargett hit tight end Dave Parks for 8 yards and the first down. Then the big New Orleans backs went to work. Don Shy bulled his way for 19 yards. Hargett came back with a pass to Tony Baker, who rolled his way for 27 more yards before Mike Bass and Rickie Harris could bring him down. Andy Livingston began the fourth period with a 15-yard run, down to the Redskin 24. Ernie Wheelwright came in and carried for 17 more. Now it was first and goal at the Washington 7. Don Shy fumbled, picked it back up, and got 2 yards before Marlin McKeever hit him.

Sam Huff came in for one more goal-line stand, one more valiant man-to-man standoff with an enemy ballcarrier. He nailed Shy for no gain. On third and five, Hargett went to Wheelwright again, and he took it in standing up. It was Redskins 17, Saints 14.

I could only hope that the offense was sufficiently rested and had had enough time on the bench to muster its forces and control the ball for a long drive.

Dyer ran Tom Dempsey's kick back to the Redskin 22. Larry Brown carried twice for 8, bringing up a third and two at the Redskin 30. The big third-down play had arrived. Jurgensen went to Charley Taylor, who made it up to midfield, for the first down yardage and then some. Sonny came back to Taylor again for 8 more, Brown carried for 1, and the Redskins had third and one at the Saints' 41. Harraway hammered out a couple of yards, and Washington had the first down, a drive in the making. Larry Brown came back for 7, Jurgensen staying on the ground to eat up the clock. Harraway banged into the middle for 2 more yards, making it third and one at the Saints' 30. Harraway bucked into the line again.

The official fished around for the ball in the pile-up and put it back at the line of scrimmage, an egregious misplacement. The fans began to stir restlessly; a few boos were sounded, either at the referee's placement of the ball or the offense's inability to move it. Now on fourth and one, Jurgensen called on Harraway again for the first down. There was no field-goal try. Lombardi was gambling to keep the drive alive, worried that his defense would not be able to contain the now devastating New Orleans backs. A ten-point margin, not a six-point one, was what the Redskins needed for security. Harraway didn't make it. No Redskin first down. The New Orleans offense came on the field, led by their diminutive rookie quarterback and their mammoth running backs. The Redskin offense trotted off, and the defense came on to a ghostly stadium silence that was soon to turn into boos.

There were five minutes left on the clock. Tony Baker ripped off a quick 11 yards to show the New Orleans running game had not gone stale on the bench. Carl Kammerer plugged Don Shy at the line of scrimmage, and Andy Livingston came in to take his place. Livingston reeled off 7 yards and then 1 more, making it fourth and two at the Saints' 49-yard line. The Saints had to go for it, in all likelihood had to try the Redskin middle again. Lombardi had all his beef on the line: Kammerer, Hoffman, Crane, Norton, McLinton, McKeever, and Sam Huff. Livingston bulled right up the gut for 5 yards and the first down. He carried for 3 more to the Redskin 43, and the two-minute warning sounded.

The Saints had all their time-outs left; the clock was pressing against them, but they still had some options and could still mix their plays. Now Hargett elected to go to the air, and the Redskins put on a rush. With Tony Baker in the clear in first-down territory, Hargett threw instead to Don Shy, and the pass was incomplete. It was third and seven. Marlin McKeever blitzed, and Hargett unloaded far short of split end

Al Dodd, forcing a fourth and seven. Once again the Redskins mounted a rush, forcing Hargett out of his pocket. He swept toward the Redskin side line and instead of turning the corner he paused to pump the ball, looking for a receiver. The Redskin secondary was hanging back deep for the pass, and by the time Hargett realized he could run for the first down, it was too late. McLinton came charging over to knock him out of bounds.

The Redskins took over, and Jurgensen ran out the clock with the help of a long and daring third-down pass to Charley Taylor.

So the Redskins went down to the clubhouse with a 17–14 win in the bank, a guaranteed winning season, and their first victorious campaign in fourteen years. Whatever the outcome in the Cotton Bowl the following Sunday, they could do no worse than 7–5–2 and might do as well as 8–4–2. There was a certain glory in that. It would seem a stolid and dogged enough accomplishment in the cold print of the NFL record book.

I could not help but think back to Mercein's claim for Lombardi's indomitable faith, his belief that any game could be won if it only went on for another five minutes. It was hard to imagine that he felt any such sensation about this game. The Redskins had played a whole half without putting a point on the scoreboard, the defense and the offense had repeatedly crumbled when the going got tough. Hargett's inexperience and a ticking clock had saved them. Another five minutes indeed! If appearances meant anything the Saints would have needed less than five to run the Redskins off the field. Lombardi seemed to sense that down in the clubhouse. His eyes were dull, his face haggard, and his lips stretched thin and stern. There would be no flashing teeth today. Had he seen something that disturbed him? Or was this some strange Spartan gesture of self-control over the urge to gloat?

Someone asked about Sonny's third-down mini-bomb to Charley Taylor on the closing series, the sheer nerve of risking an interception at that stage of the game.

"What the hell am I going to do?" Lombardi growled truculently. "What do you suggest we do on third down? Hell, the way we were moving the ball we might as well pass. We needed the first down.

"We didn't do much all day. I don't know why. I'll have to wait for the films. Why the hell Bragg ran with that punt I'll never know. Hanburger had the guy coming in blocked. No way he could have got to the punter." He paused, the bitterness welling up to the brim, perhaps suddenly scalded by the knowledge that 7–4–2 was not good enough, not commensurate to the intensity of his efforts. Then his face cleared, as if mastering the awkwardness of such unseemly thoughts, and he said, "But, hell, Bragg's a pro. He must have known what he was doing. He was out there to make the judgment, not me."

A young man cleared his throat and bent forward, parting the bank of reporters in front of him, and asked, "Coach, were you disappointed when you didn't get the first down on the fourth-down situation in the fourth period?"

Lombardi peered at the questioner. He was forever lamenting the fatuity of reporter's questions. I felt certain that he would make some withering comment. Instead, he looked at the questioner and admitted in a rather kindly voice that not making the first down had definitely been a disappointment.

Then someone wanted to know if he was disappointed with the season.

"I feel good about a winning season. I thought we could have one. I've never had a losing season," he mused.

"You haven't been here long enough," a reporter's voice rang out.

"Who said that?" Lombardi snapped. The reporters around the writer who had spoken man who said it edged away as from a leper. "You really have a lot of faith, don't you? Jesus! Thanks a lot," Lombardi said.

"You haven't lost your sense of humor, Coach, have you?" the man said, recovering well, with no loss of face.

"No," Lombardi said. "No. Listen to me." He gave a strangled, falsetto laugh.

"How would you compare the Washington press with the Green Bay press?"

"Comparisons are *odious*," Lombardi replied with delight, squeezing all the meaning he could into that last word.

The reporters started to file out of the room, and the young man who had asked the question on the fourth-down play appeared, tape recorder at the ready.

"Got time for a little interview, Coach?"

"All right," Lombardi said wearily. He put on his official after-the-game radio-TV face: humble, parsimonious of comment, earnest, and aware of posterity.

As I started to leave the room, a reporter stopped me. "See that guy getting the interview with Lombardi?" he asked.

"Yeah."

"You know who he is?"

"No."

"I'll be goddamned," the man said, his face breaking into a grin. "That guy doesn't work for any radio station. His hobby is collecting tapes of famous sports figures. He was around the Senator clubhouse all summer, until they found out what he was up to and kicked him out. Isn't that a bitch? Here's Lombardi giving his first radio interview of the season, and he's giving it to a guy who's going to store it in his bureau drawer."

We looked back at Lombardi, his face creased with sobriety as he weighed the impact of his words, honing the language he assumed would soon be flashing from coast to coast. "I hoped we could have done better," Coach was saying as we left, while his questioner was nodding encouragement.

The arc lights and TV cameras from the local television stations were set up in the Redskin dressing room to immortalize the team's first winning season since 1955. Carl Kammerer came prancing naked out of the shower room, juggling four cans of grape soda pop. The arc light suddenly snapped on. Kammerer blinked in surprise and jumped behind a pillar in the middle of the room. "Hey," he said, "is that damn thing on? Here I wait seven years to have a winning season, and as soon as we do, the first thing I do is walk out naked on national TV."

There was a plastic holly wreath hanging over Joe Rutgens's empty locker stall. Was it a garish Christmas decoration hung there by Rutgens himself prior to his departure? A boorish gesture by some teammate with a taste for the macabre? In either case, the pallid plastic holly seemed too synthetic a monument to Rutgens's career.

I remembered Rutgens telling me that he had never played on a winning team—not at Illinois, not with the Redskins. And now that the team had become winners at last, he was not in the clubhouse to celebrate, missing a winning season by forty-eight hours.

Rutgens, in spite of his anxiety to get the season over with, to get home for Christmas, had not yet left for Illinois. He was still in town, bewildered, hurt, uncertain of himself and the future. I ran into him at Maggie's Goalpost, a Redskin haunt with crudely drawn murals of football players on the wall. Old Number 9 was up there on the wall humming that pigskin. And so was Rutgens, old Number 72 bear-hugging a Los Angeles Ram runner, like Hercules squeezing the life from Antaeus.

"No," Rutgens said, "I didn't go to the Saints game. I had the tickets, but I don't know. I stayed at home and listened on the radio. Maybe I should of gone. They won. Got the winning season. I'm glad of that for them."

"It's a hell of a way to go out," I said, "just sort of disappear from sight."

"Yeah, that's the bad thing about it. I'm real disappointed. I'm going to talk to some of the guys I know, coaches around the league, see if I can land anywhere else. I don't know how to go about it, to tell you the truth."

He took a gulp of beer, slaking the brittle emotion in his voice. "I've been here nine years. I know so many people here. I've always played here. I guess I'd like to play here next year, if I can play anywhere. I guess it would have to be here. When you get to the tail end of your career, you don't have many years left, you'd like to finish them out in the place where you started."

"How did he cut you?" I asked.

"I guess I saw it coming. I don't know. Yeah, what the hell, I sensed it. He took me out after the Dallas game. I didn't think I played that bad. I thought I had a pretty fair game. I sure didn't see anybody else doing any better in the films, and I guess from what I heard they didn't do a lot better against the Saints on Sunday either. Last week, when Vinnie's shoulder popped twice at Philly, I figured they'd need another offensive guy and I kind of figured I'd be the guy to go, but I didn't figure on the waiver. I just thought they'd put me on the move list. But I guess they didn't have any more moves left."

"It's a brutal game," I said, trying to assuage his stricken look of misery, trying to suggest that the fault lay in the game, not in him. That such was the nature of the beast.

"That's for damn sure. That's for sure. I knew it was going to happen to me eventually. I took somebody else's job and I knew somebody would finally get mine. But not this soon. I thought another few years, anyhow. The guys have been saying all season long, you don't know when Lombardi's going to make his last cut. 'You never know,' they'd say, and I'd laugh. I got to say this, he keeps you on your toes.

"I guess I'm not emotionally ready to leave football," Rutgens said. "I'll give it another shot. I'm not ready to quit. I don't want to quit. I try not to think about being out of football. I guess I know for sure now it's just a matter of time. One year. Two years. But even that. I'd even take that. It's pretty hard to give up football, even when you know you have to. It's been my life. What else have I done? I'm not bitter, though. My wife's the one who's bitter. After Lombardi told me, I went back to the apartment, and she was there with the baby, and I said, 'Well, it's finally happened. It finally came.' And we just sat around the apartment all day. I just left everything in the locker room. My belt and gear, my helmet. I didn't take my helmet. I should have taken my helmet home."

Lombardi's last session with the press on the Monday after the Saints game was a drab, lifeless affair. Lombardi sat behind his desk, staring at a sheet of team statistics like a man determined to understand a Chinese road map. It was not difficult to tell where the Redskins had made the wrong turn. Jurgensen was still number one in the league, with a 62.1

passing percentage and 2896 yards. Charley Taylor was in a three-way tie for the pass-receiving lead with 65 balls. Jerry Smith was in fifth place with 51, Bob Long in seventh with 48, and Charley Harraway was tied for eighth with 47. Larry Brown was in fifth place among the league rushers with 827 yards. Rickie Harris was in second place in punt returns, but would have been in first, had the dubious clipping penalty not been called against Hanburger in the first Dallas game.

So there it was: an explosive team that could move the ball and had, in fact, moved it for 4042 yards in thirteen games for an average of 311 yards per game—good enough offensively to win most ballgames. But on the other side of the ledger, the Redskin opponents had moved it for 4143 yards, had so far run 822 plays to the Redskins' 788. It was, in short, a team that gave up more ground than it gained, that controlled the ball fewer times than the enemy. It was, you could say, the same old Redskins, masters of the invincible attack and the vulnerable defense.

But despite the similarities to past campaigns, there was a difference: the Redskins would finish with a winning record. That was clearly an improvement. Even more central, the team had survived—just barely, but it had survived. They had trembled on the brink of disaster, had crossed over a time or two, but they had come back out on the other side. As Lombardi said after the Steelers game, they had bent, but they had not broken. They had endured the "alien force" that Charley Harraway had talked about. They had faced the stress and the pressure of the most inflexible, willful man in football, and they had not snapped. They had been routed in Baltimore, disgraced at home by the Eagles, edged by Dallas, and had bent to the ground in the storm of Lombardi's pitiless pressure, yet somehow they had not broken. That victory at least was theirs, and Lombardi's as well; it had not been easy.

As Lombardi gloomily surveyed the statistics, a reporter asked, "How does it feel to be with a winner?"

He frowned, disdaining the possibilities of cheerful reminiscence that question implied. He said, "The Saints game was the first pressure game the Redskins have had. It was a must game. To win it gave us a winning season. This was when winning something meant something."

"Even if you lost to New Orleans, you could have got the winning season this week by beating the Cowboys," someone noted.

"Not the same thing," Lombardi said, shaking his head impatiently. "The Saints game meant the winning season. Never mind the second chances, the Saints game was the chance. To win guaranteed something, to lose was not to guarantee it."

"The Colts, Dallas, the Rams weren't 'must' games?" someone asked.

"Every game has pressure. Those games would have been great to win, had pressure to them, but if you lost them the season wasn't over; you could still win more games. You weren't out of anything if you lost, you still could win the next week and the next. The Saints game was bigger because it meant the difference between winning and losing."

"Now that the season's almost over, do you have any ballplayers you'd like to single out for having an outstanding season?"

"No, I don't like to single out people. You always forget some you shouldn't when you do," Lombardi explained lamely.

"I was thinking of people like Jurgensen, Taylor, Jerry Smith, maybe Mike Bass—people who might make the All-Pro teams."

"I don't hold much with All-Pro teams," Lombardi grunted. "Besides, I don't want to praise these people too much. I got to negotiate contracts with them."

"I was thinking of Williams—the way he beat the drums for his players before the All-Star team was named. The way he boosted Howard and sounded off when Eddie Brinkman didn't get any votes."

Lombardi started, as if coming out of a deep trance. "Williams on who?" he said. "Williams?" he scowled, clearly thinking of Edward Bennett Williams, wondering what the hell he was doing beating the drums, outraged at the effrontery of the man.

"Ted Williams on Ed Brinkman," the reporter said.

"Oh, him. Ted Williams," Lombardi nodded, his annoyance subsiding.

"Do you figure Dallas is going to let up for this last game, preserve their troops for the play-offs?"

Lombardi glowered at the questioner. "I would hope," he said, the emotion back in his voice, "that Dallas will play as tough as they can. If they're going to represent the East, they should play hard against us." An angry look passed across his face. For one painful moment he was alone with the notion of Tom Landry sloughing off for a game with Vince Lombardi, of thinking ahead, his mind elsewhere, not in the least concerned with Vince Lombardi's imminent arrival at the Cotton Bowl, the scene of so many "must" games between them in the past.

Lombardi prided himself on his cryptic utterances, his small fibs to throw the press off the spoor of his schemes, and his great stone face both in adversity and triumph. But it was a hollow effort, stoical play-acting. At bottom, his emotions ran too deep and his need to win was too profound to allow him to dissemble. On the important matters you knew where Lombardi stood, knew what he wanted, and knew what it was like for him to get it or not.

After the press conference was over, I met Gerry Allen outside, and we went around the corner for a cup of coffee. He had been on that move list ever since the Steeler game. Now he had come to terms with the indignity of being sent down, was outwardly as cheerful as ever, a man whose enormous animal vitality and charm could not be suppressed. He wore a windbreaker and a pair of white and green football shoes with ridged soles. "I come downtown now, man," he said, "and people see me on the street and say, 'How come you ain't playing?' And I say—well, what can I say? So I say I'm not feeling well or I got an injury. I was a star. I was a starting back for two years. On Sundays I used to feel like I was really somebody, which is the way you should feel. The fans really liked me last year, they would cheer me when I was introduced. I was an exciting runner. Truthfully now, I'm telling you, I am the second-best runner in the league. Gale Sayers is the best runner in the history of football. He is better than me by far. But I'm better than Leroy Kelly."

He ran his hand over the top of his fuzzy Afro and gave me a soft smile that seemed to say, "Go ahead, man, and tell me I'm a little cocky calling myself the second best in the league, and me on the move list with a club not known for its running backs.'

"What happened this year?" I asked.

"I thought this was going to be my year. I really did. Fast? You better believe I'm fast. I ran a 4.75 forty, but that's nothing. It's after forty yards that I really pour it on. Running is for yards, man. That's the whole idea of it. The idea is don't get tackled.

"I was ready when Lombardi came. I said, yeah, this is more like it. Lombardi had said his kind of back was 6'1", 200 pounds, just like me.

"Only," I said, "he said his kind of back was 6'1" and 215 pounds." He stared at me in astonishment. "He did? Jesus Christ, that explains it. No wonder he put me on the move list. You sure about that?"

"Positive."

"I'll be damned. Well, anyway, I went to camp with the idea that this is where it's at. Every camp I go to I'm always on the last team. I always start low as they can put me, and I always fight my way up. Lombardi's camp was the same way. But that didn't bother me. I'm a hell of a practicer and I knew I'd be up there. Mental pressure?" he gave a throaty chuckle. "Man, Lombardi really had me going. Do you know what he called me?" His eyes opened in amazement at the recollection of whatever it was Lombardi had called him.

"What?" I said. "What did he call you?" expecting some execration strong enough to curl the pages of the offender's playbook.

Allen's eyes narrowed, and he paused to give the word theatrical force. "A nincompoop," he said. "He called *me* a nincompoop. Can you believe that, man?"

I let out a sharp laugh, a horselike sound that caused heads to turn throughout the coffee shop.

"You think that's funny, do you?" Allen said. "I was running and dancing in the holes, and that's my style of running, and you don't change a man's style overnight. I remember once he told me, 'If I see you dancing in that hole one more time, you're leaving. Right now.' He stopped practice and told the defense where I was going to run the next play, told them the hole I was going to hit, and said they'd better not let me get any yards. Can you imagine that? He told them where I was coming and told them they'd better stop me. The quarterback handed me that ball and I plowed right in the hole.

"How many yards did you get?" I asked.

"None," he said with simple eloquence. "None, man."

"Then the thing I decided to myself was if he was going to cut me, he was going to have to do it with no mistakes by me. He was going to have to do it on his own. He was going to have to do it because I wasn't his kind of player, didn't run with the style he wanted. Because I made up my mind he wasn't going to get to cut me because I made mistakes or because I didn't run good. If we had a blitz pick-up assignment, for example, I'd think to myself that that incoming linebacker was Vince, and man, I'd stick it to him. Same with the lineman. I'd see those faces inside those helmets and I'd think they were all Vince, and I'd go roaring into those holes.

"It was giving me satisfaction. I started learning my assignments better, learning my plays more, and I stopped dancing. So he couldn't get his chance to cut me."

"So he found a way to motivate you after all," I grinned. "Not the easiest way maybe, but a way."

Allen laughed. "Yeah. I guess you got to say that. Nobody knows football any better'n him. I got to say if we did what he told us to, we'd be world champs right now. He's the coach. Some coaches—their title is coach, but their assistants do the coaching. You got to say that he's the Man, and it's not so often you can say that about a coach. Still, to call me a nincompoop, that still gets me. Can you imagine that?"

As we were talking, there was a man at the next table straining an ear to overhear our conversation. He had obviously heard enough to know that Allen was no ordinary man, a football star of some sort. But who? He got up, came over to our table, bent down and said in an unctuous voice, "Excuse me, but I believe I know you from somewhere. What is your name, if I may ask?"

"I'm Gerry Allen," Allen beamed.

The man's face was utterly blank. "Oh," he said, "thank you," and walked off.

Allen shook his head, not without a wan charm. "You know," he said, "that cat's gonna get out on the street and all of a sudden it's going to come to him. He's gonna think, 'Who in the hell is Gerry Allen?' " He gave a bittersweet smile.

Chapter 26

On Tuesday morning Lombardi began all over again for a game that meant nothing, a game that ended a season that had no discernible scope for further achievement. To win it would be nice, 8–4–2; to lose it would be unpleasant, but endurable, 7–5–2.

Lombardi buttered himself a piece of toast and poured a cup of coffee. It was about 8:20 Tuesday morning. He had arrived at the stadium a few minutes before, had hung his suit coat and shirt in his locker stall, and was puttering about, getting himself ready for the day, coming to terms with the week that still lay ahead.

"I'm tired, bone tired," he told me. "Let me tell you, this has been a long season. They're all long, I guess. Maybe I'm getting older, but this one has seemed longer."

He took his coffee and sat down in the wooden chair from which he lectured the press after home-games. He stirred his coffee for a while.

"Great changes have taken place in the country in the last ten years. It's the nature of the times that there's more tendency to question now than there was ten years ago. The father complex is not around any more. Yet, there are other ways to motivate people too. People want to excel, that's a human constant. And a young man, because of his body, can excel in sports. That's the reason you can get kids to drive themselves into the ground to play this sport, to go out and play hurt. I've always thought the best football player is the one who loves the glory. Like Paul Hornung. A super glory-player. Any time you got down near the goal-line you gave the ball to Paul, because he'd get it in there somehow. Whether there was no blocking, or whatever the hell happened, he was going to get it in there. Any time it was an ordinary game, Paul was an ordinary football player; the bigger the game, the more extraordinary he became. I could sense that in him."

He stopped and stared me in the eye, as if to let the force of those remarks sink in. But that was not what he was thinking about, not what was on his mind.

"I'll tell you," he said with sudden vehemence, "we had a complete breakdown in the second half against the Saints. I could see things were going wrong from the side lines, but it wasn't until I saw the pictures that I could see how bad it was. Our key people were breaking down, blowing their assignments. What does this mean? I wish I knew. Did it just happen? Or is it a weakness under pressure? I'll have to find that out. And to me, that Saints game was a pressure game. It meant a winning season. There are some games you must win. If you lose the first game of the season, let's say, you still got the season ahead of you. But if you lose the second game, then that third game becomes a pressure game, *the* pressure game. Because you don't often lose three in a row in this league and go anywhere. Anytime you're playing for more than just a win you're playing a pressure game, whether you're trying to break out of a losing streak, whether it's for the championship, or whether you're playing for a winning season like against the Saints. It's a question of extra significance."

"How are you going to get them up for this last game?" I asked.

"I don't know. I just don't know yet. Something will come to me, I guess. It usually does." He looked at his watch. "In another hour I'll be on them, oh, won't I just," he laughed. "The films won't be much fun for anyone today. Then after I've told them what they've done wrong, I'll have to wait, wait and see what their reaction is outside. I try to shut out everything negative about them after we've seen the films.

"As far as the tongue-lashing goes, it depends on what they're going to do on Wednesday and Thursday. How hard can you drive them? That's something that's got to come natural, something you've got to feel. Sometimes you don't have to say anything all week. They'll carry themselves. Sometimes you've got to whip them—well, drive them—I don't like the word 'whip.' "

"You don't like to think of yourself as a heartless man, do you?" I asked, the season close enough to the end so that risks in being blunt had vanished.

"No. Why would anybody? It's no damn fun being hard. I've been doing this for years and years and years. It's never been great fun. You have to drive yourself constantly. I don't enjoy it. It takes a hell of a lot out of me. And, Christ, you get kind of embarrassed with yourself sometimes. You berate somebody and you feel disgusted with yourself for doing it, for being in a job where you have to. Fortunately, I don't remember."

"Will you let up on a guy if you've been on him too hard?"

"Never. No carrot and stick for me. I'll never look for a way to make it up to a guy I've been on. That doesn't mean I won't push some people more than others. You've seen me on the field, and there are obviously people I push all the time and some I don't. There are many people here it took me a longer time to find out how far I could push, don't know yet what their limit is. I'll be pushing them all over again next year until I do find their limit. By the same token, there are some people I knew I couldn't push. Some people I had doubts about, and I pushed them and berated them to find out what I could about their character, their limits. Those are the things that are important to me, because this is what the game is all about."

"How about the color question?" I asked.

"I've always had good relationships with black players. I like to think the reason is I don't know they're black. Everybody is the same damn color. When I'm mad at them and when I'm not. Now racial prejudice is one of the few areas where we've got a bad record as a nation. As far as football, it's been there. No getting around it. It's hurt teams. It can destroy them. I'm not saying I don't know who's black and who's white on this club. I'm just saying that I have no sense of it when I'm dealing with my people. The Negro ballplayers in this society have got a pretty good sense of people with color consciousness, for knowing when you're treating them differently from whites, either bending over to be nice or to be critical. Even when a coach doesn't intend to see black people as black people, it shows. You can't hide it if you feel that way. I don't feel that way. I'm very grateful for that, because, first of all, to feel that way is wrong, and second, it's good football not to feel that way.

"Well," he said with a benign smile, "I guess it's time to get ready to look at some movies." He walked into the little cubicle with the locker stalls, climbed out of his pants and T shirt, and put on the thermal underwear, flannel knickers, and sweat shirt of his profession.

On Wednesday morning he buttered another piece of toast, poured another cup of coffee, and began browsing through the sports pages of the *New York Times.*

"I thought you didn't read the papers," I remarked.

"I don't," he said, still reading the *Times.* "I read the *Post* coming over in the limousine this morning. Normally I don't."

"In *Run to Daylight,* every chapter began with you stopping off to pick up the papers before you had breakfast at the drugstore," I said.

"That was early in my career. When I had some faith in what the papers said."

I laughed at that. I asked him next if he found his return to coaching as satisfying as he had thought it would be during the year of rustication in the Green Bay front office. He ignored the question and buttered another piece of toast. I repeated it.

"Satisfying? I don't know. You do what you have to do. I was unhappy out of coaching, let's put it that way. At first I thought I wanted to do something different. I was asked to run for the Senate and the governorship."

"Did that tempt you?"

"I gave it some thought. I wasn't sure my nature was right for it. You know I'm pretty sensitive about what they say about me in the sports pages. I wasn't sure I could take the beating you get in public life. At the same time I liked to think I could make a contribution to people. And then I was asked to go with a lot of big corporations, and that tempted me, too. You like to think you can rise to a new challenge. But I wasn't sure about those things. For one thing, I was under a tremendous amount of tension in Green Bay—three championship seasons in a row, twenty-two or twenty-three games a season, every game getting increasingly more tense. So I left to take a year's sabbatical, to get away from the tension and think. As it turned out, a year was too long. Six months would have been plenty of time. Funny, I've always liked golf, always figured I could play a fair amount of it and be happy, but I found out quick enough that golf's not enough. And the more I played golf and sat in the office, the more I realized I couldn't stay where I was. I felt I had to get back to the game. I'm just like anybody else. Nobody wants to be a legend, really. And you're no longer a legend once you come back, because then you're suffering defeats. You're getting beat. Not that I want to get beat, Coach, I'll tell you I don't. But I want to be alive too, no dead legend.

"The chances were small here. I want to tell you we got maybe five topflight football players. The ones in Green Bay who became topflight football players had the wherewithal to do it. They had something in them to get the job done. And I'm not too sure you can develop wherewithal.

"I did think so at one time. Maybe it was because of my ego, or whatever the hell I have—I thought I could develop it. I just don't know now. Maybe you need to start out with some inherent quality of excellence. The important thing is in having the spark in most, not just some, but most of your players. We've developed some of that spark here. But *some* is less than *most*, and *most* is what you need for a championship."

The first of the wire-service All-Pro teams was announced on Wednesday, and in the clubhouse after practice the team gathered around the newspaper that ran the list. Jerry Smith was the only Redskin to make the UPI first team. Jurgensen and Chris Hanburger made the second team. I was standing near Len Hauss's locker as the list was read off across the room, and Hauss cocked an ear. He gave a sad smile when he didn't hear his name and wandered over to congratulate Jerry Smith. Charley Taylor was looking at the list in disbelief, scarcely able to credit that he not even made second team. Roy Jefferson, Gary Collins, Gene Washington, and Dan Abramowitz were the four wide receivers who had beaten him out. They were all extraordinary receivers, had caught a few balls, had scored a few touchdowns—but to say they were in Charley Taylor's league? Perhaps you could stretch a point and say they could catch as well as he did, but which of them had drawn his double coverage, which of them blocked like Taylor, and which of them could run with the ball the way he could?

There was hurt in his eyes and he said, "Well, you can't beat city hall." Jurgensen passed by, on his way out of the locker room. "You're number one on my team, Charley," he sang out. It was a gallant gesture on the part of the Old Redhead, who led the league in passing and found himself runner-up to Roman Gabriel on the list. You had to wonder if it had all been worth it for him, to suppress his nature, to go through the hell of training camp, to break the habits he had refined during twelve years, only to end in second place in the Capitol Division, in the All-Pro lists. To have won it all, that would have been worth it, would have been the proof that he had been the best quarterback in football, after all. But that was not the way it had worked out. He had been second team to Starr and Unitas during the 1960's, and now he was second team to Gabriel. "Every morning when I drive to work, I sing 'I'm off to See the Wizard, the Wonderful Wizard of Oz,' he had told me. It had not been enough; the Wizard's magic had not done the trick.

By Thursday the lines of relief were etched on Lombardi's face. It was almost over, this six months of his life, and he wanted it to end, the weekly suspense to draw to a close.

"Is it harder to prepare for Dallas with all their multiple offenses?" I asked, mindful that the Cowboys' technological, explosive brand of football was said to be the wave of the future, while the Lombardi grind-out-the-yardage style was said to be passé. I was also mindful of the fact that Craig Morton had thrown the ball less than 300 times and Jurgensen more than 400. When it came to the stodgy offense, Lombardi was not as culpable as the critics said.

"When it comes to preparation, the difficulties are always with the teams you don't know, the teams in the other conference, where you only play them once every two or three years," he said. "We know Dallas. The Redskins have played them two times a year."

"When I was at Pittsburgh, we always did better against the teams in the other conference," Bill Austin mused from across the room.

"This year, being in the East was new for me," Lombardi went on. "I didn't know them. Maybe next year I'll know them better—Atlanta, the Eagles, the Giants, teams like that. Of course, I know the Cowboys all right, even though we weren't in the same conference," he grinned.

With the end of the season at hand, the talk turned to the college draft.

"I looked at the pictures of this Bradshaw yesterday and, boy, is he something," George Dickson said.

"Yeah, did you see the touchdown he threw, with those guys hanging all over him?" Austin said. "Looked like Gabriel." He shook his head in admiration.

"Bradshaw's got to go first," Lombardi said.

"Probably Phipps will go first," Austin said. "Phipps plays in the real class football league. Phipps looks like a sure bet to me to make it, what do you think, Vince?"

"You know, I saw the *Look* All-Americans on the Bob Hope show," Lombardi said. "Damn, that McCoy is big." He gave an appreciative whistle. "He is big."

"We'll be seeing him next year," Austin said. "He'll be playing against us. That's the only way we'll get to see him."

"Yeah," Lombardi grunted. "I wouldn't mind getting a draw at him. We could use him up there in the line."

"I told you, Coach, I put him on the scale at Notre Dame last year, and he went 287½," Dickson sang out.

Lombardi turned accountably glum. "I'm telling you, he'd

be nice to have," he said. "And the most impressive one of the whole bunch is this Walker Gillette. This is a hell of a year not to have a first-round choice," he lamented.

The thought was too depressing to dwell on, and the other coaches returned to their charts. Finally Lombardi said, "How long can Jurgensen play? That's the question for us. How long will it take to find a quarterback to take his place? That's what worries me. How long? You need a couple of years to groom one. And you don't have a team without a quarterback." He shook his head, contemplating,1970, 1971 ... How many more exceptional years did Sonny have? You could say a year, or two. Only a fool would say five. And Lombardi was no fool. The season was almost over, but 1970 had already begun.

Out in the dressing room, I found Leo Carroll on the chair in front of his locker. He was obviously in low spirits.

"What's the matter? Your weight still going down?" I asked. "No," he said, infinitely morose, "I've got to get my hair cut. Goddamn, only two days to go, and he catches me." Forty-eight hours of anonymity would have seen him through until the 1970 training camp. Now he would have to have those locks shorn and would have to face the gang back in San Diego with a Lombardi-style haircut.

"Well," Flea Roberts chirped from the locker stall next to Leo's, "football's like the Army. Those bastards make you get your hair cut the day before you're released. You're going back to society and you got to go get yourself a baldie," he chuckled.

"I'm just going to get myself a little trim," Leo pouted. "He'll never notice, just a little trim. Damned if I'm going to get it all cut off. There are guys around here with more hair than me," he said, his voice now almost crying with anguish.

"If you got to get you hair cut, they ought to make Flea shave his moustache," I said. "Ssshh," Flea said. His moustache, a barely visible tuft of wiry hair on his upper lip, had only just come to Lombardi's attention. A few days before, Flea had run a crisp little pass pattern, and Lombardi had told him, "That's a hell of a catch, Coach. By the way, what's that growing over your lip there?"

Leo moped off to the shower room. "If Leo gets his hair cut," Jim Norton laughed, "he'll drop down to 228. A defensive end playing in this league at that weight?" He shook his head. "And that's it, he's not playing."

Leo arrived for practice Friday, his head visibly shorn, his sideburns raised an inch or so, and a scowl on his face large enough to intimidate a Cowboy tackle. But that was not to be. All-American boy or not, Leo was too light to figure in Lombardi's plans for Dallas. It seemed a charateristic touch, however, that Coach had not overlooked the tonsorial grooming of a superfluous defensive end.

Lombardi was sprawled out in a wooden folding chair in the coachs' dressing room, Christmas carols sounding from the stereo speakers. He bent forward, pressing his palm to his back, and a grimace passed his face. "I'm telling you, every time I sit down I get pains," Lombardi grumbled. "It's been a long time since I've had a day off, I want to tell you. The season doesn't bother you much, it's just every day, every day out there. It's the constant grind, you just wear out. Every other profession you get some time off, a Sunday or something. Monday, Saturday, I don't care, but some damn day or other. Even the players are so bushed they can't keep awake, and they're just youths."

One of the coaches looked up from a table where he was diagramming goal-line defenses. "Maybe we ought to flash a picture of some dame up on the screen to keep them on their toes at the film sessions," he said.

"That's what we used to do in Green Bay," Lombardi reflected. "Flash one of those calendar babes up there on the screen; that ought to keep them awake. You know," Lombardi laughed, "I got a feeling we'll see about four Dallas passes, so they can get the game over quick as hell."

"Do you know how long that football is actually in play in a game?" Svare suddenly asked. "Fourteen minutes. A guy going one way, he is actually in play five minutes. You take the special teams out of there and your defense and offense are playing five minutes apiece. You wouldn't think it would be that tiring, but what the hell, you run a mile in four minutes and it takes all your energy to do it."

"Football kills you emotionally," Lombardi said. "The ten- sion'll tire you out more than the physical exhaustion will. You know why football is so popular? Those people running around hitting each other? Hell, no. It's because of the huddle. Every time the clock stops, every time the play is over, the huddle forms, and the fan puts himself in the same situation, tries to figure what he would do. Football is situation as much as action."

"That's right," Svare said, "you got to give the man in the stands time to think. Colonel Frank Burke used to tell me about professional wrestling, that when you get upset in the ring and you want to put the other guy away, you have to wait a second and give the fans time to react. Because if you move too fast, they don't know what the hell is happening."

"That's what baseball overdoes," someone said. "Hell, ev- eryone in the ballpark knows what's going to happen long before it actually does. No damn suspense left in the game that way."

"We got the best game of all," Lombardi said. "No game like it."

It was bitterly cold outside in the stadium that Friday morn- ing. Plumes of vapor snorted from the mouth and nose of the players who climbed up the dugout steps onto the frozen RFK Stadium turf for their last practice of the season.

Lombardi, for the first time that year that I had seen, led off the calisthenics. He was swaddled like a bear in a great-coat, and his short arms and legs were barely visible as he did his jumping jacks, turning around in place and bestowing his huge, yet somehow shy and awkward grin on the whole team. There was no reason for the gesture to be touching, yet some- how it was. You could feel a certain electricity in the crisp winter air. It was, no doubt, the mood Lombardi sought; a sense of affectionate bondage would be the motivational key to Dallas. The team would play to win for Coach, and he would coach to win for the team. They would be playing this one as a tribute to their season together.

On Saturday, as we all sat in the mobile lounge at Dulles Airport, waiting to be driven and coupled to the Redskins' chartered jet, Lombardi spied a mod electric shirt on one of the players. "You guys are really something, you are," he sang out. And then, grinning widely, looking from side to side for approval, he blushed. The team roared with laughter. "You guys are really something, you are, Mister," they all echoed with great pleasure. It seemed to me the Cowboys wouldn't have a prayer.

Chapter 27

Down in Dallas it was beautiful football weather at the Cotton Bowl. It was the first day of winter, the sun was out in the pale blue Texas sky, and the temperature was in the fifties, with a gusty wind blowing out of the north. The Redskins won the toss and elected to receive.

Jurgensen went to work from his own 20-yard line, pressing the team forward into the wind and experiencing some difficulty. A quick opener to Charley Taylor, some short yardage from Brown and Harraway, a Cowboy penalty, and the Redskins had a first down on their own 46. Jurgensen went back to the air, and Mel Renfro picked off the ball and brought it back to the Washington 39. Dallas drove for a first and goal at the Redskin 7 and the Washington line stiffened, holding Calvin Hill and Walt Garrison to 2 yards on consecutive rushes. Morton then overthrew Lance Rentzel in the end zone, and Dallas had to take the field goal for a 3–0 lead.

Now the Redskins took over on their 22 and the Dallas front four left Washington with a fourth and eleven at their 21. Mike Bragg's punt boomed into the wind, made scant headway, and dropped out of bounds 25 yards upfield, once again giving Dallas good field position. Working on a second and three from the Redskin 26, Morton found tight end Pettis Norman in the clear, and Norman lugged it in for the touchdown, putting Dallas up 10–0.

There were still four minutes left in the quarter, and neither team showed an inclination to do much with the time or with the fifteen minutes of the second period, for that matter. Dallas appeared content to sit on its lead; the Redskins seemed re-

signed to be sat on. The drives fizzled, the offenses were sluggish, and the game settled down to a punting duel in the wind.

Mike Bragg uncorked a 14-yard boomer on fourth and ten.
Dallas promptly worked the ball to fourth and twenty and
punted one about 70 yards in the air, right out of the playing
field. Early in the second period, the Redskins worked the ball
to a fourth and four on the Cowboy 27-yard line. With the
wind at his back, Curt Knight put the Redskins on the scoreboard, trailing 10–3.

Now both teams found themselves in feckless fourth-down
holes. Dallas punted on fourth and thirty. The Redskins came
right back with a Bragg kick on fourth and fifteen. The Cowboys then kicked on fourth and eight. Bragg came in to kick
on fourth and thirty-three. Then suddenly, Morton's passes
began to click. Three passes and a draw worked the ball from
the Dallas 20 to the Washington 15-yard line and a first down.
Dallas then reverted to form, got a fourth and twelve and had
to settle for a field goal and a 13–3 lead, as the gun sounded
to end the half.

With lowered heads, the Redskins trotted off the field and
up the ramp to the dressing room. Lombardi scuffed along
behind them, his head down, looking from side to side, as if
to spot a tin can to kick. In the press box, the public-address
system announced that at the half in New Orleans, Roy Jefferson had been blanked on the pass-receiving front, and Dan
Abramowitz had caught four. So had Charley Taylor here in
Dallas, and the pass-catching derby had come down to Taylor
and Abramowitz with thirty minutes of football left in the
season. How often in the past had the Redskin season come
down to a forlorn quest for some personal triumph? A passing
title for Sonny? A receiving title for Charley? It seemed a
pattern that no exercise of will could rearrange.

The two teams came back onto the field as spiritless as they
had left it. They pushed the football up and down the gridiron
with the perfunctory motions of street cleaners. Passes were
dropped, blocks missed, penalties called, and Curt Knight
even had a field-goal attempt blocked from his own 27 with
a tail wind at his back. The third quarter stretched into the

fourth, and the action continued at a desultory pace, neither team demonstrating any great eagerness to win. Lombardi looked disgusted down on the side lines, and Flea Roberts and Dave Kopay were sent in to catch the ball in place of Bob Long and Larry Brown. Jurgensen finally staged a drive that carried from his own 23 down to the Dallas 16-yard line, with the Flea catching three straight balls for 44 yards. The momentum of first and ten was going for him, but Jurgensen was nailed for a loss of 8 by Jethro Pugh. Kopay ran for a yard, bringing up third and seventeen. Jurgensen went back to throw and was sacked for a loss of 11 by Bob Lilly and George Andrie. Knight's field-goal attempt from the Dallas 42 was wide to the right. There was a little less than ten minutes to go in the game, the Cowboys' ball first and ten on their 20, the Redskins down ten points and their wad seemingly shot.

Then Calvin Hill fumbled the first play from scrimmage, and Chris Hanburger scooped it up on the 19 and carried it in standing up. Preposterous as it seemed, the Redskins had a chance to win, could redeem themselves with a last-minute effort. Knight's kick into the wind fluttered down at the Cowboy 10-yard line, and rookie Richmond Flowers returned it to the Dallas 40. Sam Huff came in for a last do-or-die defensive effort, his second retirement from football all but announced. He stopped Calvin Hill for a yard gain. Then Morton hit Lance Rentzel for 18 yards, the first pass Rentzel had held onto all day. Garrison carried for 9 yards up the middle to the Redskins' 32. He came back for 3 more yards off guard and a first and ten at the 29. It seemed more a matter of a soggy, dispirited Redskin defense than of a suddenly invigorated Dallas offense. The ball was progressing downfield with a marked lack of resistance. Hill ran around the right side for 5, then Garrison around the left side for 2 and Hill to the left side for 4 more and the first down on the Redskin 18. Morton hit Bob Hayes for 3, and Pat Fisher belted him on the spot. Calvin Hill swept the left side for 9 more, making it first and goal on the Redskin 6. On the next play Hill went in standing up around the right side. Mike Clark's kick was good, and the Cowboys had a 20–10 lead with three minutes remaining.

Clark's kickoff carried out of the end zone and the Redskins put the ball in play on their 20, but a holding penalty spotted it back on their 10. Jurgensen hit Charley Harraway for 9. Cornell Green picked off Sonny's next pass, and I climbed into the press-box elevator for the trek to the dressing room. When I reached the runway at the southern end of the field, the Redskins had the ball some 50 or 60 yards to the north, deep in Dallas territory. The scoreboard still said 20–10, and there was less than a minute to play.

"What are we doing with the ball?" I asked a reporter. "I left the press box when Green intercepted."

"It was ruled pass interference on Dallas, so the Skins got the ball back and first and ten." I peered downfield, but there was little to see from my angle and less to hope for, given the elements of time and score now posted on the Cotton Bowl clock. The maroon jerseys and gold pants of the Redskins swept to one side of the field's crown; blue and white, Cowboys pursued. Jurgensen was throwing swing passes to his backs, but I didn't even bother to watch whether they were complete or not. I watched him release the ball, go down under a wave of Cowboy linemen, and get back up again to try again.

The clock was ticking away, and finally a time-out was called, with three seconds on the board. Jurgensen unloaded another swing pass and went down, smothered for the last time by the Cowboy line.

It was 20–10. The season was over. The two teams filed up the runway, the Cowboys smiling and chatting as they passed, their fans yelling down good wishes, an occasional Redskin trotting across the runway to pat a Cowboy on the rump and wish him luck against the Browns. Tom Landry came up the ramp, his face as blank and expressionless as a pan of dough. Then Lombardi passed by, his eyes narrow slits of smoldering anger, his lower jaw grinding away, and an urgent bounce of revenge in his steps.

He was, after all, the last of the poor losers. But, on the other hand, he was the last of the big winners too. There were not many men who had won three of anything in a row in the

1960's. Lombardi had had occasion to do just that—those five NFL crowns, those two Super Bowl rings. He hadn't, after all, put his winning streak on the line for the hell of it. He cared so much about winning that he did not dissemble the ulcerous rage of defeat.

The dressing-room doors remained shut for some time. "What did he say?" I asked a player in the dressing room. "He said he was ashamed of us as men. He said the Cowboys didn't come out to win today, and we showed we weren't men enough to teach them a lesson."

"He's got a point there. About the Cowboys at least," I said.

"Yeah, he does. Got something to say on the other point, too. You got to face that. We weren't any tigers out there today."

The reporters tracked Lombardi down in the hallway.

"Did you achieve what you set out to this year, Coach?"

"Somewhat."

"What did you, and what didn't you?"

"That's for me to know," he said with a tense grin, ending the season as he had begun it back in February on one of those cryptic throwaway lines.

Yet the answer was obvious enough. The seven wins were what he had set out to achieve. The five defeats and the two ties were what he didn't have in mind.

The carpeted Cotton Bowl dressing room was littered with tape and soggy towels. The Redskins drifted out into the parking lot and the large red duffel bags were loaded into the belly of the chartered buses for the last ride of the season. A police motorcycle escort led the way onto the Dallas freeway, a courtesy for champions and Presidents. And the team deserved that. They were average football players perhaps, but they were a company of strong and honorable men. What team had faced greater pressure, worked harder, and struggled longer with their own doubts and anxieties? They had played for a man who never yielded, who never stopped driving them. They had almost broken, but in the end they had held and had come out on the winning side at 7–5–2. Certainly, they could face the off-season, even July 1970 in Carlisle, with some measure of self-esteem. For the first time in recent memory, they had ended a season less diminished than they had begun it. I sat next to Gerry Allen on the bus. "Man," he said, "do you know what the Coach told me? Do you know what he said?"

"No," I admitted.

"He told me I am the best runner on this team, the best back he has got. Does that make any sense to you? The best runner he's got on the move list? It's like you write your book and you show it to your publishers, and they say, man, you wrote one hell of a book here, but we ain't going to publish it. We're going to publish this other cat's book. Yours is better, but we are going to put out this other one here that ain't as good. How would you like that, man?"

"He's getting you ready for next year already," I said.

"Maybe so," he allowed, with a pleased grin. "We'll go somewheres with me in there, I'll tell you that."

I asked Flea Roberts about the team. "It's like this," he said, "if you've won in the past you've got a certain class about you. It's like a rich old lady. She doesn't have to tell you she's rich. You watch the way she crosses her legs and folds her hands, the way she speaks. All of this tells you she's rich. Well, the Redskins don't have that class. Ain't any players in the league dying to come to Washington. Now the Rams, the Colts, the Browns, the Vikings, the Jets, the Chiefs, those teams have class. You know it. When you come to Washington, you know you're not going to be any world-beater. Hell, you feel you been shortchanged. That's the way I felt when I came here. And I didn't figure Lombardi would make any difference, though I know now he's changed my feelings about the Redskins. Teams hold us a little bit higher than they held the Redskins before. I know my friends on other clubs tell me we're playing better football. They know it, their coaches know it from the films.

"I've played on losing teams and championship teams, and I've seen all kinds of breeds of coaches. There's an average coach who just has knowledge, and then there's a good coach who has knowledge and can get it across; then there's an

excellent coach—aw, hell, a great coach—who has the knowledge, the ability to get it across, and the fire to make a group
of people go into their beyondness, to make them play above
their level, and there's no doubt Lombardi has that quality.
Everything with him is just pushing, pushing, pushing toward
a goal. He never stops and he's gonna have it. He's gonna have
it. He's gonna get it here. I don't know who's gonna be around
to share it with him, but he's gonna get it because he never
lets up. It's hard, hard on players. Like warfare. You get close
to a guy on this team, and the next thing you know, he's got
a bullet in his head.

"You know," the Flea went on, "you hear about the great
people in the world, and it's seldom you have the chance to
work with one, and I can say I've worked with a real great
man. Not just because he's the former coach of the Green Bay
Packers, but because he's a man who never stops. He's a hard
man, he does what he has to do, he gives it all he's got, and
he's a fair man. Hell, I don't think you can ask anything more
than that, anything more of any profession in the world."

I wandered up and down the aisle of the tourist section,
saying good-bye to the players, knowing that I had only seen
a small part of their lives, had only experienced a fraction of
what they had gone through. It was not the same as knowing
it for yourself or feeling the exhilaration and despair of the
action itself, but I had tried to get as close to it all as I could,
had tried to see what it was like in the round. For me, this
flight home was the end of the line; there was no next season.
The finality was there, and I knew as much as I ever would.

Frank Ryan asked, "What are you going to call your book?"

"I don't know yet."

"Well, if it's about football, tell what you know and call it
'The Nature of the Beast.'"

"There's a double meaning there," I said.

"Oh my God, yes, I forgot about that," he laughed.

The plane was nearing Washington, and I went back to the
first-class section to beard the beast. Lombardi was sound
asleep, an almost beatific smile on his face, the taut flesh of his
grimacing lower face loose and relaxed—a stern Italian *pater-*

familias, perhaps a stonemason from the old country, a hewer of men down in the gridiron quarry, his job now finished, as good a piece of work as trying could make it.

What did he make of it all, I wondered. Later he would tell me, "I think I have to say I am a teacher first and a coach second. The difference between teaching and coaching is selling yourself, being involved right up to your neck. You got to live it all day long, in the car, at home, at night, looking at the pictures, out on the practice field. And to be a teacher you got to win their hearts. Once you win a team's heart they'll follow you anywhere, they'll do anything for you. I haven't won this team's heart yet, maybe. But it's not for lack of trying. And I'll keep trying."

I had said, "You finished this year 7–5, the same record you had your first year in Green Bay. Yet, then, at the end of '59 you must have known that the Packers were ready, were good enough to go all the way the next year. You don't have that same expectation about the '70 Redskins, I guess."

He had made an indistinct sound in his throat, a sort of rasping acknowledgment that this was so. "The Packers were young and they were deep in talent. It was all there. You could see it, you could feel it. The Redskins? They're not that young, not that talented. But we'll be there, we'll be giving it what we've got. Hell, there's no other way."

So now Lombardi was napping, and I went back to my seat. The jet was nearing home. The lights of suburban Washington were flickering on the ground below us. The pressure of descent was beginning to squeak in the eardrums. I got out of my seat and stood in the aisle. Lombardi, a man who always reacted to pressure, had just woken up, was stifling a yawn. The beast, always a pretty noble creature, now looked tame as well, the flesh in his face softened, at peace.It was as if the man he had been for the last six months was a creation of the imagination, an act of his own will. Now he looked to be a good-natured, short, middle-aged Italian-American with graying wavy hair and a mouthful of big square teeth, but, perhaps also, a man who could really be something, he could, when he put his mind to it.

I thanked him for his kindnesses, for the enjoyment I'd had in these last months and the chance to learn what I had.

Lombardi gave a weary smile, we shook hands and I went back to my seat, as the plane dipped over Dulles.

In a few minutes the jet would land and the Redskins would leave the terminal for the darkened parking lot. They would disappear, many of them to come back to play another day and many never to be heard of again. This was for them a homecoming and a diaspora. The 1969 Redskins were all over. In 1970 there would be new people, a new schedule, a new league, in the end a new fate based on a new won-lost record.

As a team, the '69 Redskins had done their best. It was not good enough, but it was better than they had ever done together, better than many thought them capable of. As men, they had quality and character. As a team they lacked a soul, would never really be happy and able to win until they found the soul Lombardi wanted. There was no room for compromise there.

Lombardi, for his part, had a soul, but he lacked a team. He had been the great winner, the champion of the sixties in a game that had no other standard of excellence, or even meaning, beyond winning. He had put it all back on the line, and now he would enter the 1970's as an underdog, as a man just a shade above .500.

You had to admire that. The gall of it, the daring, the need to prove himself afresh. He was no fool, he could size up the prospects of the 1969 Redskins as well as anyone. Better than anyone, perhaps, for he was by nature a pessimist and a realist. Why had he done it, then? I had to believe that, for all the doubts and the bleak assessments of what was and could not be altered, he was a man who believed in himself, and accordingly sought risks and great odds to reaffirm that faith.

Football was a profession ideally suited as a testing ground for that faith. When you won, it was beyond dispute. The record proved it, the diamond rings attested to it. It was a profession that offered a man complete control and the knowledge that he had done it himself. There had to be pride in that. Lombardi was a man strongly moved by pride, by the sense that he alone was responsible and that he alone had made it possible. There was some pride at 7–5–2. The next step was glory, and he was a man who believed in that as well, had waited a long time for it to come in the days before Green Bay, and was willing to wait and to keep pushing in Washington until it came again.

Once Lombardi had asked Paul Hornung whether he wanted to be a playboy or a football player. "Both," said Hornung, and Coach was said to have laughed. On another occasion, Hornung had climbed aboard the Packer team bus prior to a game, his collar smeared with lipstick, his eyes a trifle red. "Where you been?" Lombardi grunted. "To church," Hornung answered in a dulled voice. "To church, to church, he's been to church," Lombardi chuckled to himself all the way to the stadium, rocking back and forth in his seat at the head of the bus.

That was glory to Lombardi, the merger of these two worlds: playboydom and football, the church and a night on the town, the saint and the sinner. That was why Paul Hornung was for him *the* football player, the only one I had ever heard him mention with something like passionate approval. Hornung perhaps possessed both sides of Lombardi's own character, the need to prove himself by winning and the grace to do it the easy way without the unpardonable cruelties of the will. Perhaps he was the man that Lombardi longed to be. "The Golden Boy," not just one of "The Seven Blocks of Granite." Hornung had had the glory and the pleasure young; it had come easy to him and had arrived without the need of discipline, those "twenty-five years of apprenticeship." To Lombardi it had come late in life. He was forty-five when the big break came, when he got a team of his own. The years of obscurity must have grated on him, the dreariness, the mortification of being someone else's assistant. The discipline must have cost him. But he had suffered it, and, as he liked to say, he was willing to pay the price.

When I first met Lombardi, back in May, he had told me of Hornung, "I don't know why Paul was the type of pressure player he was. Maybe it was because he knew the tougher the situation, the more glory there was for him in it. Inside the 20-yard line, Paul was the greatest player I've ever seen—just average downfield, but inside the 20, the greatest."

Lombardi clearly had that quality. Perhaps, like Hornung, he sought risks and pressure because there was greater personal glory in it. At midfield Lombardi was harsh, merciless, egoistic, inconsistent, and often even mediocre, but within the 20-yard line he had greatness. He did what he had to do. His life was an extraordinary act of will, of discipline, of ceaseless driving. The yardage inside the 20 was always tough; for Lombardi in 1969 it had been tougher than for most, but he had never flinched, had just kept pushing. Hell, there was no other way.

Washington Redskins

Name	Pos.	Ht.	Wt.	Age	Yr. in NFL	College
Bragg, Mike	P	5-11	186	21	2	Richmond
Knight, Curt	K	6-2	190	26	1	C. G. Academy
Jurgensen, Sonny	QB	6-0	203	35	13	Duke
Ryan, Frank	QB	6-3	215	33	12	Rice
Beban, Gary	WR	6-1	195	23	2	UCLA
Owens, Brig	S	5-11	190	26	4	Cincinnati
Wade, Bob	S	6-2	200	24	2	Morgan State
Vactor, Ted	CB	6-0	185	25	1	Nebraska
Harraway, Charley	RB	6-2	215	25	4	San Jose State
Dyer, Henry	RB	6-1	230	24	3	Grambling
Fischer, Pat	DB	5-9	170	29	9	Nebraska
Kopay, Dave	RB	6-0	225	27	6	Washington
Bass, Michael	DB	6-0	190	24	2	Michigan
Taylor, Charley	WR	6-3	210	27	6	Arizona State
Brown, Larry	RB	5-11	195	21	1	Kansas State
Harris, Rickie	S	5-10	182	26	5	Arizona
Roberts, Walt	WR	5-9	163	27	5	San Jose State
Didion, John	LB	6-4	245	21	1	Oregon State
McLinton, Harold	LB	6-2	235	22	1	Southern University
Roussel, Tom	LB	6-3	235	24	2	Southern Mississippi
Hanburger, Chris	LB	6-2	218	28	5	North Carolina
Hauss, Len	C	6-2	235	29	5	Georgia
Schoenke, Ray	T	6-4	250	27	6	SMU
Duich, Steve	G	6-3	248	23	2	San Diego State
Promuto, Vince	G	6-1	245	31	10	Holy Cross
Kammerer, Carl	DE	6-3	243	32	9	Pacific
Grimm, Dan	G	6-3	245	28	7	Colorado
Huff, Sam	LB	6-1	230	35	13	West Virginia
Rutgens, Joe	DT	6-2	255	30	9	Illinois
Bosch, Frank	DT	6-4	246	23	2	Colorado
Snowden, Jim	T	6-3	255	27	5	Notre Dame

Name	Pos.	Ht.	Wt.	Age	Yr. in NFL	College
Rock, Walter	T	6-5	255	28	7	Maryland
Crane, Dennis	DT	6-6	260	24	2	Southern California
Long, Bob	WR	6-3	205	27	6	Wichita State
Norton, Jim	DT	6-4	255	27	5	Washington
Hoffman, John	DE	6-7	260	26	1	Hawaii
McKeever, Marlin	LB	6-1	235	29	9	Southern California
Smith, Jerry	TE	6-3	208	26	5	Arizona State
Richter, Pat	TE	6-5	230	27	7	Wisconsin
Carroll, Leo	DE	6-7	250	25	2	San Diego State

HEAD COACH: Vince Lombardi

ASSISTANTS: Bill Austin, Lew Carpenter, George Dickson, Harland Svare, Mike McCormack, Don Doll, Sam Huff.

SOME REDSKINS WHO ALSO SERVED

Name	Pos.	Ht.	Wt.	Age	Yr. in NFL	College
Gerry Allen	RB	6-1	210	28	4	Omaha
Tom Brown	DB	6-1	195	28	6	Maryland
Bob Brunet	RB	6-1	205	23	2	Louisiana Tech
Dave Crossan	C	6-3	245	29	5	Maryland
Eugene Epps	DB	6-1	185	21	1	UTEP
Charlie Gogolak	K	5-10	165	24	4	Princeton
John Love	WR	5-10	185	25	2	North Texas State
Chuck Mercein	RB	6-2	220	26	5	Yale
Joe Rutgens	DT	6-2	255	30	9	Illinois
Bob Shannon	WR	6-2	200	24	1	Tennessee A & I
Fred Sumrall	DT	6-2	258	21	1	Tennessee State
Danny Talbott	QB	5-11	185	24	1	North Carolina
Harry Theofilides	QB	5-10	180	25	2	Waynesburg
A. D. Whitfield	RB	5-10	210	25	5	North Texas State
John Wooten	G	6-3	250	32	11	Colorado